Welcome to

Astronomy for Beginners

You don't need letters after your surname, an encyclopaedic knowledge of the skies or even a telescope to get into stargazing. That's the beauty of astronomy: armed with nothing more than your eyes and a basic grasp of where to look in any given location, you can embark on one of the most accessible and infinitely rewarding hobbies in the world. Planets, stars, constellations, nebulas, asteroids and many other celestial objects are within reach of the naked-eye beginner. And for those with telescopes, the universe – with its myriad colours and awe-inspiring sights – is your personal gallery of a trillion cosmic wonders. Our easy-to-follow guides will give you all the basic skills you need to take yourself from stargazing hobbyist on your first night to an astronomy enthusiast, fully equipped with the right telescope and tools of the trade on a stellar journey of a lifetime.

Astronomy for Beginners

Imagine Publishing Ltd
Richmond House
33 Richmond Hill
Bournemouth
Dorset BH2 6EZ
☎ +44 (0) 1202 586200
Website: www.imagine-publishing.co.uk
Twitter: @Books_Imagine
Facebook: www.facebook.com/ImagineBookazines

Head of Publishing
Aaron Asadi

Head of Design
Ross Andrews

Edited by
Ben Biggs

Senior Art Editor
Greg Whitaker

Design
Ali Innes

Photographer
James Sheppard

Printed by
William Gibbons, 26 Planetary Road, Willenhall, West Midlands, WV13 3XT

Distributed in the UK & Eire by
Imagine Publishing Ltd, www.imagineshop.co.uk. Tel 01202 586200

Distributed in Australia by
Gordon & Gotch, Equinox Centre, 18 Rodborough Road, Frenchs Forest, NSW 2086. Tel + 61 2 9972 8800

Distributed in the Rest of the World by
Marketforce, Blue Fin Building, 110 Southwark Street, London, SE1 0SU

ISBN 978-1-909372-88-7

Part of the All About Space bookazine series

IMAGINE PUBLISHING

Contents

©NASA
66
In-depth sky charts

41
Navigate the sky
PLANISPHERE

148
Report a discovery

22
Telescope guides
©Alamy

What to observe

Astrophotography

The next step

Glossary & Directory

Getting started

32 Equatorial mounts

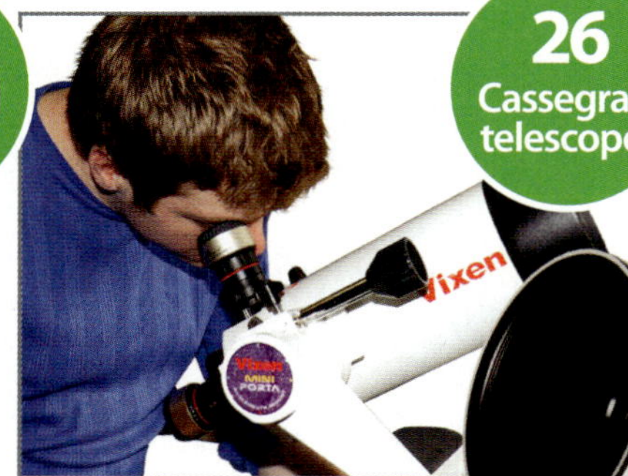

26 Cassegrain telescopes

16 Telescope guide

36 Learn to use binoculars

34 Pick the best eyepiece

MEADE ETX-125
CELESTRON

An introduction to astronomy

Ever wanted to explore the night sky but didn't know where to start? Our beginners' guide is here to help

There's a treasure trove of astronomical objects brimming from near enough every degree of the 20,000 square degrees that make up the night sky above your head at any one time. Standing under a dark cloak pitted with a vast number of twinkling stars, galaxies and planets along with the occasional appearance of the Moon and satellites which navigate their way through the vast blackness on their orbit around Earth, we are almost looking out of a great dome-shaped window whose fixed constellations and stars seem to wheel from east to west as our planet pirouettes on its orbit around the Sun. As it turns, our planet slowly takes these stellar patterns out of sight as evenings draw on before bringing them back into view again the following night. This imaginary sphere, which envelops our world in a night sky printed bubble and stirs awe and wonder from amateur to professional astronomer, is known as the celestial sphere.

Of course, as the seasons change, so does the night sky and as you gain a familiarity with the stars and planets you will notice new constellations and astronomical objects belonging to our Solar System creep into view from winter through to autumn.

Stepping outdoors into a clear night armed with layers of warm clothing and a hot drink as well as an optional deck chair, you have all you need to learn your way around the night sky for your very first evening's session. You might not realise it, but your eyes alone are a wonderful device when it comes to taking in what nature has to offer.

Understand the celestial sphere

North celestial pole
The northern point in the sky about which all of the stars seem to rotate – around the North Star, or pole star, Polaris.

Ecliptic
The Sun's path on the celestial sphere as seen if you were at a central point on the Earth's surface.

Celestial equator
A great circle on the celestial sphere which lies in the same plane as the Earth's terrestrial equator and is tilted at roughly 23 degrees to the ecliptic.

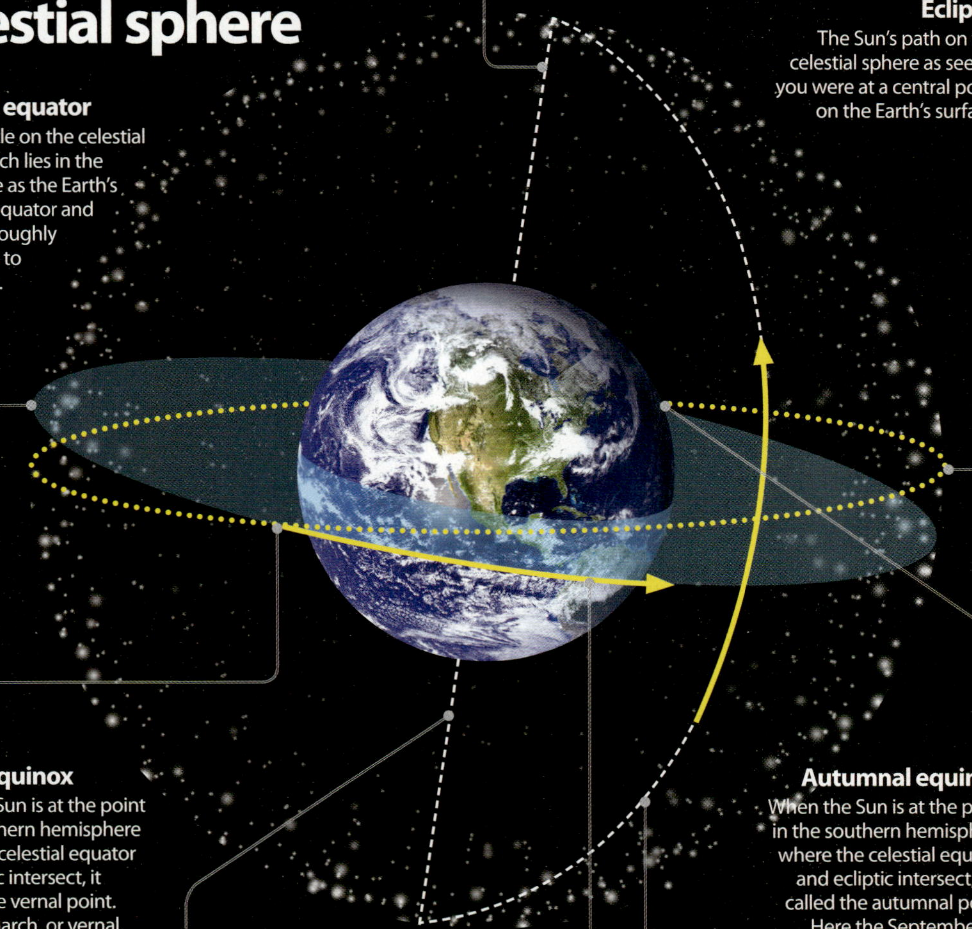

Earth ©NASA

Vernal equinox
When the Sun is at the point in the northern hemisphere where the celestial equator and ecliptic intersect, it is called the vernal point. Here the March, or vernal, equinox occurs.

Autumnal equinox
When the Sun is at the point in the southern hemisphere where the celestial equator and ecliptic intersect, it is called the autumnal point. Here the September, or autumnal, equinox occurs.

South celestial pole
Only visible from the southern hemisphere, stars rotate around the dim south pole star, Sigma Octantis.

Right ascension (RA)
The celestial equivalent of terrestrial longitude projected on to the celestial sphere. Measured in hours (h), minutes (m) and seconds (s).

Declination (Dec)
Comparable to the geographical latitude of the Earth which is projected on to the celestial sphere. Measured in degrees (°), minutes (′) and seconds (″).

Measuring the skies

1 degree
If you extend your arm and hold out your little finger, you can measure the distance and apparent size of an object equivalent to 1°. A full moon is equivalent to 0.5°.

5 degrees
By stretching out your arm and holding up three fingers, you are able to measure a distance between objects and an object's apparent size equal to 5°.

10 degrees
Your fist measures approximately 10°. For example, if you can stretch out your arm and fit your fist between Jupiter and the Moon, then the pair are 10° apart.

20 degrees
By holding out your arm in front of you and spreading out your fingers, you are able to measure a distance of approximately 20°.

Four naked eye sights

Discover four space objects you can see without any kit at all

Astronomy isn't just for people who own telescopes and binoculars. There are plenty of objects to see and identify in the night sky with the naked eye. Go outside on a clear night and you'll probably already be able to name some of the more famous constellations, but you might not be aware there is so much more waiting to be observed with your eyes alone. It's not just stars, though. Planets, comets and galaxies are all visible to an observer without any fancy equipment. Sometimes, seeing and identifying an object with just your eyes can be a more rewarding experience than using a telescope to find it. Below we've highlighted four great sights you can see while out and about on a dark and clear night. For things like the Milky Way, you'll need to be in an area of low light pollution, but find one and the night sky is there for you to behold.

©NASA

Ursa Major

Constellation: Ursa Major **Right ascension:** 10.67h
Declination: +55.38°

Also known as the Great Bear, the Big Dipper or the Plough, Ursa Major can be seen from most of the northern hemisphere throughout the year. The middle star is actually a famous double star comprising Mizar and Alcor. Ursa Major is easily found in the northern night sky, and the outside of the Big Dipper's bowl also points towards Polaris, the North Star, with the helpful 'pointer stars' Merak and Dubhe.

©NASA

The Quadrantid meteor shower

Constellation: Boötes **Right ascension:** 15h 28m
Declination: +50°

Start the new year with the Quadrantids as they shoot from their radiant in the constellation of Boötes during 1 to 5 January. On average, up to 40 meteors per hour can be seen at the shower's peak on 3 January and through to 4 January. Since the Moon's near last quarter will hide fainter meteors with its glare, best viewing will be in the darker hours after midnight, in a dark spot away from light pollution.

©NASA

The Orion Nebula (M42)

Constellation: Orion **Right ascension:** 05h 35m 17.3s
Declination: -05° 23′ 28″

The Orion Nebula is a bright star-forming nebula and is situated at a distance of around 1,340 light years away making it the closest region of great star birth to Earth. To find the nebula, locate the three stars that make up Orion's Belt. From the left star of Orion's Belt (Alnitak), move south in the direction in which Orion's sword points, hanging from his belt, with the nebula visible clearly as a naked eye object at the sword's tip.

©NASA

Centre of the Milky Way Galaxy

Constellation: Towards Sagittarius **Right ascension:** 17h 25m 40.04s
Declination: -29° 00′ 28.1″

Our galaxy weaves through the night sky as a powdery band of light from billions of stars. Because we are a part of it, we can only see a portion of our galaxy, which is roughly 100,000 light years in diameter. Few have seen the splendid view of the Milky Way because of light pollution from streetlights in towns and cities. However, from a dark spot, the form of such a huge abundance of stars becomes immediately apparent.

Essential equipment

The basic kit every beginner needs

The hobby of astronomy can be bewildering for the beginner without advice to guide them. There are so many types of telescope, not to mention mounts, eyepieces, filters and other assorted accessories that it's easy to rapidly become confused. Hopefully though, we can help you navigate your way through and make choosing the right instrument an enjoyable experience rather than a daunting one.

A lot of people think that to be an astronomer you must have a telescope. This is far from the truth! The unaided eye can show you constellations, the Moon, bright planets, even the odd galaxy. Binoculars are an inexpensive option to increase the range of what you can see. The most recommended are a pair of 10x50s, which, with a lens diameter of 50mm and a magnification of 10x, can show you the moons of Jupiter, the craters on the Moon, the brightest galaxies and star clusters, even the stars of the Milky Way. The minimum size and magnification of binoculars for astronomy is 7x40, which may suit older observers – as you age the diameter of your dilated pupil shrinks, which means some observers will not get the benefit that larger diameter 10x50 binoculars offer. Of course, if you decide astronomy isn't for you, then at least you haven't spent a fortune on binoculars and they can still be used for terrestrial objects.

If you do go for a telescope, the most important quality to look out for is the aperture diameter, not the magnification. Beware cheap 'toy' telescopes that are small but claim '500x magnification!' To see faint objects your telescope needs to be able to collect as much light as possible, and so the wider the aperture (ie the wider the diameter of the telescope tube), the fainter the object you can see. A minimum aperture is around 100mm for a refracting telescope and 100-150mm for a reflecting telescope like a Dobsonian. Refractors use lenses to focus the light; reflectors use mirrors. You may also want to consider spending a little more on a computerised GoTo mount, which features a hand controller that can direct your telescope to any astronomical object you wish to have a gander at. A good beginners' telescope should cost between £200 and £500. They are available from reputable dealers (a quick web search will display a range of options) to manufacturers such as Celestron, Meade and Sky-Watcher.

■ You'll need a few pieces of kit to get the most out of your astronomy experiences

Three great beginner telescopes

TAL-100RS (EQ5) 100mm Refractor

Cost: £490 ($780)
Supplier: Harrison Telescopes
Website: www.harrisontelescopes.co.uk

Supplied with 6.3mm and 25mm Super Plössl eyepieces, this telescope offers sharp resolution views of objects including the Moon and planets and will reveal deep sky targets. Portable and practical, the TAL-100RS features engraved aluminium setting circles and manual slow-motion tracking controls.

Meade StarNavigator 102mm Refractor with AudioStar

Cost: £299 ($480)
Supplier: Telescope House
Website: www.telescopehouse.com

Learn as you observe with this GoTo telescope which features a database of over 30,000 objects and AudioStar with Astronomer Inside digital audio technology, which, with the use of an in-built speaker, allows you to listen to interesting facts on over 500 celestial objects.

Meade 8" Lightbridge Dobsonian

Cost: £499 ($800)
Supplier: Telescope House
Website: www.telescopehouse.com

This reflector telescope makes finding astronomical objects a doddle with its four-reticule red dot viewfinder and adjusts to your observing needs with brightness controls. With a built-in battery-powered cooling fan, this telescope is kept at an ideal temperature even when observing galaxies 50 million light years away!

Choosing the right telescope

Make sure you get the best start in amateur astronomy by buying the right telescope for your needs

Images of the universe and its amazing array of objects are to be found everywhere but it's natural for people with an interest in astronomy to want to see celestial objects for themselves, and this can be achieved by obtaining a good telescope.

First, let's tackle the issue of the beginner's expectations. Those remarkable bright, colourful images of the cosmos obtained by the likes of the Hubble Space Telescope have been secured using sensitive CCD chips and subjected to computer enhancement.

The human eye isn't nearly so good at producing images. Only bright objects like the Moon, planets and certain stars produce an instantaneous 'wow' factor. The larger the telescope's primary mirror or lens, the more colour and detail you will see.

Choosing the right telescope can be a tricky prospect, but the most important thing to be aware of when buying any telescope is its optical quality.

So which telescope should you opt for? A Newtonian reflector on a simple undriven altazimuth mount (known as a 'Dobsonian') offers the best value in terms of aperture. Dobsonians are ideal if you want to learn your way around the skies the 'old-fashioned' way. They collect lots of light and deliver knockout views.

Newtonians (and refractors) become much more costly with an equatorial or computerised mount. Computerised mounts come in several forms – Dobsonian (push-to or go-to), single tine-mounted (tracking or go-to) and German equatorial (go-to). A computerised push-to Dobsonian costs about twice as much as a manual one, while a high-end Newtonian on a driven German equatorial mount may cost ten times more.

For ease of use a short focal length refractor of up to four-inches in diameter or catadioptric (Schmidt or Maksutov-Cassegrain) up to five-inches on a computerised mount may fit the bill. Both will show many deep-sky objects as well as revealing detail on the Moon and planets. Achromatic refractors of short focal length display a degree of false colour around the edges of bright objects. The best views, however, are to be had through apochromatic refractors, which are about four times more costly than an equivalent-sized achromat.

Whichever telescope you choose, there's nothing stopping you from taking your first steps and reaching for the stars.

> "The larger the primary mirror or lens, the more colour and detail"

There are many different types of telescope on the market

Reflectors and refractors explained

Reflectors

There are two main types of telescope: reflectors and refractors. The former use mirrors to gather and focus light. The primary mirror is parabolic in order to focus incoming light rays, while the secondary mirror reflects light into the eyepiece. They are generally cheaper than refractors but they are sensitive and can be easily knocked out of alignment.

1. Primary mirror
2. Secondary mirror
3. Corrector plate/meniscus

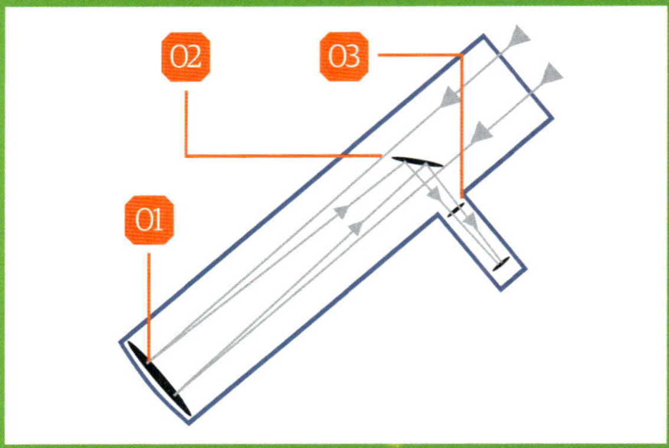

Refractors

Refractors bend, or refract, light as it enters through the front, with an objective lens gathering and focusing the light. They are more resilient, keeping their alignment even when knocked. However, refractors are usually longer than reflectors in order to minimise the occasional visual impairment induced by refraction.

1. Objective lens
2. Dew cap
3. Tube

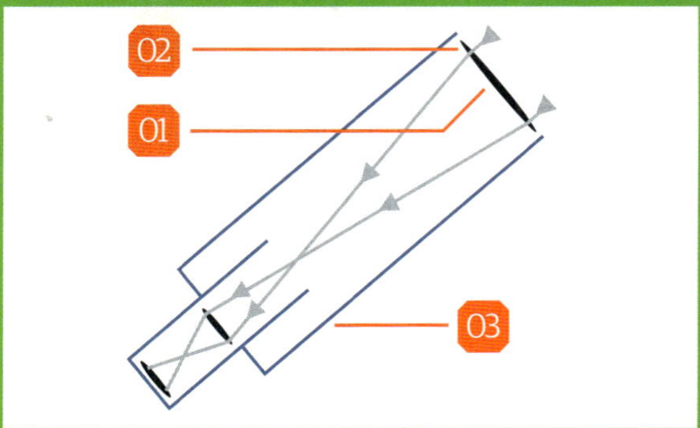

Anatomy of a telescope

Find your way around your new equipment

Aperture

A telescope's aperture indicates the size of its primary mirror or objective lens. Larger apertures deliver sharper and more detailed images and reveal fainter objects.

Focuser

When an eyepiece is inserted into the telescope it needs to be moved in or out to achieve sharp focus using the focuser. There are various kinds, including elementary push-pull friction focusers, basic rack-and-pinion and helical types to more advanced Crayford and electronic ones.

Mount

The telescope's mount holds it steady when viewing. The user can also freely move the instrument – either by pushing the tube manually, by turning clamps or via an electronic handset – to keep an object centred or to move to another object in the sky.

Finder

Attached to and aligned with the main telescope, the finder is a low-magnification instrument used to point the instrument so that the desired object can be centred in the telescopic field of view. Types of finder include naked eye (red-dot or crosshair) reflex finders and telescopic finders with crosshairs.

Eyepiece

The eyepiece magnifies the light focused by the primary mirror or lens to produce an image. Eyepieces come in various configurations (the Plössl is the most commonly used) with different focal lengths, apparent fields of view and tube diameter (either 1.25-inch or 2-inch).

"The power of any given telescope is directly relative to the diameter or aperture of the objective lens or primary mirror"

Five top telescopes

Buying a telescope can be mind-boggling to the uninitiated so be sure to read this before making a decision

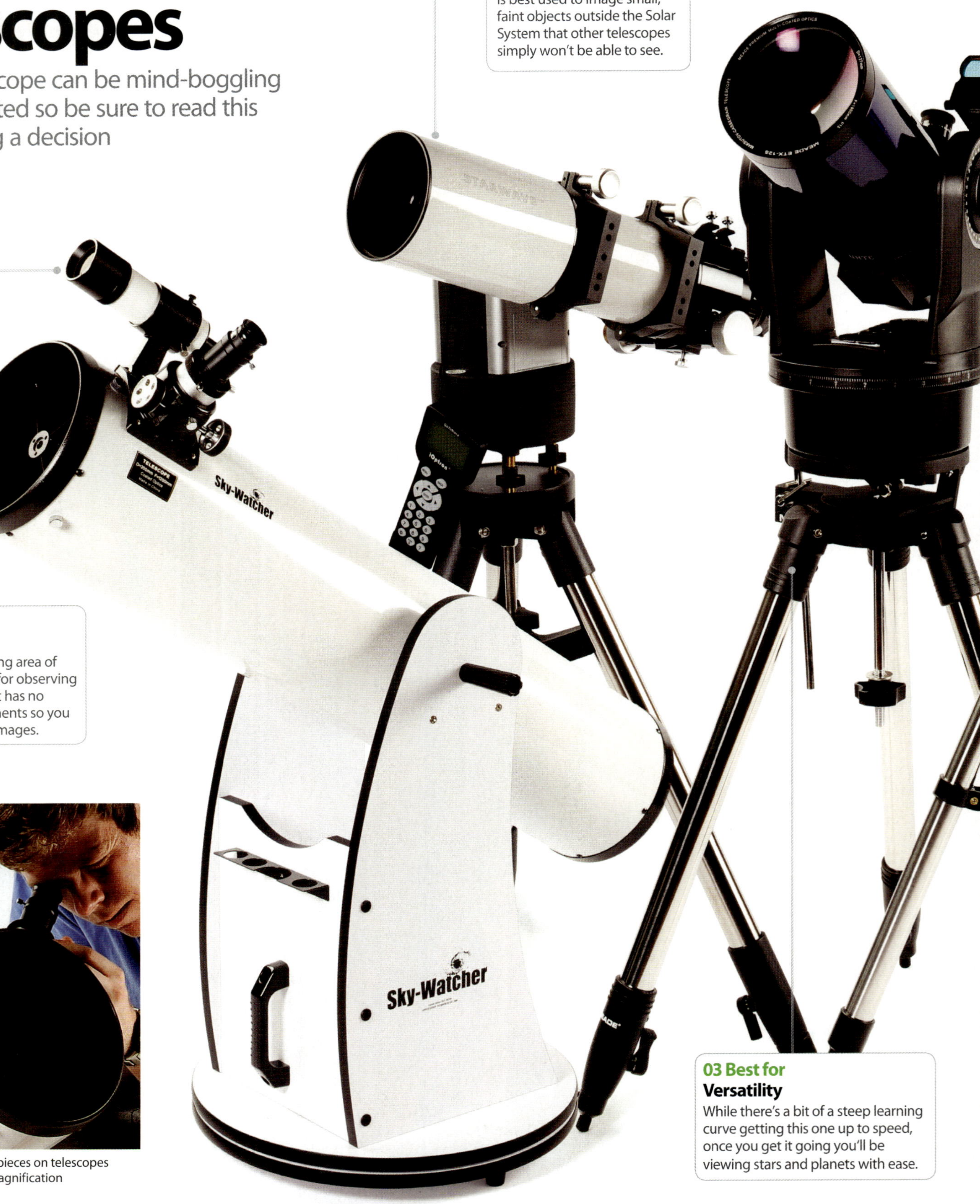

02 Best for
Astrophotography
This gorgeous glass telescope is best used to image small, faint objects outside the Solar System that other telescopes simply won't be able to see.

01 Best for
Deep sky objects
The large light-collecting area of the Dobsonian is best for observing deep-sky objects but it has no computerised components so you won't be able to take images.

03 Best for
Versatility
While there's a bit of a steep learning curve getting this one up to speed, once you get it going you'll be viewing stars and planets with ease.

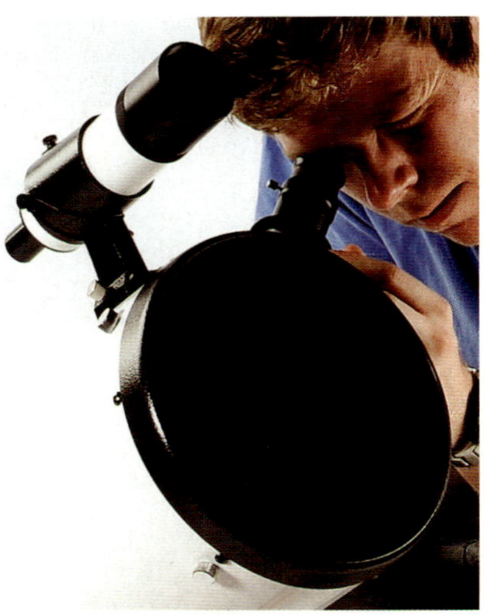

■ You can use various eyepieces on telescopes to get different levels of magnification

05 Best for
Planetary photography
For images of planets in the Solar System and other objects like the Moon this is a good telescope to use, especially as focusing is a breeze with the dual-speed focuser.

04 Best for
Complete beginners
If you're looking for an entry-level telescope that'll provide you with great observations of the cosmos then this scope with its wide field of view is a great choice.

■ Most modern telescopes are computerised

01 Sky-Watcher Skyliner 200P Dobsonian

Cost: £315/$489
From: www.astronomia.co.uk

With an eight-inch f6 primary mirror, this versatile telescope gulps in light, allowing faint objects to be seen and wide-angle views to be enjoyed using the 25mm (48x) eyepiece provided; more detailed views of the Moon and planets are given by the 10mm (120x) eyepiece provided. Being a Dobsonian it's easy to use, but there's no tracking – a generous 9x50 finderscope helps locate your celestial quarry.

02 Starwave 80 ED Refractor

Cost: £329/$511
From: www.altairastro.com

An excellent choice for those who want a portable medium field (f7) refractor capable of producing excellent astro-images as well as being a great visual performer. Known as a semi-apochromat, its colour correction lies between that of a standard achromat and an apochromat. Note that the optical tube assembly only is provided, but tube rings and a Vixen-format dovetail bar are supplied so that it can be attached to the mount of your choice.

03 Meade ETX-125 PE f15 Maksutov Cassegrain UHTC

Cost: £649/$1,000
From: www.telescopehouse.com

A top performer, this five-inch Maksutov provides pin-sharp, high-contrast views that approach apochromatic quality. With its Autostar go-to controller, this Premier Edition (PE) automatically levels the telescope and points it north, making setup even easier. Fork-mounted, it can be used in altazimuth mode or equatorial mode for astrophotography and is extremely portable.

04 Celestron NexStar 102 SLT

Cost: £399/$620
From: www.astronomia.co.uk

A complete package for the beginner, this four-inch f6.5 achromatic refractor is mounted on a single tine atop a lightweight but stable tripod. The NexStar handset offers go-to functionality and great tracking. Good views of both Solar System and deep-sky objects are delivered, but being a short focal length achromat it displays some false colour on bright objects. Comes with 25mm (26x) and 9mm (73x) eyepieces and a red-dot reflex finder.

05 GSO eight-inch F5 Newtonian

Cost: £369/$573
From: www.altairastro.com

Despite its low price, this eight-inch reflector has some high-end features, including a mirror cooling fan, dual-speed Crayford focuser and 10x50mm finderscope. Note that it isn't supplied with a mount or tripod, but suitable ones are available from Altair Astro and other suppliers – tube rings and Vixen-format dovetail bar are included in the package. When equatorially mounted, this is a great instrument for deep-sky observing and astro-imaging.

Refractor telescopes

The instrument of choice for many first-time astronomers, refractors offer fantastic views of the night sky

The magnifying abilities of lenses have been known for centuries. In the late 16th and early 17th Centuries this knowledge was refined and in the hands of a few talented opticians, lenses were combined and the telescope was born. This instrument was then turned on the sky, most famously by Galileo Galilei who observed Jupiter and its moons, the lunar surface and spots on the Sun.

It was well understood that glass could bend (refract) light and that it had a magnifying effect. As optical technology improved so did the telescope, although it remained fundamentally the same; using an objective lens to gather and focus the light and a series of smaller lenses near this focal point to magnify the image. Nowadays, the lenses have become bigger and developments in optics introduced doublet or even triplet lenses; in other words the placement of two or even three lenses close together as the main or objective lens to reduce and correct problems noticed when using a single piece of glass. Primarily, these compound lenses help to reduce 'chromatic aberration' (see Jargon Buster boxout). A single lens doesn't focus all the colours of the spectrum at the same point, but this can be corrected considerably, by using two lenses of different shape and type of glass put close together. This type of telescope lens is called an 'achromatic lens', or just an achromat. These are found in just about every type of refracting telescope made today, from the cheapest to the more expensive. The effect of chromatic aberration is to make bright objects appear to have a coloured halo around them. This can be completely eradicated by using a triplet lens, but due to high costs these are only ever used in the more expensive instruments.

Because refractors are particularly good at giving highly magnified and high contrast images, they are ideal for observing the Moon and planets. If you are thinking of buying one, then there are a couple of things you need to look out for: very cheap refractors have poor quality lenses which manufacturers try to improve by introducing a masking ring a short distance behind the main lens that helps to reduce the false colour effect. It also reduces the effective aperture, so don't be tempted to buy one of these. Make sure that all the lenses are 'fully multi-coated' in the technical specification. This helps to make sure that all the light is passed through the lens system and reduces flares and other unwanted artefacts. Also ensure the focuser is smooth and that it is supplied with a diagonal mirror which makes viewing more comfortable. If eyepieces are supplied, check they are of decent quality. If you are hoping to see stars and nebulas as well as planets, then go for an instrument of a moderate focal ratio. Finally, avoid purchasing a telescope which is too big, making it unwieldy. You'll see more with a telescope that you can handle. Remember, quality nearly always costs a little more.

Anatomy of a refractor telescope

Lens
The refractor lens is the 'eye' of the telescope. It gathers the light from objects and directs it down the tube to the eyepiece at the other end.

Dew shield
As the name suggests, this part of the telescope tube extends beyond the lens to prevent dew forming on it. Ideally this should protrude 10-15cm (4-6in) in front of the lens.

Eyepiece
The eyepiece is the lens which magnifies the image and puts the focused image where your eye can see it. Telescopes are often sold with two or three eyepieces which are usually interchangeable with other telescopes.

Diagonal
This is used to make viewing more comfortable as it turns the light coming through the telescope through 90°. It is either made from a prism or a flat mirror which is preferable as mirrors absorb less light than prisms, important as starlight is often very faint.

Focuser
This is the mechanism which smoothly moves the drawtube in and out to obtain a good focus of the image. Each eyepiece will have a slightly different point of focus and it's important that the focuser is smooth and does not cause the drawtube to wobble as it moves.

■ Many telescopes feature go-to mounts that guide you to many sights

■ Refractors offer great views of the Moon and planets

©NASA

"Remember, quality nearly always costs a little more"

A perfect view

The refractor is frequently the instrument of choice for the first-time amateur astronomer, as they're easy to use and set up and don't need a lot of maintenance. There are, of course, different designs of telescope including reflectors, which use mirrors, and compound telescopes, which use lenses and mirrors. Each has its advantages and disadvantages, however, some designs seem to work particularly well when viewing certain types of objects. Refractors are very good for viewing the Moon and planets due to their very good contrast, which allows faint and subtle detail to be more easily seen, and also because they often come in longer focal lengths. This allows for higher magnifications; just what's needed to make the object look bigger to allow for observing those intricate details. It tends to cost more to make a lens rather than a mirror, though, so refractors usually have a smaller aperture.

Reflector telescopes

The reflector telescope is an amazing instrument. We take a look at their history and how they work…

The great 17th Century scientist Sir Isaac Newton is credited with the invention of the reflector telescope, although there were others who came up with a similar idea for such a device at around the same time.

The only type of telescope in use by astronomers in the early-1600s was of course the refractor which used glass lenses in a tube in order to gather and focus light. Several scientists were aware, however, that there was another way to achieve this, using a mirror. In 1668, Newton produced a small telescope which used a spherical mirror made of polished metal that bounced the light reflected from it up the tube to a much smaller flat mirror at an angle of 45 degrees. This in turn reflected light through a small hole made in the side of the tube where it could be focused and viewed through an eyepiece lens. This type of telescope soon became known as the Newtonian reflector and it is still very much in use today, although its size and method of construction has taken a great leap from Newton's first production. However, the problem with making metal mirrors, made from a material called 'speculum', an alloy of copper and tin which can be highly polished, meant that they did not become popular for nearly another 100 years when the technology was improved such that the mirrors could now be made of glass.

It was quickly realised that reflecting telescopes had many benefits including less optical problems, known as aberrations, than refractors at the time. And, probably the greatest advantage of all, the fact that mirrors could be easily made much larger than lenses. As construction methods and technology improved, mirrors and therefore telescopes, became larger. This in turn meant that fainter objects could be discerned and detail, known as resolution, could be greater. Because it is cheaper to manufacture mirrors of a given size than lenses of the same size, reflectors also have an advantage on a cost/performance scale. Due to this and some of its inherent optical advantages, Newtonian reflectors are popular for astronomers wanting to study deep sky objects which are, by their nature, faint. Newtonian reflectors don't hold all the aces, though. Due to the secondary mirror effectively blocking some of the light entering the tube, contrast in images can be affected, although this is usually minimal. It can be enough though, to make a difference to planetary and lunar studies where contrast and detail can be critical.

Over time the Newtonian reflector was joined by other designs of telescope, some of which tried to combine the advantages of both the reflector and the refractor. The 'compound' telescopes now come in many guises and can be useful for certain types of observation and study, but the Newtonian reflector is still ubiquitous, being used as an effective and less expensive solution by both amateurs and professionals the world over.

Anatomy of a reflector telescope

"Reflectors require a little more maintenance than a refractor"

Focuser
The focuser consists of a tube which can be adjusted towards and away from the telescope tube to give a sharp focus in the eyepiece of the objects being viewed.

Secondary mirror
Tilted at an angle of 45°, this small, flat mirror has an elliptical shape which looks circular when viewed through the open focuser tube.

Spider
The spider is the device which holds the secondary mirror centrally over the primary. The vanes have to be thin so as not to block light coming down the tube.

Primary mirror
The primary mirror in a Newtonian reflector should be of good quality and preferably parabolic in shape, as this will give cleaner, crisper images. The diameter governs how much you will see.

Tube
The cylindrical tube which makes up the body of the telescope holds the mirrors, the 'spider' and the focusing mount. Its size is governed by the diameter of the primary mirror.

■ Reflectors have come a long way since Newton's time

■ Reflectors are ideal for viewing the Moon, planets and deep sky objects

A versatile option

Newtonian reflectors make great amateur telescopes as you get a good aperture for your money. They are versatile so can be used for viewing the Moon, planets and deep sky objects. However, they do take a little more maintenance than say a refractor as the mirrors have to be aligned in the tube, with each other and with the focuser in a process called collimation. Although this can seem daunting at first, providing the user is careful and methodical it is usually straightforward and with practice, quite quick to perform and only needs doing once in a while. Because the telescope tube is open to the sky, mirrors can become tarnished and dirty; they can be cleaned, or every few years re-coated professionally. This is relatively inexpensive and is like having a brand-new telescope once the mirrors are reinstalled. Therefore the first-time purchaser needs to consider carefully if this is the right kind of telescope for them.

Maksutov-Cassegrain telescopes

There are many types of telescope designs available to the amateur astronomer. Here is an explanation of a type now in common use…

As the name suggests, the Maksutov-Cassegrain telescope is a hybrid or compound design of instrument which uses both lenses and mirrors. At first glance a 'Mak', as this type of telescope is often affectionately known, can look very much like its cousin, the Schmidt-Cassegrain. There are, however, some important differences.

Both Maksutov and Schmidt-Cassegrain telescopes use a spherical primary mirror. However, because a spherical mirror does not bring all the light rays that reflect from it to exactly the same point – which is necessary for a sharp, clean image – the light entering the telescope needs to be altered a little to account for this and give the user the good image required.

The Russian optician Dmitri Maksutov in 1936 designed a telescope which uses a spherical primary mirror with a small hole cut centrally, similar to a Cassegrain telescope, and a lens which would give the necessary correction to the light path. The lens had the shape of a meniscus. If you look closely at a glass of water, you'll notice that the water seems to cling to the sides of the glass through a property known as surface tension. This gives the surface of the water a curved profile – this is the meniscus. Maksutov found that this steeply curved shape was needed to give the proper correction and had the added benefit that it was possible to silver a small circle on the back of this lens to produce a secondary mirror. This curved secondary mirror would further correct the light rays and reflect it back through a hole cut in the centre of the primary and out to the focal plane where the image is formed. This design had the advantage of offering a fairly long focal length telescope in a compact package as the light was being reflected up and down inside the tube. You can find this type of optical design used not only in telescopes, but also in longer focal length camera lenses.

The design has been developed further to add versatility. For example, by using a secondary mirror inserted through the meniscus lens allowing the secondary to be shaped slightly differently for even more optical corrections, as well as allowing the designer to produce differing focal ratios and so producing differing fields of view, while still keeping the advantages of the basic optical layout of Maksutov. The addition of the meniscus lens though, with its thick piece of glass, makes these instruments quite heavy, but nevertheless, compact. Because glass can take a long time to cool down to ambient temperature, larger aperture Maks often have cooling fans built in to aid the process.

Are there major advantages of Maksutov-Cassegrain telescopes over say Newtonian reflectors or simple refractors? One of the major advantages of these systems is the longer focal lengths available in a compact tube. This leads to Maksutovs being excellent telescopes for viewing and imaging the Moon and planets. Such telescopes are now manufactured and sold to beginners and advertised as being good for just this type of observing.

"Maksutovs are excellent telescopes for viewing and imaging the Moon"

Anatomy of a Maksutov-Cassegrain telescope

Meniscus lens
This is the lens at the front of the telescope which alters the light rays to compensate for the aberrations introduced by the spherical primary mirror.

Secondary mirror
In a Maksutov-Cassegrain, the secondary mirror is often seen as a small silver circle on the reverse of the meniscus lens. In larger instruments it can be held in a 'cell'.

Cooling fan
In larger commercially made Maksutov-Cassegrain telescopes one or more cooling fans are built in to the body of the instrument to get the glass to cool down more quickly, which helps stabilise the images.

Visual back
In many Maks, the hole at the back of the telescope is threaded to accept a variety of accessories including the eyepiece. Cameras can also be added using adaptors.

Spherical primary mirror
Unlike a Newtonian telescope, the Maksutov-Cassegrain primary mirror is made to a spherical curve cross-section. The aberrations this produces can be easily corrected to give a good image.

■ The meniscus lens can be seen here at the front of a Maksutov-Cassegrain telescope

Easy observing

Maksutov-Cassegrain telescopes make great instruments for observing the Moon and planets in particular. That isn't to say that they aren't any good for deep-sky observations – they are, but due to their longer focal lengths they can give a restricted field of view. This isn't a problem for planetary viewing because of their relatively small size on the sky. The longer focal length also allows for increased magnification potential; again this is beneficial to lunar and planetary observing. Because of the design of the optics, Maks have hardly any optical aberrations and produce a nice flat field of view.

On the down side, due to the larger pieces of glass, they can take longer to cool down to ambient temperature than say a Newtonian reflector or a similar-sized refracting telescope. In larger aperture instruments, this process of cooling can be aided by the addition of small electric fans.

Using Dobsonian telescopes

There is a lot of misunderstanding about Dobsonian telescopes; what they are and what they can do. This should help clear it up...

The Dobsonian telescope is a Newtonian reflecting telescope on an altazimuth mount. It is the mount that distinguishes it from any other type of Newtonian reflector and this was popularised in the Sixties by avid amateur astronomer John Dobson. It's thought that Dobson invented the design for the mount, but as he freely admitted, the idea had been around for many centuries as cannons were mounted in such a way and wars fought using them. However, he developed the idea that Newtonian reflectors could be mounted on a simple platform using household parts and therefore made very cheaply, and so his name was attached to the now ubiquitous amateur telescope.

It is their simplicity of design and cheap parts that made these telescopes so popular. There were many differing variations on the theme, some being very sophisticated and rather getting away from the humble and inexpensive materials and design. The popularity was quickly appreciated by commercial telescope manufacturers and so you can find Dobsonians as mass-produced products of varying size and quality, as well as in kit form.

Dobsonians are often known as 'light buckets' as they are an inexpensive way of owning a relatively large aperture telescope - most of the money you spend is put into the optics rather than the mount. In other words, the amount you pay for say a ten-inch aperture Dobsonian may only buy you a six-inch Newtonian on an equatorial mount. One of the advantages of the Dobsonian therefore, is the 'bang for your buck' in terms of aperture. When homemade, they are often built from plywood and other lightweight yet stable materials and usually disassemble easily for transportation and storage. Indeed, it is possible to have a 16-inch aperture telescope that fits into the back of a small family car. This means you can travel to a dark sky site and take advantage of it with a large telescope. They are, however, not suitable for some forms of observing.

Because the user has to constantly move the telescope to follow objects, observing anything at more than moderate magnifications can be awkward. Teflon bearings are used to give frictionless movement but there is still the inertia of the telescope to overcome. Dobsonians are not very suitable for anything other than basic astrophotography due to being on an altazimuth mount rather than equatorial. It is possible to get motor drives and 'GOTO' systems for 'Dobs' nowadays and even equatorial platforms, but this rather goes against the original idea of the Dobsonian telescope as being a cheap alternative for avid amateur astronomers.

The appeal of the Dobsonian telescope is unlikely to diminish any time soon, though, as they make a great introductory telescope for beginners and are ideal for experienced observers on a budget.

Anatomy of a Dobsonian telescope

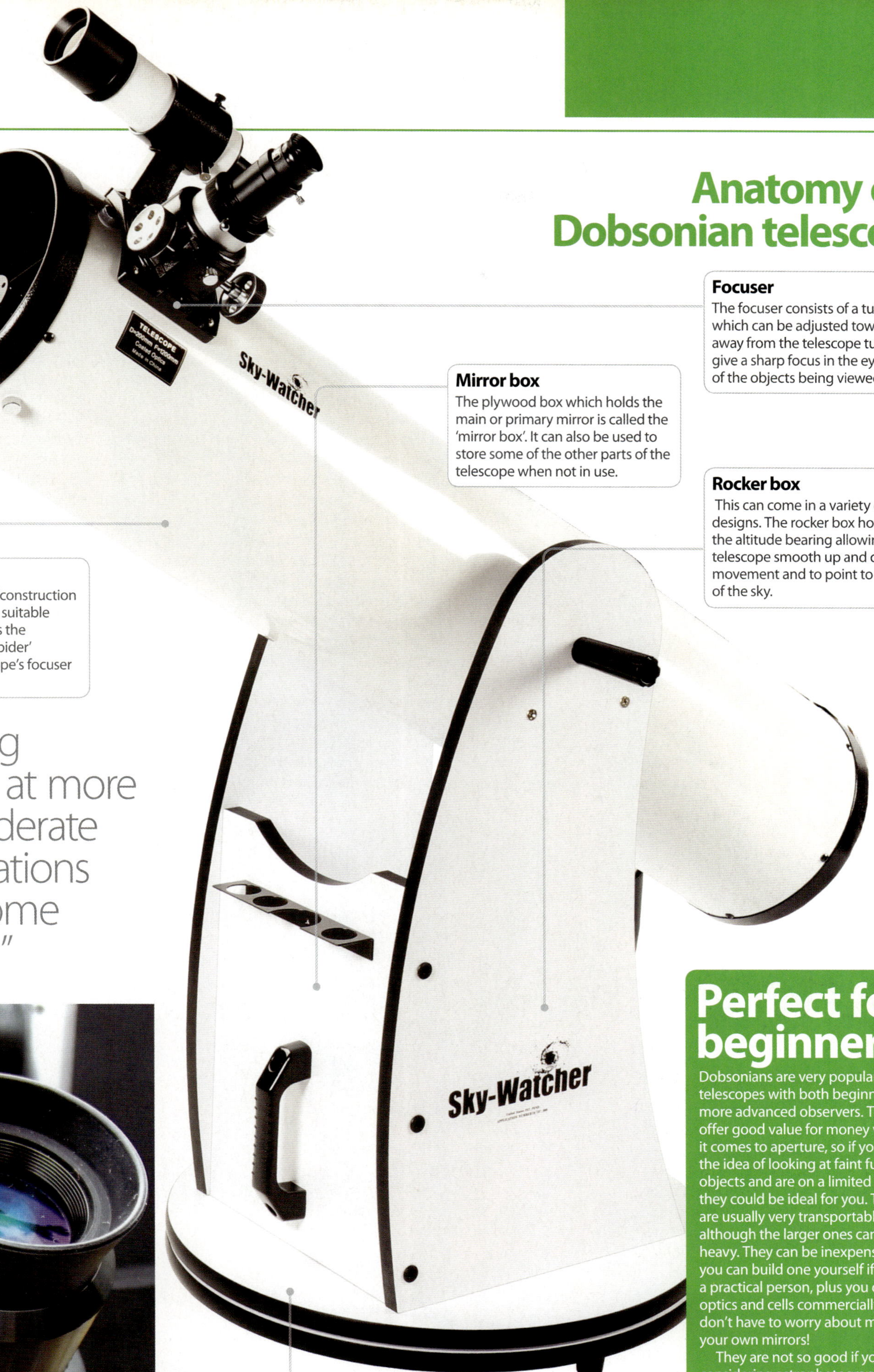

Focuser
The focuser consists of a tube which can be adjusted towards and away from the telescope tube to give a sharp focus in the eyepiece of the objects being viewed.

Mirror box
The plywood box which holds the main or primary mirror is called the 'mirror box'. It can also be used to store some of the other parts of the telescope when not in use.

Rocker box
This can come in a variety of designs. The rocker box houses the altitude bearing allowing the telescope smooth up and down movement and to point to any part of the sky.

Tube
This can be made from 'construction tube', plywood or other suitable material. The tube holds the secondary mirror, the 'spider' support and the telescope's focuser and finder scope.

"Observing anything at more than moderate magnifications can become awkward"

■ Dobsonian telescopes are a cheap option but not ideal for astrophotography

Azimuth bearing
The bottom bearing of the telescope is the azimuth bearing, which allows the telescope to rotate smoothly, often in the form of plywood or MDF discs with Teflon for friction-free movement.

Perfect for beginners

Dobsonians are very popular telescopes with both beginners and more advanced observers. They offer good value for money when it comes to aperture, so if you like the idea of looking at faint fuzzy objects and are on a limited budget they could be ideal for you. They are usually very transportable too, although the larger ones can get heavy. They can be inexpensive as you can build one yourself if you are a practical person, plus you can buy optics and cells commercially so you don't have to worry about making your own mirrors!

They are not so good if you are considering astrophotography and you do need to know your way around the sky a little to use them effectively. Also, when objects are near the horizon, you will need to bend over to view them, not so good if you have a bad back.

Cassegrain telescopes

The Schmidt-Cassegrain is one of the most popular telescopes for the more serious amateur astronomer

The Schmidt-Cassegrain telescope, as the name suggests, is a hybrid. It is the merging of two designs of telescope by a German optician (Schmidt) and a French optician (Cassegrain). To get a proper understanding of how the telescope works, it is best to have a look at the original designs from which it grew.

The Schmidt telescope, sometimes called the Schmidt camera, was designed in 1930 by Bernhard Schmidt to produce a wide, flat field of view. A photographic film was placed at the focal plane of a spherical mirror as this design of telescope was never meant for visual use. Because the mirror is spherical, it distorts the image and so the light entering the telescope has to be altered in such a way as to counteract this distortion introduced by the spherical mirror. This is done by something known as a 'corrector plate', a specially shaped window of glass that fits in the front aperture of the telescope.

The Cassegrain telescope, unlike the Newtonian, doesn't reflect the image to a focal point through the side of the tube, instead it reflects it back down towards the main or primary mirror and on through a small hole cut in the centre of this mirror to come to a focus behind the telescope tube.

The hybridised Schmidt-Cassegrain telescope was invented in 1940 by James Gilbert Baker and combines the spherical optics and corrector plate of the Schmidt camera with the Cassegrain's central hole in the primary mirror and the field-flattening effects of the secondary mirror to produce a visual and photographic-capable system that is compact and relatively inexpensive to produce. This has proved popular with amateur astronomers as it offers a telescope with a moderately long focal length which is good for lunar, planetary and much deep-sky viewing and imaging, all in a compact 'package'.

It was the commercial telescope manufacturer Celestron who helped to promote its popularity in the Sixties and Seventies by placing it on an easy-to-use fork mount. The American optical company Meade also quickly realised this telescope design's potential and so it set up the manufacture of a rival scope to Celestron, but with similar features. This proved beneficial for the would-be purchaser as the competition kept prices very keen and also prompted both companies to innovate ideas to enhance the user experience with their respective telescope offerings. This included computerised 'GoTo' systems and various optical and mechanical additions to both the telescope and the mount. Various-sized apertures were produced by both companies with a very popular eight-inch as the starting point, going up to a very substantial 16-inch aperture for the Meade products.

Because of the various aperture sizes, the good quality optics and the plethora of accessories for these telescopes as well as the easy adaptability of the scopes for both visual and imaging use, the Schmidt-Cassegrain has become a byword in amateur astronomical circles for versatility and affordability. Some of the best amateur astronomical photographs and images have been produced using these incredibly popular instruments.

Anatomy of a Schmidt-Cassegrain telescope

Secondary mirror
This mirror reflects the light from the primary mirror back down the tube to the focuser. Because of this the telescope is effectively 'concertinaed' up, producing a relatively short, compact tube.

Visual back
The hole at the back of the telescope is threaded to accept a variety of accessories including the eyepiece. Cameras can also be added using adaptors made for the purpose.

Spherical primary mirror
Unlike a Newtonian telescope, the Schmidt-Cassegrain primary mirror is made to a spherical curve. The aberration this produces can be easily corrected to give a good image.

Focus knob
In most commercially made Schmidt-Cassegrain telescopes the focuser knob turns a screw which moves the primary mirror up and down the tube to obtain good focus.

"The Schmidt-Cassegrain has become a byword for versatility and affordability"

Schmidt-Cassegrain telescopes often come with built-in computerised 'GoTo' systems

A great advanced option

Schmidt-Cassegrain telescopes have, for a long time, been the choice of both the serious beginner and the more advanced amateur astronomer. This is primarily because they have tended to be made in larger apertures and usually come with sophisticated computerised 'GOTO' systems allowing the telescope and therefore the observer to find and easily track thousands of different objects in the night sky. They are also very versatile and can be used both visually and with cameras very effectively. They also provide a moderately long focal length telescope in a compact tube. They do have fairly large secondary mirrors though, which increases the obstruction for the light in the aperture of the telescope. This can reduce contrast in the final image a little although it is often considered negligible compared to the advantages of the design. All in all, they make a good all-round telescope for the amateur astronomer at any level.

Telescope mounts

It's all very well having a telescope, but which is the best mount to use?

Mounting a scope

There are essentially only two ways to mount a telescope, either alt-azimuth or equatorially and each way has its pros and cons. If you are looking for a quick to set up and easy to use mount, then some form of alt-azimuth would probably suit you best. However, if time is an issue for you, avoid the more sophisticated instruments with computer drive systems as these can take a while to set up. Alt-azimuth mounts are not very well suited to any form of astro-imaging other than simple shots of the Moon, so here you'll need an equatorial mount. These tend to be much larger and heavier and require a lot more setting up. The advantages are that they can be used for long exposure astro-photography and even for visual observing you only need to guide the telescope around the one polar axis rather than in both altitude and azimuth.

Alt-azimuth

The simplest mount has the most complicated sounding name, which actually describes how this mount works. It has two axes of movement, the first is in altitude or up and down, the second is in azimuth. This is a circle describing 360° around the horizon taking the north cardinal point as 0° and south as 180°. The azimuth axis then simply allows for movement around in a circle parallel to the ground. Most camera tripods are in fact alt-azimuth mounts. You can find various types of alt-azimuth mounts, but their axes of movement will always be the same.

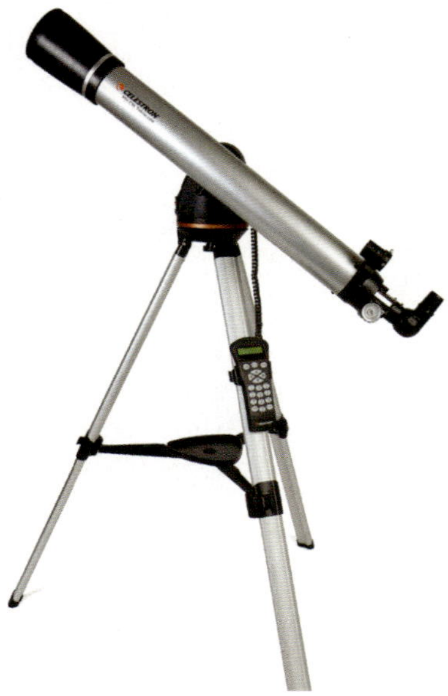

Dobsonian mount

Originally conceived by the American astronomer John Dobson, from who the mount gets its name, the Dobsonian is another form of alt-azimuth mount. The whole point of this type of mount is to provide a cheap, stable platform for larger telescopes and to have very smooth motion in both axes. This is achieved by using frictionless Teflon bearings so that the user can gently nudge their telescope without the object being studied flying off out of the field of view. This is a very popular mount due to it being inexpensive and a good DIY project for many amateurs.

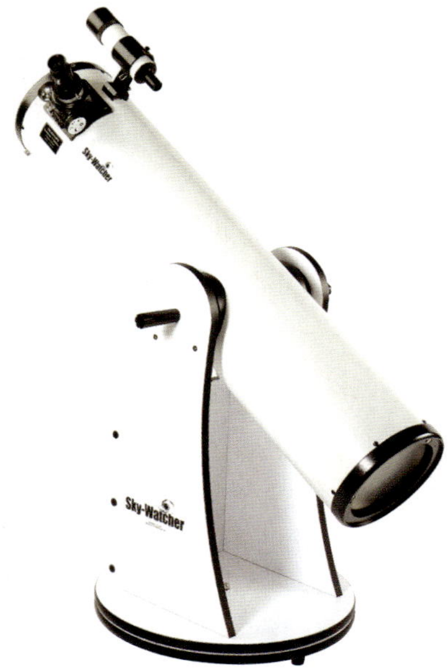

German equatorial mount

The German equatorial mount is the most common type of mount designed to allow one of the axes of the mount to be polar aligned. Looking a little like a letter T, the upright of the letter is the polar axis and is tilted to become parallel to the Earth's axis. This means that it is only necessary to track the telescope, which is positioned at the end of one of the arms of the T, around this polar axis to follow the path of the stars as they rise in the east and set in the west. Perfect for tracking a specific object in the sky.

Fork equatorial mount

Usually used with commercially produced Schmidt-Cassegrain and similar telescopes, the fork equatorial mount performs a similar function to the German equatorial mount in that it allows the telescope to be driven around the polar axis. In this case, the polar axis is formed by the fork itself; this looks like a letter U. The tilt of the axis is created by an equatorial wedge which usually can be added to an alt-azimuth fork mount as an accessory. This enables long exposure photography and imaging.

Alt-azimuth fork mount

Most commercially made Schmidt-Cassegrain and Maksutov-Cassegrain telescopes are supplied on an alt-azimuth fork mount. This describes where the telescope is slung between the tines of the fork of the mount. Where the telescope pivots is the altitude axis and the azimuth axis is provided by the rotating base. These instruments are usually provided with either electronic drives to both axes or computer systems which will allow the telescope to be set up to point to and track many thousands of objects in the night sky.

Single arm alt-azimuth mounts

This mount suits smaller refractor and catadioptric telescopes as the tube is attached to one arm as opposed to being slung between two. With small instruments this keeps the weight of the system down, making them portable. It is a type of mount favoured by the telescope manufacturer Celestron for its smaller range of instruments. They are motorised mounts and frequently supplied with a 'GOTO' computer tracking system, making them versatile and appealing as a family telescope.

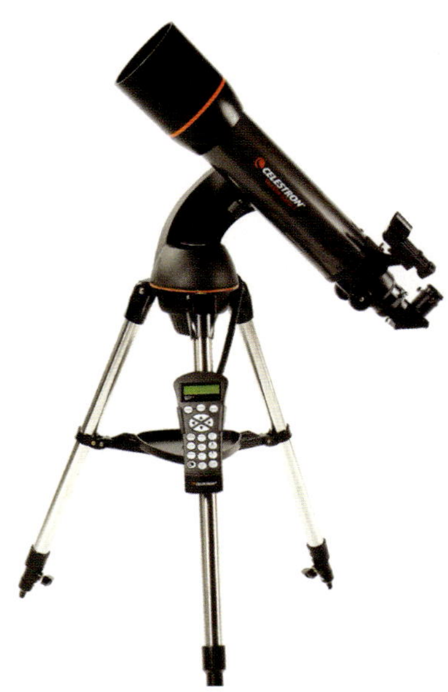

Set up a Dobsonian mount

Discover how to get up and running using one of the easiest mounts for beginners to start with

With plenty of stability yet having finger-touch, silky-smooth ease of movement, the Dobsonian mount provides one of the easiest and most enjoyable ways to point a telescope.

Back in the Sixties, a California-based amateur telescope manufacturer named John Dobson wanted to mount his Newtonian telescopes in a simple, inexpensive and user-friendly way. At the time, virtually every Newtonian telescope was mounted on a hefty German equatorial mount – these are neither cheap nor easy for a beginner to use, and they are also far from portable. Dobson's genius was to revisit an old idea – that of the simple altazimuth ('up-down') mount – and to construct it with easily obtained modern materials. Innovations included the use of Teflon and Formica for the load-bearing surfaces, materials which offer silk-smooth motion. Telescopes with this kind of plastic bearing have 'stiction' – they will only move while being pushed, and won't drift after pointing.

Dobson's design grew in popularity during the Sixties and Seventies, but by the Eighties they were becoming increasingly manufactured commercially. Today the Dobson-mounted Newtonian, the 'Dobsonian', is among the most popular of designs. They come in various sizes: diminutive four-inchers to 30-inch light buckets.

"The Dobsonian mount provides one of the easiest and most enjoyable ways to point a telescope"

01 Choose a spot

Although Dobsonians have a fairly small 'footprint' in comparison with a sprawling tripod, their wooden ground boards are flat with small corner feet, so they need a fairly solid, dry and level surface upon which to rest.

02 Get the balance right

Make sure that the telescope balances with the accessories you intend to use. A heavy eyepiece or digital camera may need to be counterbalanced at the other end of the tube.

03 Align the mirrors (collimation)

Moving a telescope can cause it to become misaligned, so check your telescope's collimation before observing. This is best done in the light. Finderscopes and reflex finders also need to be checked while in the field.

04 Adjust the tension

Many Dobsonians have an altitude or azimuth clutch, which changes the amount of pushing or pulling pressure required to point the telescope. Adjust the clutch tension to follow objects with the least amount of effort.

05 Take care with heights

Viewing through some telescopes can get you on a high – quite literally! Getting to the eyepiece of a big Dobsonian when it's pointed high in the sky may require climbing steps – so make sure they are safe and secure.

06 Point effectively

In terms of ease of pointing, Dobsonians are at their least effective when they are aimed at objects near the zenith. This area, directly above the observer, is often called 'Dobson's hole'.

Learn to set up an equatorial mount

The Earth's rotation can be a headache for astronomers, but an equatorial mount is the cure

Since its creation in the early 19th Century, the German equatorial mount (GEM) has helped astronomers achieve perfectly steady tracking, even at high magnifications. Whether it's for following a planet single-handedly while at the eyepiece, or capturing pinpoint stars in long-exposure photographs of the universe, there's no denying that the GEM platform is the most accurate and rewarding basis for an amateur observatory today. It's not without its drawbacks, though. When considering the relatively heavy bulk and complicated set-up procedure associated with these mounts, the prospect of buying a full-size GEM can be daunting for the casual observer, and imagers will need to take several time-consuming steps to ensure they get best results in really deep photographs. Still, the appeal of mirroring the Earth's rotation with a purely mechanical device holds strong, even among first-time buyers, and perhaps a large part of this is down to the sheer classical beauty of an equatorially mounted telescope on its tripod. With today's designs, it needn't be scary for the beginner. After all, the setup is the only part that requires practice; once that's out of the way, the intuitiveness of the GEM shines through.

"The GEM platform is the most accurate and rewarding basis for an amateur observatory today"

01 Assemble the mount

Start by assembling the mount head and counterweight shaft on top of the tripod. Make sure the central bolt is securely attached through the top of the tripod. Some mounts require you to loosen this bolt to rotate the head.

02 Adjust the weight

If your mount doesn't have a polarscope, you'll need to put your weight on first, then the telescope. Tighten the Declination axis and loosen the Right Ascension. Adjust the position of the weight until the two are balanced.

03 Hunt for the pole

Now find the celestial pole. In the northern hemisphere, Polaris is close to the pole. In the southern hemisphere, the pole lies in the constellation of Octans. Familiarise yourself using a star chart.

04 Set the axis

Use the latitude bolt on your mount to 'prop up' the polar axis to your local latitude. Then, sighting along the mount, set this axis to point north or south, depending on your hemisphere.

05 Zero-in

Centre your telescope on the pole with RA and Dec locked. If you have a polarscope, rotate its reticule to match the sky's orientation, and set Polaris in the right spot by using the latitude and bearing axis of your mount.

06 Swap the axes

With Polaris in the right spot, your mount is aligned. Now you just need to lock the latitude and bearing axis and unlock your RA and Dec. Using the RA slow-motion handle, you can now smoothly track the sky single-handedly!

Eyepieces

You can't look through a telescope without an eyepiece. Let's get familiar with the different types

"The higher power eyepieces work well for lunar and planetary viewing"

Kellner

One of the simplest designs of eyepiece, the Kellner has been around since 1846 and is still a useful lens. This is an achromat lens, which means that it's designed to correct any false colours caused by refraction or bending of light in the eyepiece. Because they are relatively inexpensive, Kellners are often included with starter telescope kits. Although they can vary in quality, they are still a useful eyepiece.

Orthoscopic

The orthoscopic design of eyepiece was invented in 1880 by Ernst Abbe and gives a near distortion-free image. It uses four elements of glass, three of which are cemented together. Although considered old fashioned and harder to find, the orthoscopic is still a useful design of eyepiece for the amateur astronomer. They make very good lenses for observing planets, partly due to their clarity and relatively narrow field of view.

Plössl

Plössls used to be regarded as one of the best design of telescope eyepiece available. They are often now included in commercial telescope kits. The design uses two sets of identical lenses and is sometimes known as a symmetrical eyepiece. Plössls give a reasonably large, flat field of view. They can of course vary in quality; but the chances are that you'll keep the best ones, even though you might change your telescope.

Wide-Angle

The talented optical designer Al Nagler, who started the company known as Tele Vue in the USA, introduced his concept for a wide-angle telescope eyepiece in 1992. It was a big hit, due to its outstanding quality and the impressive vistas it offered. A number brands including Celestron produce equivalents as it's an excellent eyepiece for low power, deep sky viewing. As you might expect, they are not inexpensive.

Long Eye Relief

Another cleverly designed eyepiece from Al Nagler, the Radian series was made for spectacle wearers! Other brands have created similar eyepieces that provide 'long eye relief', meaning you can use them comfortably without having to take off your glasses. They have quite a wide field of view and the higher power eyepieces are good for lunar and planetary viewing; a great benefit if you need to use your glasses all the time.

Nagler-style

With a breathtakingly wide field of view, Al Nagler gave these superb lenses his own name. With a superb 82° apparent field of view, this range is beloved of serious deep-sky observers. These have a price you would expect of the very best optics. There are several other companies who have emulated the design (like Luminos). As optical technology moves on, there are even wider-field eyepieces coming onto the market.

■ Telescopes are also available in a binocular variety, as is the case with this Vixen BT81S-A

Choosing the right binoculars

Binoculars come in all shapes and sizes, so which ones are best for astronomy?

There are lots of different types and makes of binoculars on the market, some sold as being good for sports or general purpose and some have special coatings or other features designed to persuade you to buy them. When it comes to using them for viewing objects in the night sky however, what are the best ones to use and what do those features actually mean?

Binoculars are essentially two refractor telescopes bolted together. To make the tubes shorter, prisms are used internally to fold up the light path. There are two types of prisms which are used in binoculars; roof prisms, which mean that the binoculars tend to have straight, short tubes, (most compact binoculars use this type) and porro-prisms, used mostly in what are called field glasses. It's the latter type which are generally best for astronomy, often because they are used in instruments with larger objective lenses; that's the lens at the front. This isn't to say that you can't use binoculars with roof prisms for astronomy; it's just that the porro-prism type tend to be a better size.

Binoculars are described using two numbers, for example 10x50. This is a type of shorthand describing the magnification as being 10x and the diameter of the front lenses being 50mm. It's this objective lens diameter which is the most important, as this governs the amount of light entering your binoculars, in other words how faint and well resolved the objects you'll look at will be. Interestingly enough, the magnification is less important. Any binoculars with an objective lens diameter of less than 40mm will not show objects particularly well; much larger and they will be heavy and difficult to hand hold. Likewise, too high a magnification will also make them difficult to hand hold and the image too faint. For example, 16x50s will also magnify your handshake 16x! Ideally you should use binoculars rated at 7x50 or 10x50 as these will be the easiest to hand hold and give you enough aperture to show you hundreds of objects in the night sky.

Binoculars explained

"It's this objective lens diameter which is the most important..."

■ A good quality pair of binoculars can last a lifetime, so keep those lenses capped and scratch-free when you're not using them

The benefits of binoculars

Compact binoculars are often too small to be useful for observing the night sky. The front lenses need to be at least 40mm in aperture. The quality of the optics is important too. Better quality lenses and coatings will let through more light and therefore you'll get a brighter, sharper image. Of course this comes at a price.

Binoculars using porro-prisms usually have larger objective lenses although they can vary in quality considerably. Using 7x50 or 10x50 binoculars will normally give you the best results as these don't magnify your hand shake too much and give you a reasonably wide field of view, important when you are trying to find objects in the sky. One of the many benefits of using binoculars is the upright image, the same as your naked eyes would see, and because the lenses are so much bigger than your eyes you will see thousands of objects that you can't without them.

Astronomy basics

©SPL

©NASA

©NASA

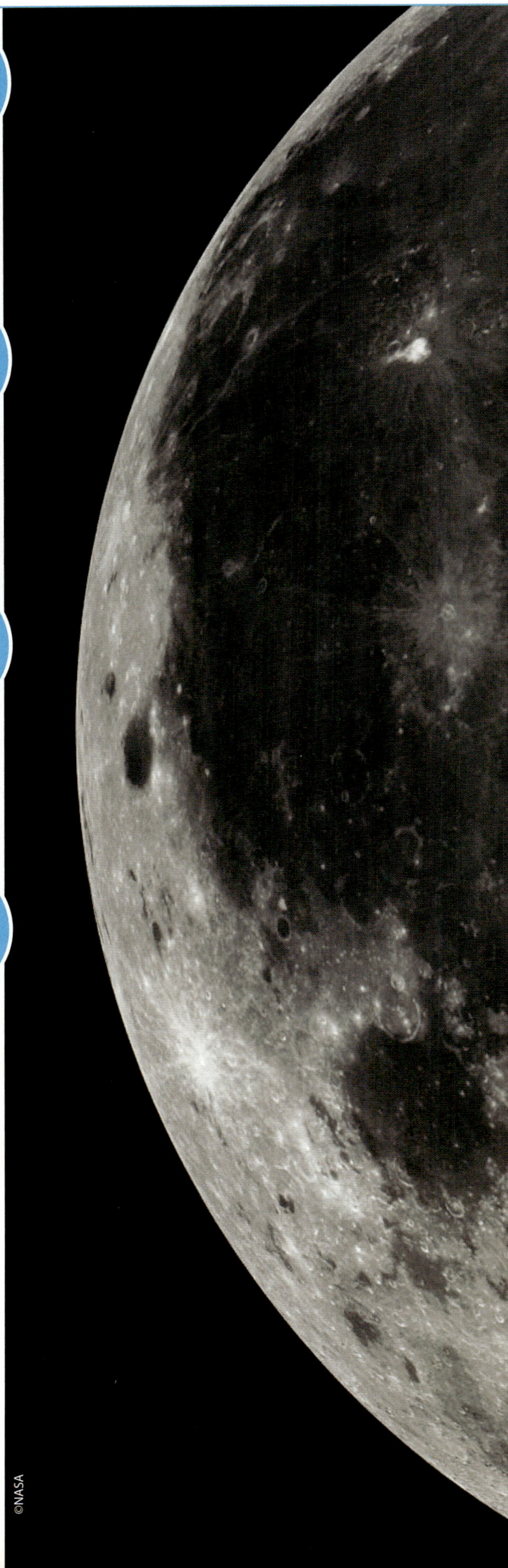
©NASA

"Mastering the basics will help you see more, and develop the knowledge you need to have the confidence to take things to the next level"

48
The Moon up close

Using a sky chart

How to find your way around a map of the stars

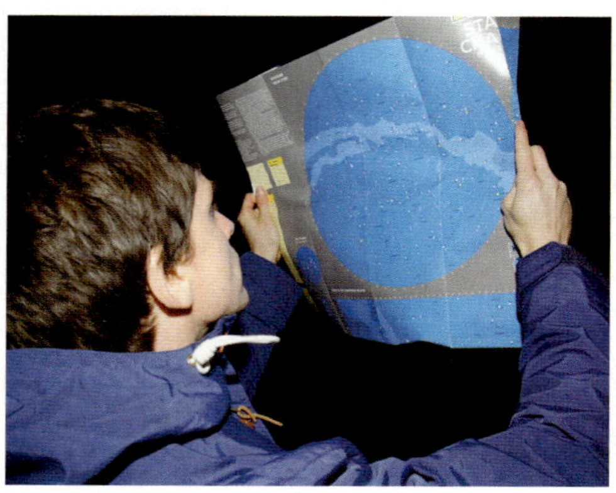

01 Find your way

In the northern hemisphere hold the chart above your head pointing south, and vice versa for the southern hemisphere. Orientate the chart with the compass points and use a red light to view it.

02 Track the sky

You'll be familiar with constellations after a few nights. To find planets, learn where the ecliptic line is. All the planets, and the Moon, sit close to this line, so you'll be able to find them here.

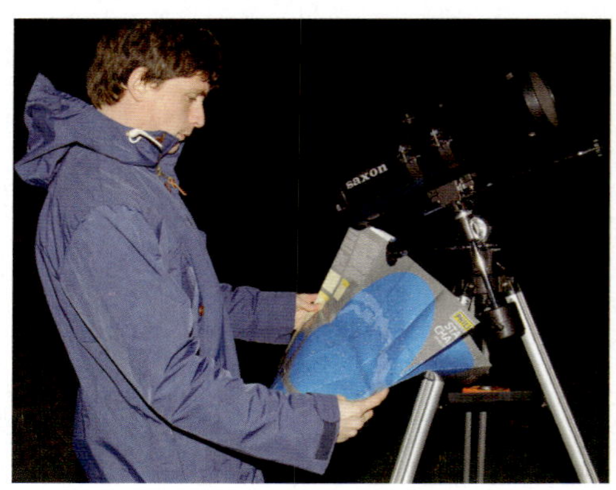

03 Star hopping

Once you've mastered the basics, you can use the star hopping technique to find more objects in the sky. Find a bright star and use it as a reference to locate dimmer deep sky objects nearby.

Navigate the night sky

Use celestial co-ordinates to find your way around the night sky

Modern astronomy can seem a world apart from that of just a few decades ago. While the ultimate goal might be the same, the methods through which celestial objects are observed have changed somewhat drastically. Many have replaced the instruments and tools an astronomer would once require to traverse the night sky with computerised equipment that instantly locates an object.

This, of course, isn't necessarily a bad thing. Making astronomy easier and opening it up to a wider audience is a great way to get more people involved in a fantastic hobby. Some, however, prefer the halcyon days of declinations and coordinates, so let's take a look at just how you can navigate the night sky without some fancy new software.

Astronomy revolves around the celestial co-ordinate system, devised millennia ago when our understanding of the universe was much less than it is now. Earth is defined to be at the centre of a celestial sphere that rotates, with stars and planets occupying positions on the sphere at a given time much like terrestrial longitude and latitude lines.

This sphere appears to rotate daily (in actuality it is Earth that is rotating), and so objects change their position. Depending on your location on Earth, you will be standing on a different declination line, sort of like latitude. At Earth's equator you are at 0° declination, while at the North Pole you are at a declination of +90° (and vice versa for the South Pole).

Declination is broken down into arcminutes (there are 60 in one degree, denoted as 60') and arcseconds (60 in one arcminute, written as 60"). Polaris, for example, was found at a declination of +89° 19'8".

Similarly, right ascension is used to measure the effective longitude of a particular star. Right ascension is measured in hours from 0 to 24, with one hour corresponding to 15 degrees of the circle that is the spherical night sky. It is broken down in units of time, rather than arcs or degrees, and written as hours, minutes and seconds. So, for example, you may see an object written as having a right ascension of 18h 36m 56.3s.

The right ascension and declination are the same for any observer anywhere on Earth, as they use Earth's north and south celestial poles as orientation. By using both, you will be able to find the location of almost any celestial object in the night sky.

What is a planisphere?

A planisphere is a star chart that can be rotated to show the positions of stars at any time and date of the year. As the Earth rotates, and the whole sky is not always available for viewing, you can rotate the viewable 'window' of a planisphere to a particular time and date to show you what you can currently see in the night sky. They are a useful tool for astronomers who want to identify objects quickly and easily.

A planisphere will give you the right ascension and declination for objects in the night sky

To perform astronomy without computerised equipment you'll want to get to grips with the celestial coordinate system

Learn to star hop

If you've ever wanted to know how to find your way around the night sky with binoculars or a telescope, here's a straightforward method

Determine your field of view for star hopping

Finding your way around the sky when you are looking through binoculars or a telescope can be a nightmare, as you are looking at a very small part of the sky. If you're searching for a particular object, a star cluster for example, it can seem nigh on impossible. But if you use a traditional method and are systematic in your approach, you'll soon discover you can find your targets easily and have fun on the way.

Before the advent of computerised 'goto' systems on telescopes, astronomers had to find interesting objects to look at the hard way. It didn't take them long to work out that by using a simple system it was possible to do this reliably every time. It's known as star hopping, literally hopping from one view to an adjacent view to track down a desired object. In order to use it, you'll need to get to grips with a couple of things and have some equipment to hand.

First of all you'll need a star chart, preferably one which shows stars and objects clearly and accurately. There are several of these available which should fit the bill, or alternatively you may have some software from which you can print star charts. You'll also need a red light torch so you can read the chart in the dark.

You'll then need to know the field of view of your binoculars or the finder scope of your telescope. Some binoculars will have this written on them, for example 'seven-degree' field' or something similar. A telescope is unlikely to tell you this. To work out the field of view of your scope or binoculars, you can divide the magnification into the aperture. Equipment with a 10x50 scope will give a field of view of five degrees. The finder scope has a much larger field of view than your main telescope, so to give yourself a helping hand still further, always start with the lowest magnification eyepiece you have. This will give you the largest field of view once you have acquired your target in the finder scope.

It can be helpful to create a field of view template to use with your star chart. You can do this with just a few square centimetres of clear plastic and by using a drawing compass and felt tip pen. The quick method here is to find a star on your chart and centre it as carefully as you can in the field of view of your binoculars or finder scope. Next check the stars at the edge of the field of view and relate them to the stars on your chart. Draw a circle on the clear plastic with the compass point on the star in the middle of the field of view. Make this wide enough to just encircle the stars which you can see at the edge of the field. Don't forget that most finder scopes invert the image. To find a target, start with a bright or easily recognisable star in the middle of the field of view. Note the stars at the edge of the field heading towards your quarry. Move the scope so that the stars at that edge of the field are now seen near the other. Keep heading towards your target by doing this until you find it. You're likely to find lots of other interesting things to look at on your journey.

"Before computerised systems, astronomers had to find interesting objects to look at the hard way"

Use the star hop technique to embark on a voyage to the Andromeda Galaxy

©NASA

Star hop to the Andromeda Galaxy

1. Your jumping off point
Centre a known nearby star in the field of view, in this case Alpha Andromeda or Alpheratz.

2. First hop
Move one field of view along the northern 'arm' of Andromeda. Make a mental note of any patterns of stars as you go.

3. Halfway there
Hop another field of view. If you get lost backtrack to the pattern of stars in the previous field and try again.

4. Almost there
Hop once more, check your star chart and centre the brightest star in the field of view.

5. You're there!
As you move towards your quarry, you will see a misty patch of light coming into view. Congratulations, you have now made it to the Andromeda Galaxy!

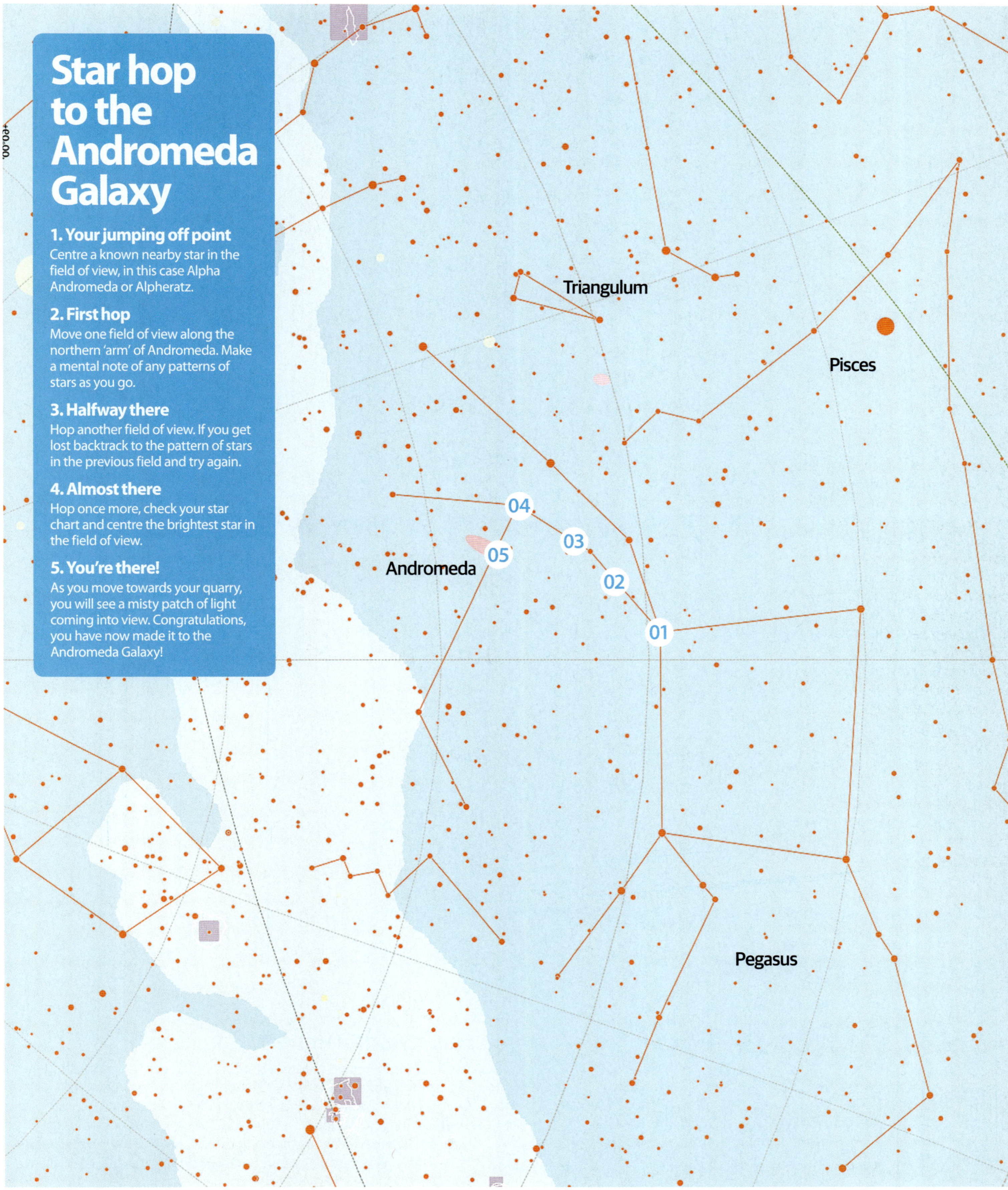

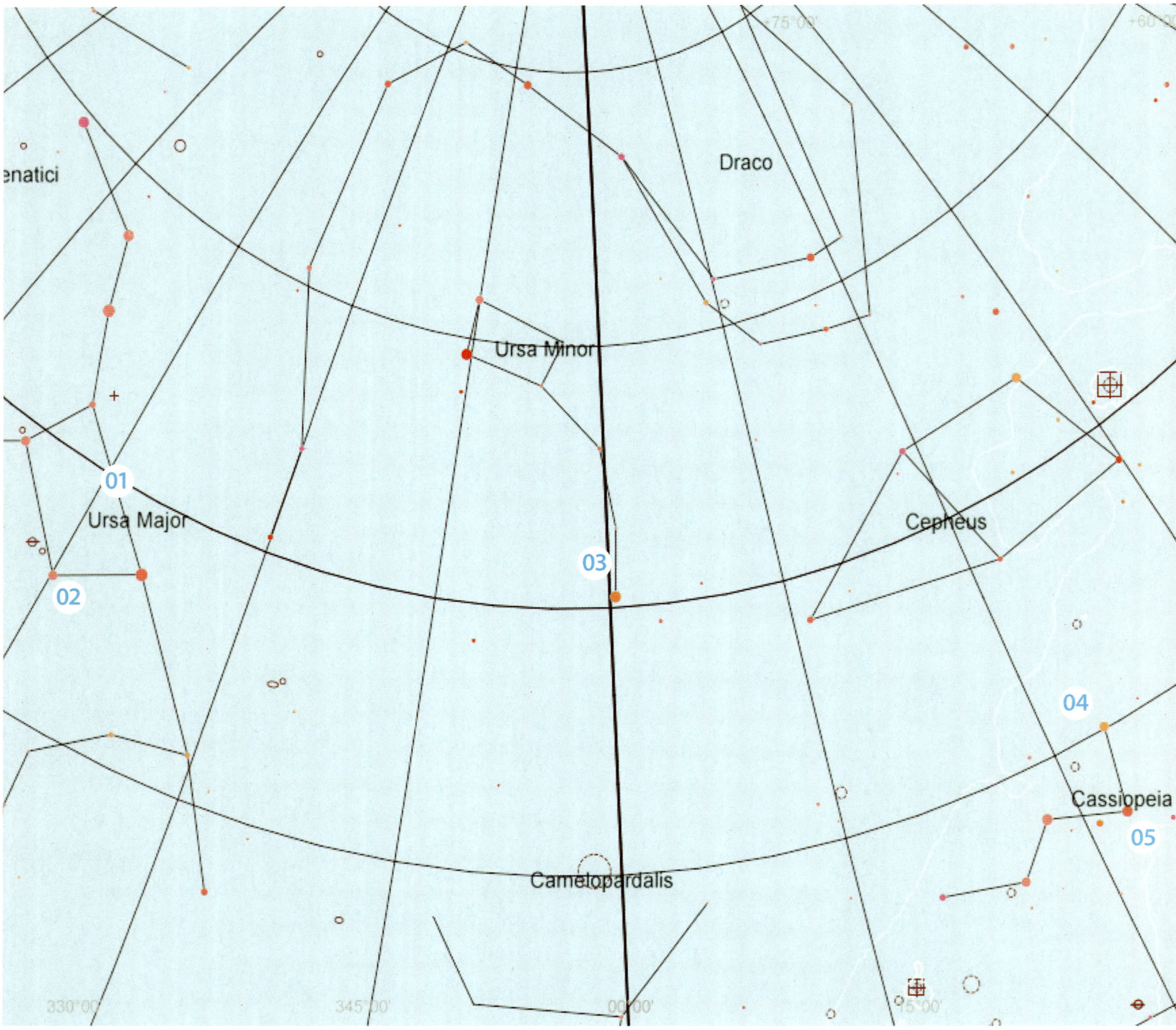

A quick hop to Cassiopeia

1. Starting position
Locate the Big Dipper, made up of the seven brightest stars in Ursa Major. The bowl shape at the end is what we're interested in.

2. First, to the North Star
Follow the line of the two stars that make the lip of the bowl past the big dipper. This should get you straight to Polaris, the North Star.

3. Ursa Minor
Polaris is part of Ursa Minor, which looks like a mirrored, small dipper. Trace the constellation to make sure you're in the right spot.

4. Carry on
Continue with the line you made to Polaris to reach the edge of Cassiopeia in about the same distance.

5. Cassiopeia
Cassiopeia has a distinctive 'W' shape. Make sure to trace the constellation again, to confirm where you are.

> "Starhopping is a great way to get to know what you're looking for with the naked eye"

Basic starhopping to Cassiopeia

Starhopping between constellations is a great way to not only find them, but also to get to know what you're looking for when you go out with the naked eye. Be careful if you're doing it through a telescope with an inverted image though, as the guide images may look a lot different to how you'll perceive the sky. At the very least, each of the constellations have a fairly recognisable pattern, so it will be good practice for when you want to find something a bit trickier.

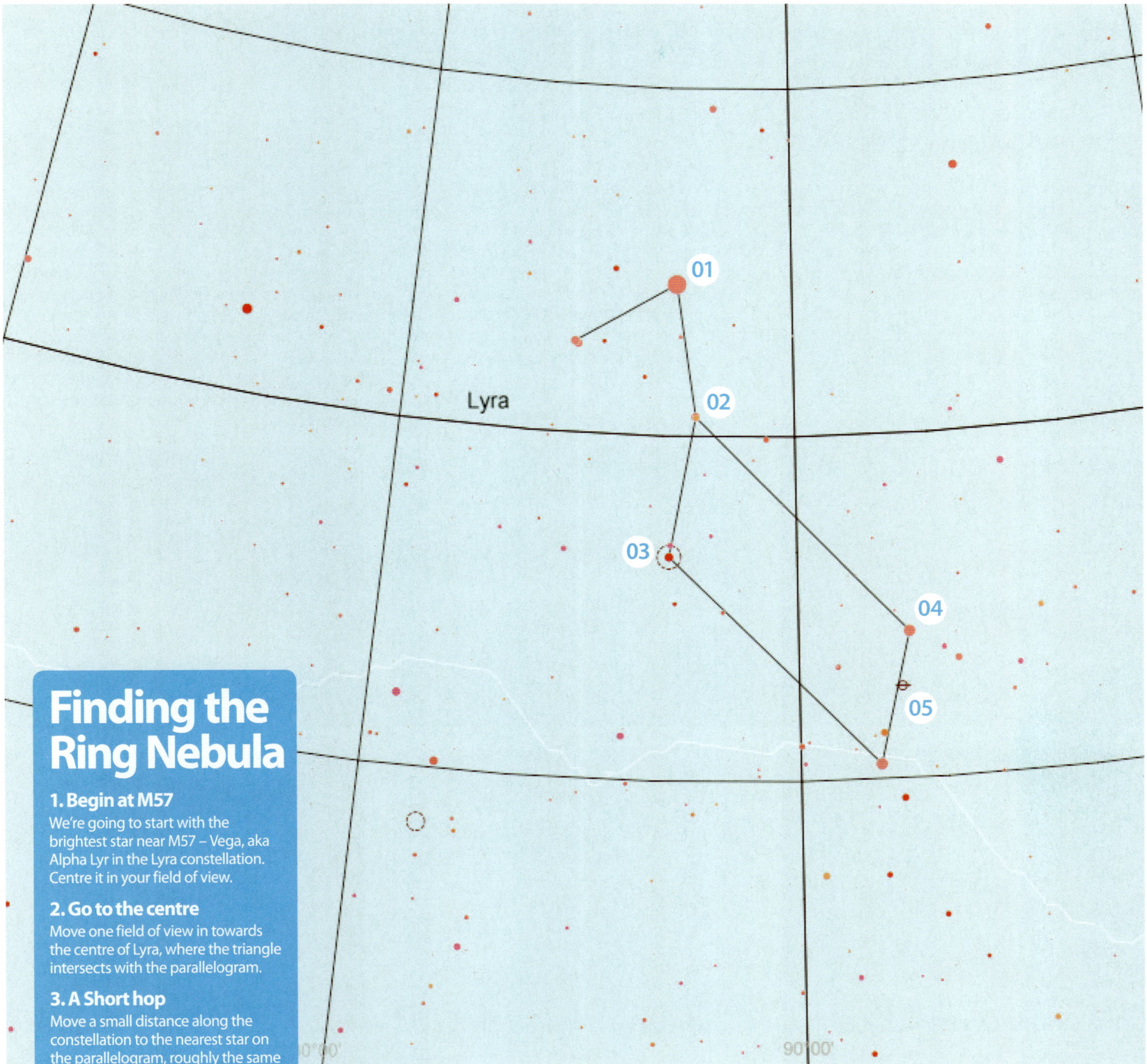

Finding the Ring Nebula

1. Begin at M57
We're going to start with the brightest star near M57 – Vega, aka Alpha Lyr in the Lyra constellation. Centre it in your field of view.

2. Go to the centre
Move one field of view in towards the centre of Lyra, where the triangle intersects with the parallelogram.

3. A Short hop
Move a small distance along the constellation to the nearest star on the parallelogram, roughly the same direction we moved from Vega.

4. Cross Lyra
Now take a right-angled turn counter-clockwise and cut across Lyra to hop to two stars on the other side of the parallelogram.

5. Between the stars
Between these two stars is the Ring Nebula. Centre your view finder between them, and search slightly up and down the line for the blue and violet cloud.

Locating Andromeda

The Andromeda galaxy is one of the brightest objects in the night sky, and our galactic neighbour. Finding it is easy if you know how. Start by centering on Alpha Andromeda, aka Alpheratz, then make a field of view hop along the northern arm of Andromeda. Make two more hops, and then centre on the brightest star in the field of view. Take another hop along the arm coming off the one you're on, and look out for the misty patch that signifies Andromeda.

Starhopping to the Ring Nebula

The Ring Nebula is one of the most interesting sights in the night sky, and due to the brightness of Vega, one that is easy to locate if you know the right star-hopping pattern. The Ring Nebula itself is a planetary nebula 2,300 light years away, and about as large as Jupiter in the sky, albeit slightly less bright. Its size makes it fairly easy to spot once you're looking for it, and through a telescope you'll be able to see the same kind of colours as produced from Hubble photos.

Measuring magnitudes

Celestial objects have varying levels of brightness – just how is that measured, and what does it mean for you?

In astronomy, you'll usually hear terms relating to how bright a cosmic body is in the night sky. The Moon is the brightest object in the night sky, and the ISS surpassed Venus as the second brightest object in 2009 when its solar panel array was completed. This brightness, while a good gauge for the naked eye, doesn't go far enough for serious study, which is where the magnitude scale comes in. Allowing for a more accurate reading of brightness, the apparent magnitude of a star measures the brightness of an object in the visible spectrum as if there was no atmosphere.

The scale is not straightforward, though. Not only does a lower number indicate a higher brightness, five points on the scale is equivalent to a difference of 100 times the brightness. The Sun, for example, is measured at about -27 magnitudes, while the Moon is -13 when it's full. Venus, the brightest planet in the night sky, is -4.9 at its most visible. Zero on the scale is usually described as Vega, and most of the brightest stars are around this number, with Sirius rated at -1.4 as the brightest star in the sky.

All of which is very interesting, but how do the magnitudes relate to you? Well, they can be used as a guide to figure out what kind of equipment you'll need to view them while star gazing. With the naked eye, you can make out around 8,500 stars, with good eyes able to pick up stars with as little as +6 magnitude. Between the range of +6 and +8, you'll need to use binoculars to properly make out Neptune, some nebula and brighter deep sky objects. Going even further, amateur telescopes will be able to pick up objects with a minimum brightness of about +11, allowing for better clarity of other deep sky objects, but just not strong enough to pick up Pluto.

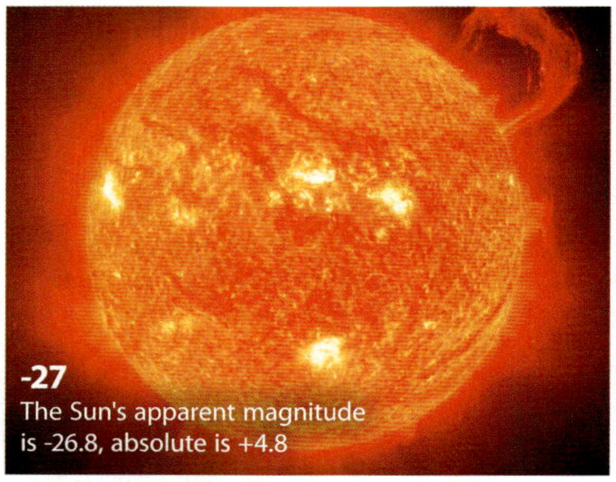
-27
The Sun's apparent magnitude is -26.8, absolute is +4.8

-2.9
Jupiter at its brightest and closest to the Earth

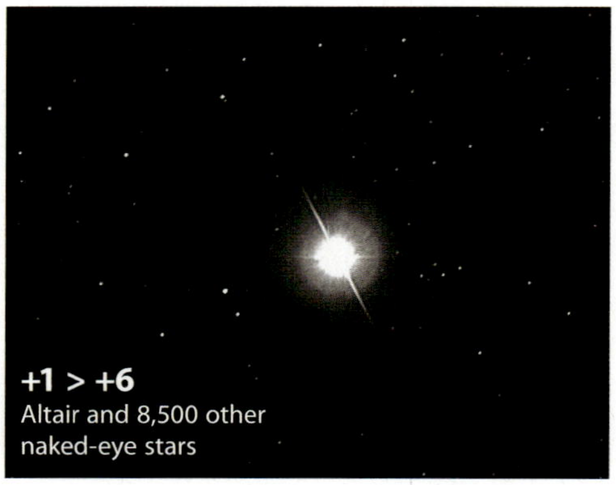
+1 > +6
Altair and 8,500 other naked-eye stars

-13
This magnitude is for when the Moon is full

-1.4
Sirius, the brightest star in the night sky visible from Earth

+6 > +8
Dark nebula and other bright deep-sky objects (binoculars)

-4.9
Venus is at its brightest during its crescent phase

0 > +1
Canopus and the 14 brightest stars in the sky

+6 > +11
Bright deep-sky objects (amateur telescopes)

Your first night: what to do

Top tips for your first foray into the field

On stepping from a well-lit room to your spot under the stars, you might notice that you can't see much at first. The stars that you do see are the brightest and so your eyes do not need to adjust very much to collect light from them. The faintest, on the other hand, stay hidden until your pupils adapt to night vision. This can be a problem especially when you want to look at a star map or a planisphere and using a dazzling torch can be more of a hinderance than a help! Your eyes react to white light more than red light, so whether you're hunting for your ideal telescope, binoculars or are just planning on unaided observing, add a red light torch to your shopping list. You can pick them up from many astronomy instrument dealers.

To get the best views possible, you need to take care where you place your telescope. A stable surface is essential, so that rules out bumpy lawns. Concrete provides a stable surface but it also retains heat that has built up during the day and, as a result, this warmth is emitted at night – this creates air currents that can cause shimmering images through your telescope. Remember if kept indoors before use, your telescope also needs a good half an hour to cool down to the ambient temperature outdoors.

Pick a spot with a good southern view. The 23 degree tilt of the Earth means that more can be seen towards the south than the north from UK latitudes. Have an idea of what you want to view before you go outside – this will help direct your evening's observing and if you have taken the time to print off sky charts or find charts in books or magazines like this one, it will speed things up.

Don't expect too much from your first night. Forget notions of seeing things like what the Hubble Space Telescope sees through your telescope – there's a reason why deep sky objects like galaxies and nebulas are called faint fuzzies. However, there are things you can do to make these faint objects seem more visible. A clever tactic is to use something called averted vision. In your eye, there are two different types of receptor – one type being the cone cells, which are concentrated mostly in the middle of your eye and give you colour vision, whereas the other are rod cells, which are on the periphery of your eye and are more light sensitive than cones, providing you with night vision. When looking at a faint object through the telescope eyepiece, if you just look off to one side of the object through the eyepiece while keeping the object on the periphery of your vision, it will appear brighter because the rod cells around the outside of your eye are more sensitive to the dim light of the object.

Experiment with the magnification on various eyepieces – you will find that different magnifications work better on different objects. Try out different filters: an Oxygen III filter is often called a 'nebula filter' as it blocks out all the light except for that wavelength of light emitted by oxygen atoms. It can also double up as a light pollution filter, blocking that annoying light blight you may encounter in an observing session!

> "If kept indoors before use, your telescope will need a good half an hour to cool down to the ambient temperature outdoors"

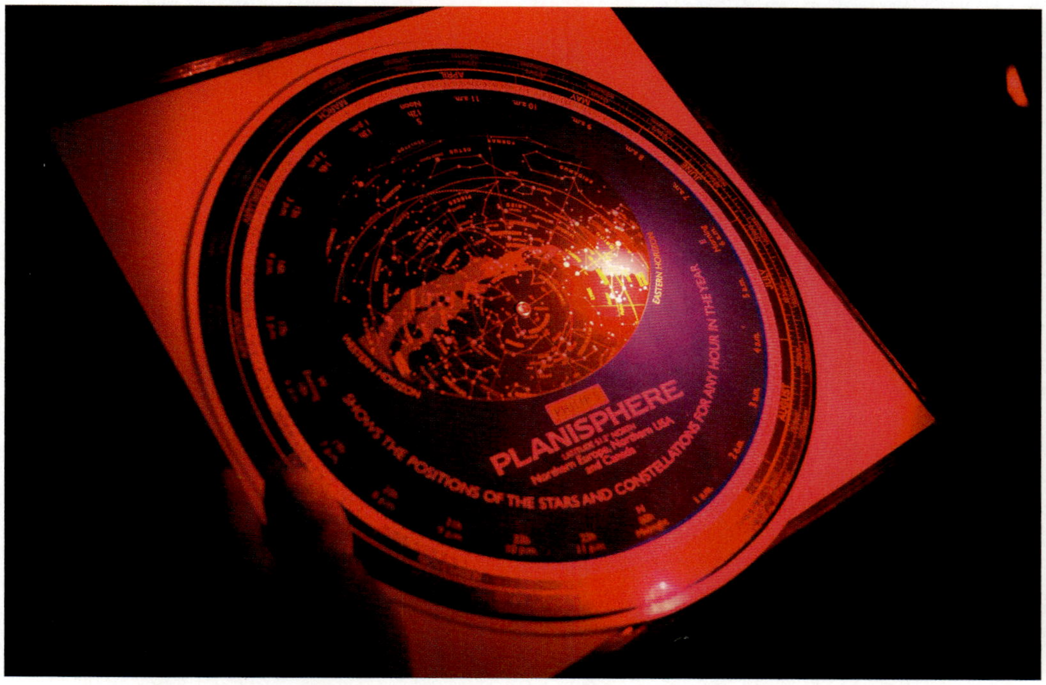

More can be seen towards the south in the UK latitudes

Use your peripheral vision when observing dim objects

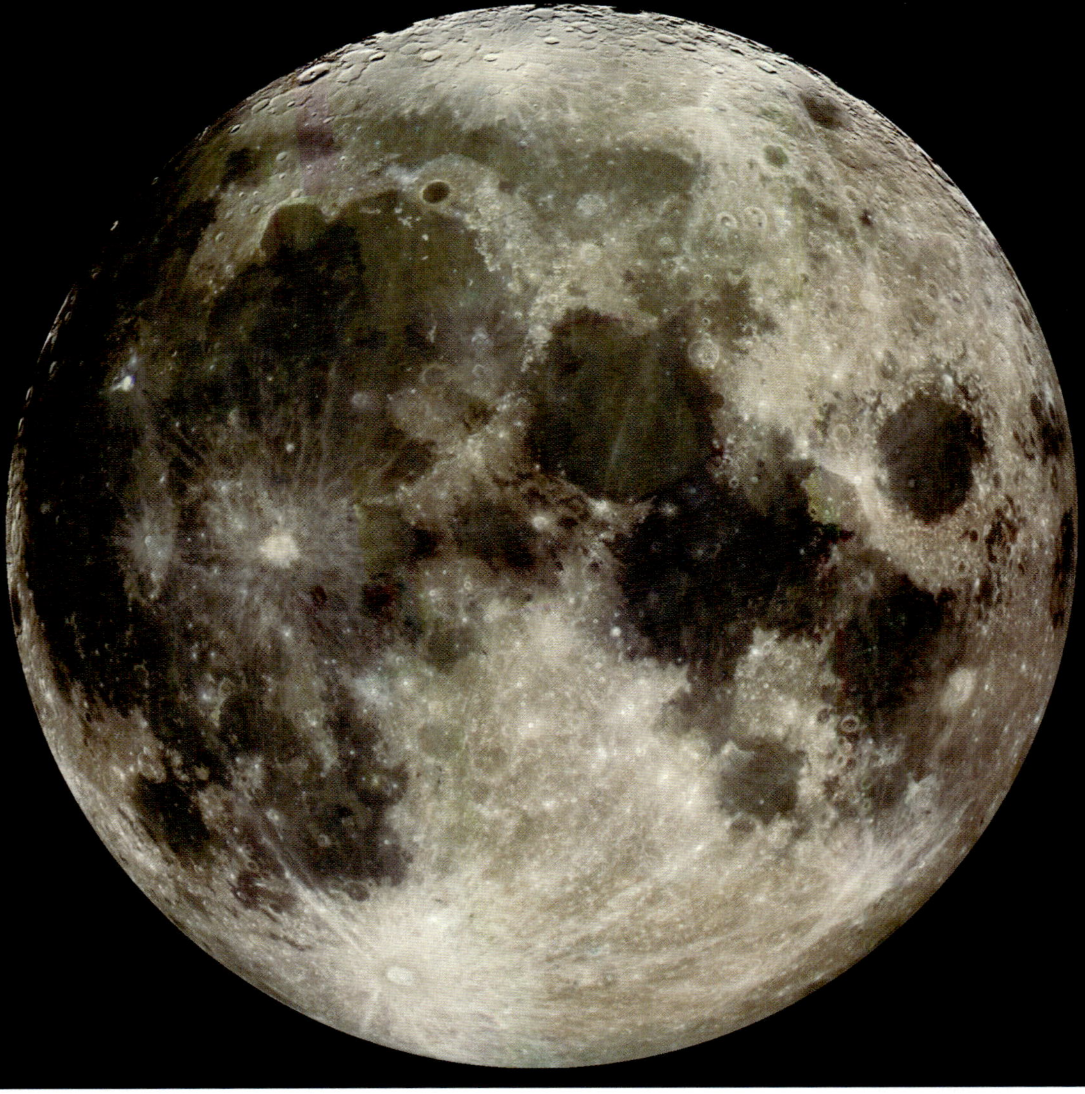

©NASA

Discover how to view the Moon

Find out how to get the best out of your views of the Moon whether using your eyes, binoculars or a telescope…

The Moon is an object with which we are all familiar; however there are ways to observe it that will make your time spent looking at it more worthwhile.

Everyone has noticed the phases that the Moon passes through – from the thinnest sliver to a bright 'full Moon' – but when and where can we see these phases and what sort of view can we expect to get when viewing the Moon through binoculars or even a telescope?

The starting point for the cycle of the Moon's phases is when it's 'new', that is to say when we can't see it as it's between us and the Sun. As it moves along its orbit around the Earth the phase increases as the sunlight illuminates more and more of the disc and it can be seen later in the evening. It's fun to try to see the Moon when it is only a few hours old, just after the Sun has set below the horizon. Once the Moon is one day old it is easier to see and over the next few evenings you'll also perhaps notice another phenomenon that's easy to pick up with just your naked eyes called 'Earthshine'. This is where the part of the disc of the Moon which isn't illuminated by the Sun is still visible, glowing faintly due to light being reflected off the Earth onto the Moon and then back to us again. This is sometimes known as the 'old Moon in the new Moon's arms'. If you've got binoculars or a small telescope turn them on to the Moon and notice that all of a sudden you can see features which weren't easy to spot with just your eyes. Darker and lighter areas suddenly stand out and you will almost certainly see some craters. You'll notice there are shadows cast by the mountains and crater walls which make these features really stand out and look three dimensional.

As the Moon phase increases you will be able to see more of the surface and the so-called 'seas', properly termed Mare (pronounced ma-ray from Latin meaning 'sea'), stand out as darker regions of the surface. Run your gaze around the edge of the Moon and you'll spot it isn't smooth but broken up with the jagged edges of mountains. Take a look at the terminator line, the division between the light and unlit area of the surface, as this is where you can see the longest shadows and some of the most interesting lighting effects. Crater walls cast long shadows where peaks can catch the sunlight. You could even have a go at taking pictures. You can point a camera into the eyepiece of your telescope and see what you get, but if you want to do it more seriously, then you will need a DSLR camera and telescope adaptor, or 'webcam' to image the surface. The results of this can be spectacular.

> "Gaze around the edge and you'll spot the jagged sides of mountains"

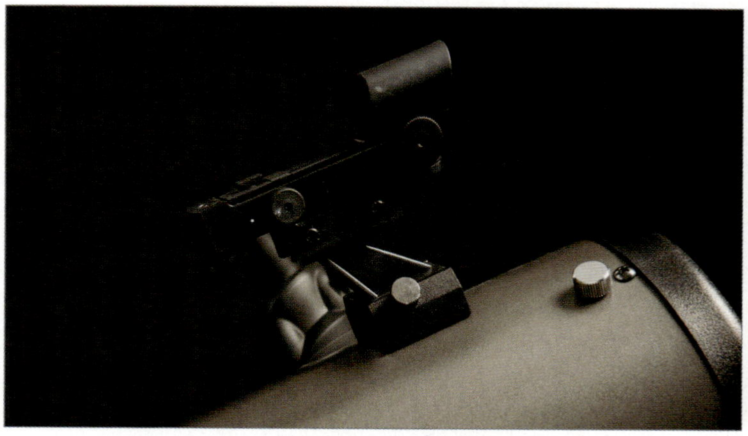

01 Align your finderscope

Make sure the finderscope on your telescope is aligned with the main scope. This will help you more easily find the Moon in the eyepiece and also 'zero in' on interesting parts of the surface.

02 Improve your disc viewing

Use a low-power eyepiece to start with for your observations. This will help you see the whole disc and orientate yourself with the view. You can increase the magnification later.

03 Reduce glare

A Moon filter is really helpful to dim down the brightness of the Moon, especially when it is near 'full'. This is a grey (neutral density) filter which screws into the telescope's eyepiece.

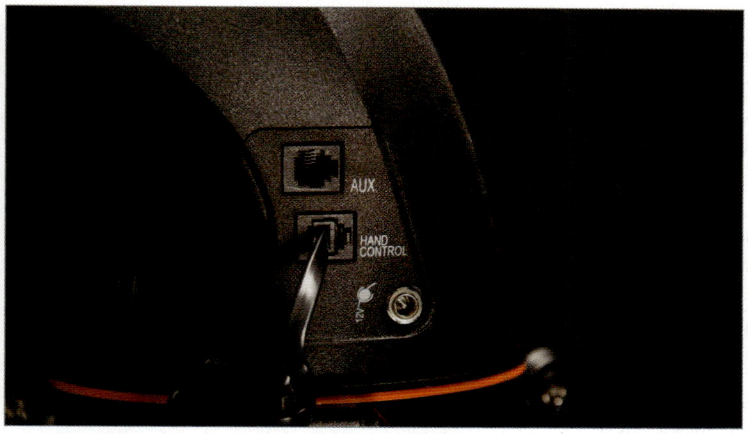

04 Use your motor drive

If your telescope has a motor drive, make sure that you have it switched on. The Moon will appear to move swiftly across the field of view and especially at higher magnifications.

05 Find the terminator

Direct your scope on to the 'terminator', the line dividing the light and dark areas of the Moon. This is the most interesting place to look. Look out for sunlight catching crater rims and mountains.

06 Locate the lunar highlands

Another very interesting area to explore with your telescope is the 'highlands', especially in the northern and southern regions, as they show up well due to shadows, even near full Moon.

8 great sights to see on your first night

01 The Andromeda Galaxy (M31)

The Andromeda Galaxy is the nearest spiral galaxy to the Milky Way.

02 The Moon

One of the most popular destinations for both amateur and experienced astronomers, the Moon has always been an object of fascination in the night sky. A good telescope will allow you to view some of its fantastic craters and features, such as the Sea of Tranquility in the east where Apollo 11 made its landing. Even binoculars or just the naked eye will allow you to observe some of its crisper features on a clear night. Make sure you have a chart of the phases of the Moon, however, so that you can plan for a Full Moon, when the lunar surface is at its best.

03 Jupiter

The planetary king of our Solar System along with its four largest moons Io, Ganymede, Callisto and Europa are visible from November through to April in the constellation of Taurus before moving close to the horizon in May. Jupiter appears as a bright whitish star to the unaided eye but through a telescope or pair of binoculars the moons that flank its limbs along with storms that rage on the planets surface, which take the shape of bands and the Great Red Spot, are visible.

04 The Orion Nebula

Conveniently located within the Orion constellation, the Orion Nebula is the nearest 'star nursery' to Earth, and is easily recognisable in the winter sky. Not only can you make it out quite clearly through a telescope, you can also see a few of its amazing colours.

05 Mars

Our neighbouring planet is visible to the naked eye, but it's when you get a telescope pointed at it that you can start to really get a good view. With a steady hand, you can even make out the polar ice caps.

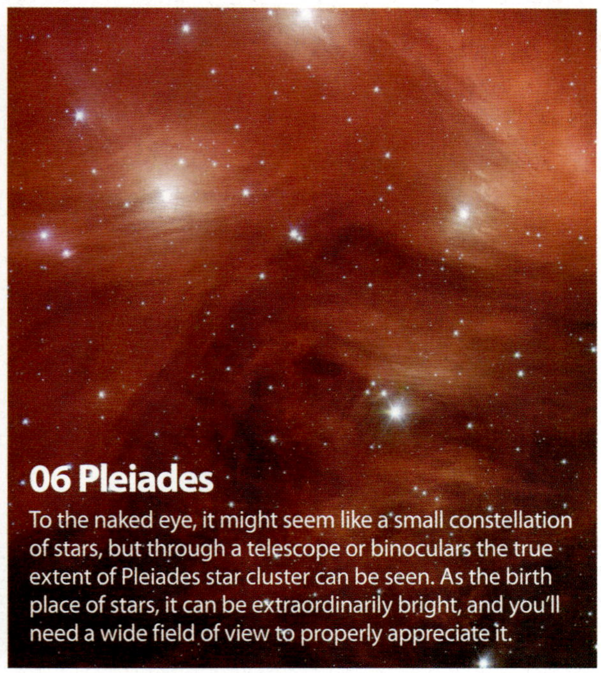

06 Pleiades

To the naked eye, it might seem like a small constellation of stars, but through a telescope or binoculars the true extent of Pleiades star cluster can be seen. As the birth place of stars, it can be extraordinarily bright, and you'll need a wide field of view to properly appreciate it.

07 Sirius

Not only is Sirius the brightest star in the night sky, it's also a binary star system. Pointing your telescope at Sirius is easy enough, but pay attention and you'll see the much smaller Sirius Beta at the edge of Alpha's glare.

08 Lagoon Nebula

This summer sight is located within Sagittarius, and is a giant interstellar cloud that has a star cluster super imposed on it when seen from Earth. It will look a bit greyish at first, but it's a great target for astrophotography.

10 tips to minimise light pollution

If you live in or near a town or city you know the effects of stray light dimming down and ruining your view of the stars. Here are some tips to help...

01 Get into shadow

If you have street lights shining into your garden, do your best to find a spot that's not illuminated by these and which can give you a good view of the sky. Getting into the shadow of a brick wall or a tree can help here. The side of a building can help too, but this can of course block your view of a large part of the sky, so you may need to hunt around for the best spot in your garden.

02 Wait for the right conditions

Artificial light is shone into the sky and is reflected back to us from dust and water vapour and atmospheric pollution. High humidity or prolonged dry spells when dust can be thrown up into the atmosphere will seem to make the situation worse. Check weather reports and wait for stable conditions with low wind speeds.

03 Get out of town

While we can appreciate that this might be easier said than done, if you have really poor views of the stars most of the time, it really might be worth the effort to pack up your equipment and drive a few miles out of your town or city to find darker skies. You will be amazed at the difference this makes, and you'll find that it's definitely worth the extra effort.

04 Shade your optics

If you can't shield yourself from stray light, then you can at least shield the equipment you are using. Dew shields on telescopes if short, can be extended using thick card, black or dark in colour, while telescope and binocular eyepieces can also be shielded using flexible 'wings' which can usually be obtained from dealers. These will help reduce stray light entering your eye from the side.

05 Cover your head

Another way of shielding yourself from any intrusive light is by covering your head with a dark cloth. This is surprisingly effective in getting your eyes 'dark adapted'; allowing the pupil of your eye to dilate as fully as possible. This in turn will mean your eye is as sensitive as it can be to light and will help you see those faint stars and other objects through your telescope. Don't worry if you think it makes you look daft, no one can see you in the dark, and it will be well worth it when you see the results.

06 Be nice to your neighbour

This may seem like an odd thing to suggest, but a lot of stray or unwanted light these days comes from security lights. If you have them, turn them off while observing and make sure they point at the ground at other times and, if on timers, make sure they are on for as short a time as is practical. If your neighbour's security lights are troublesome, then be polite and ask them to turn them off while you observe. Bring them over to show them what you are looking at; you never know you might convert them to your hobby.

Find a dark sky site

You don't have to travel to the Australian outback to see the stars in all their glory. Very often there are fantastic, light-pollution free sites just hours drive outside of town. In the UK, the website **www.darkskydiscovery.org.uk** will allow you to finds sites near you. Otherwise, check out our guide on page 156.

©Science Photo Library

07 Coloured filters

Coloured filters screw into the bottom of the eyepiece of your telescope. They have lots of good uses in observing. They can also be helpful when it comes to reducing the effects of light pollution. This is because they are only allowing through the wavelengths of light of the specific colour of the filter and blocking out the other colours, such as the orange/pink glow of street lights.

08 Stay out late

It is a fact that stray light reduces as the night wears on. If you are able to stay out late, you'll probably find that after midnight the amount of stray light around seems to be less than earlier in the evening. This is due to people going to bed and turning things such as outside lights off. Also some local authorities will turn street lighting down or off after midnight.

09 Specialist filters

There are various filters that are designed to help reduce the effects of light pollution. These often go by the name of City Light Suppression (CLS) filters or Anti Light Pollution filters (ALP). These are narrow band filters that 'tune out' the wavelengths of light emitted by low-pressure sodium street lights. These can make a difference when you are viewing through your telescope.

10 Take up imaging

The beauty of modern digital cameras is that it's easy to manipulate the image produced in software and reduce the orange glow with a few clicks of a mouse. This is the most expensive option, unless you already own a DSLR camera. However, because of the sensitivity of these cameras they can often 'see' more than the human eye in light-polluted conditions.

Observing the Milky Way

Acquaint yourself with some of the astronomical sights awaiting you in the galaxy we call home

Welcome to the Milky Way. It's funny; you live here, but how often do you go out to see the sights? Just like any great city, our galaxy is replete with iconic historical monuments, relatively young creations, and some quirky curiosities. Naturally we consider a handful of these to be the absolute best for observers and photographers, just as we do with the Colosseum, Forum and St Peter's in Rome, for which holidaymakers have plenty of information available to get clued up on before they travel.

There's an entire industry surrounding the research and sale of travel guides for Earth, but what if intergalactic tourism was viable? Suppose we astronomers could tour the universe and sample different skies. If travel-writers visited us from another galaxy, say the neighbouring Andromeda spiral, what might they pick for their absolute must-see objects? Unfortunately our perspective on the galaxy is limited, some of it is completely hidden from us but if we were Andromedans backpacking through the Solar System, these popular gems would most likely be on our bucket list… and we thing they should be on yours too!

Orion Nebula (M42)

Equipment: Binoculars / telescope

Often more appropriately dubbed the Great Orion Nebula, this cosmic cloud of gas and dust is a majestic reminder of the ongoing process of star birth, as it surrounds a bright young stellar nursery 1,500 light years from Earth. The blazing infant stars have carved out an intricately decorated bowl with a very distinctive shape seen through binoculars or a telescope. Notable is the 'Trapezium' of four bright stars in the cluster, best seen with a telescope.

Jewel Box Cluster (NGC 4755)

Equipment: Binoculars / telescope

"A casket of variously coloured precious stones," wrote John Herschel about this cluster. This object seems unremarkable in binoculars or a small telescope,but train a large aperture instrument on it and the colours of those 'stones' leap out of the eyepiece to produce a very fine sight, which Herschel likened to "a superb piece of fancy jewellery."

Omega Centauri (NGC 5139)

Equipment: Binoculars / telescope

Well all right, it's not quite in the Milky Way, but this massive globular cluster is currently the property of our home galaxy thanks to the immense gravitational attraction between the two. Some 16,000 light years away, this tightly bound swarm of millions of stars is the largest of its kind near the Milky Way, and is just visible to the unaided eye. Through binoculars or a telescope, it's an unforgettable sight – like an explosion of stars with many individually resolved.

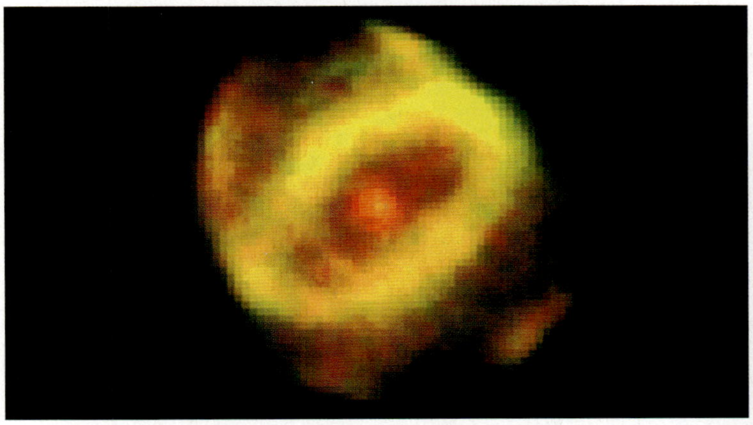

Ring Nebula (M57)

Equipment: Telescope

Like a perfect puff of smoke, the Ring Nebula lives up to its name at the eyepiece. Although binoculars can tease it out, you'll need a telescope of at least 3" aperture and at least a low-medium magnification to resolve the ring shape. It's really just a cross-section of a rugby ball-shaped gas cloud gently shrugged off by a dying star not dissimilar, in its middle age, to our Sun.

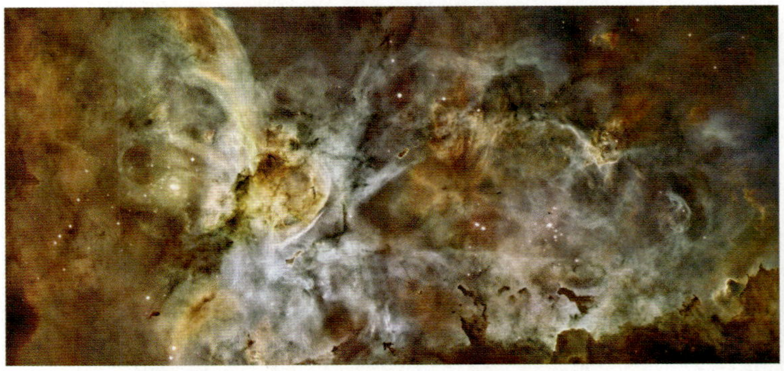

Carina Nebula

Equipment: Binoculars / telescope

You could spend half your holiday studying the impressive Carina Nebula. It's a sprawling complex of gaseous structures, including the Keyhole and Homunculus nebulae, and also contains one of the most striking stars in the galaxy: Eta Carinae. This unstable hypergiant is incredibly bright, about four million times more luminous than the Sun, and its powerful winds are shaping the gas around it with the force of a young star cluster!

Double Cluster (NGC 869 & NGC 884)

Equipment: Binoculars / telescope

These two clusters are beautifully framed in binoculars or a rich-field telescope, and both have a unique appearance. The two clusters each contain some hundreds of very young stars – just a few million years old! – and, in relatively close proximity to each other, they cruise the Milky Way together at a similar pace. The Double Cluster was thought to be just a patch of light until Sir William Herschel observed it in the 19th Century.

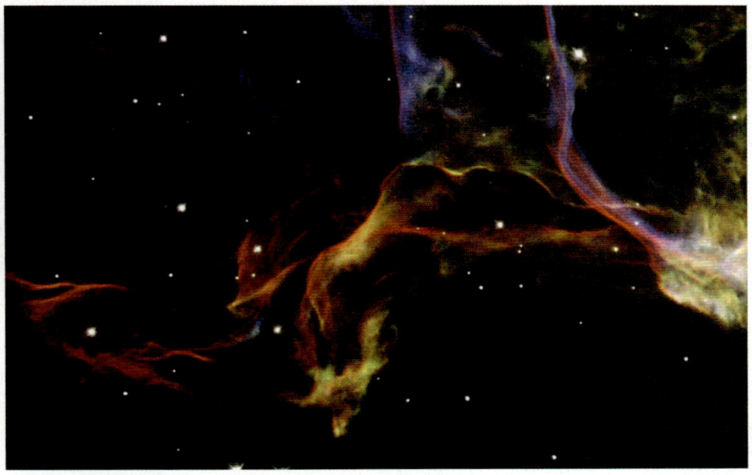

Veil Nebula

Equipment: Binoculars / telescope

Thousands of years ago, a massive star exploded in a colossal supernova event, scattering its atmospheric material far and wide into the galaxy. You'd never gauge the violence of this blast today when looking at the peaceful Veil Nebula it created. Just visible in binoculars, it has a near photographic appearance through a large aperture telescope, but the huge apparent size of this 100 light-year wide cloud requires you to enjoy it piece by piece.

Pleiades Star Cluster (M45)

Equipment: Naked eye / binoculars / telescope

Resembling a group of fireflies caught in a web, it is readily seen with the unaided eye even in light-polluted skies. This thousand-strong, young star cluster has been admired since antiquity, as our ancestors pondered over their heavenly nature. Today we gaze upon them as they were over 400 years ago.

Viewing galaxies

The Milky Way is far from alone in its voyage across the cosmos. Hundreds of billions of island universes drift through space and, with a little practice, you can see some from your garden

Strewn across the cosmic void as far as time's eye can see, innumerable galaxies bespeckle the cold black of space with a gentle radiance. On the grandest of scales, these glowing lights form a delicate, web-like structure of wispy tendrils, punctuated with enormous cavities and, since they appear to permeate the universe as we know it, we suppose that the view would be equally serene from anywhere we could imagine. It's nice to know we're not missing out! The galaxies sing to us from the distant past. Their signals are not dissimilar, in the eyes of astronomers, to fossils as studied by the enthusiastic naturalist. Each individual galaxy we see is, from our perspective in space and time, a snapshot of the history of the universe, and some are so distant, they shine in our night sky tonight as they did not long after the Big Bang. Of course, at such immense distances, these are too faint for the amateur observer, but many more lay near enough to our Milky Way to be glimpsed – a small few even by the naked eye. However, a reasonable pair of binoculars, or a rich-field telescope, is certainly the best way to start. Here are some suggested targets for the budding intergalactic voyager.

M31

Constellation: Andromeda

Without a doubt the most conspicuous galaxy in the whole sky, M31 (the Andromeda Galaxy) is also the closest. At a mere 2.5 million light years, its light left at around the same time that the genus of hominids that humans belong to first appeared somewhere in Africa. M31's core is visible in binoculars, and large telescopes will show hints of its spiral structure. With sufficient light grasp, you might also glimpse its two largest satellite galaxies, M32 and M110. Though much smaller than the giant Andromeda, it's quite a sight to see three galaxies all in one go. Try it!

How to find it:
Find the star Mirach (Beta Andromedae) and from there sweep towards Mu Andromedae. Continue along this trajectory for almost the same distance again, and there you have the magnificent M31.

M87

Constellation: Virgo

This titan of the deep sky is a real monster. Best classified as a supergiant galaxy, the elliptical M87 harbours at least a trillion stars as well as a supermassive black hole. A scientifically fascinating object, this colossal star city is also a great observing target when Virgo sits high in the sky. In binoculars, it appears as a fuzzy star, but a telescope of 8" or more will reveal a surprisingly large extent of M87's suburbs, around a noticeably brighter core. The view is not unlike that of a globular cluster, but the distance to M87 is a whopping 50 million light years!

How to find it:
M87 (sometimes denoted 'Virgo A') is nestled among the myriad galaxies of the Virgo Supercluster, about halfway between Denebola (Beta Leonis) and Vindemiatrix (Epsilon Virginis). It's slightly closer to the latter.

All space photos ©NASA

M81 & M82

Constellation: Ursa Major

M81 and M82, spiral and irregular type galaxies, respectively, are a popular pair among amateur astronomers. And why not? Their apparent separation allows this striking couple to be framed beautifully in binoculars and telescopes. Moreover, it appears that M82 was once a well-formed spiral galaxy, quite recently undergoing a catastrophic transformation, owing to a gravitational interaction with M81. So there is a great deal of scientific interest here, too. M81 and M82 are both about 12 million light years distant, and are undergoing active star formation. M82 in particular, is in a state of starburst, probably a rather self-explanatory term.

How to find it:

To locate this pair sweep from Phad (Gamma Ursae Majoris) to Dubhe (Alpha) and continue for the same distance again. M81 is the more conspicuous of the two, which are separated by less than one degree.

M104

Constellation: Virgo

29 million light years away in the constellation of Virgo, the beautiful spiral galaxy M104 (also known as the Sombrero Galaxy) tilts 'away' from us at a most fortuitous angle, presenting an opportunity to see it nearly edge-on. Most remarkable of all is the conspicuous 'dust lane' seen in large aperture telescopes; a silhouette, from our perspective, of the galaxy's disc structure cutting in front of its brilliant core. At the centre is an unusually large and dense 'bulge', and, somewhere within, a supermassive black hole. M104 may once have been a giant elliptical galaxy like M87, eventually crafting its own marvellous spiral.

How to find it:

Like M87, M104 occupies the Virgo Supercluster of galaxies. It's easiest to find by sweeping about three degrees northeast of Algorab (Delta Corvi) roughly in the direction of the bright star Porrima (Gamma Virginis).

Peripheral vision

It might seem difficult to believe, but the best way to see a galaxy is actually by not looking at it. Galaxies are among the faintest things we can challenge ourselves to see at the eyepiece and, as with most of astronomy, we need to take precautions to maximise our chances of getting that unforgettable view. One of the best ways to get started is by allowing our eyes to become adapted to low illumination. When our pupils dilate, our eyes can harvest more of the incident light and the image appears brighter to us. Also, our colour vision virtually switches off as a more sensitive, monochromatic system begins to warm up. This second adaptation is very useful, but also presents us with a problem, as each eye introduces a blind spot. This is because there is a patch in the centre of each retina where the more photosensitive cells are very thinly spread. Does this really mean that when we look directly at a faint galaxy in a telescope it seems to disappear? The answer, unfortunately, is yes. However, with practice, you can teach yourself a new skill: 'averted vision'. By moving the blind spot off the object, you can use your peripheral vision to really 'see' what you're trying to see! Observers report best results when looking away from their own nose (ie if you're using your right eye, look to the right of the galaxy).

Observing something without looking directly at it is a fine art that requires patience and determination. With perseverance it'll become second nature to use averted vision to your advantage. You'll be amazed how often a friend will fail to see the galaxy you're trying to show them, while declaring that they're looking right where they should be! Well, now you know why.

Blind spot

Faint galaxies can look like they've disappeared when you look directly at them.

Averted vision

The most effective way to see a faint object is to look slightly off to the side.

10 amazing daytime astronomy sights

Don't let the longer days during the summer spoil your astronomy – here are ten sights you can see even when the Sun is in the sky

Safety first

Warning! If you are attempting to view any of the objects mentioned here, you need to be very careful especially if using a telescope or other optical aid, as even a glimpse of the Sun through any optics, unless properly filtered, including a camera lens, can severely damage your eyesight!

"Venus is often seen in twilight either soon after sunset or shortly before dawn"

The Moon

Yes, you can see the Moon in the daytime! In fact, you've probably noticed it and wondered why you can. Because the Moon is quite reflective it is bright enough to be seen during daylight hours, when the Sun is low in the sky. Turn binoculars or a telescope on to it and see it in all its glory. It will give you the opportunity to see phases that perhaps you wouldn't normally get a chance to view otherwise.

Venus

The planet Venus is often seen in twilight either soon after sunset or shortly before dawn. Depending on where it is in its orbit it will either appear as a partly illuminated globe or a crescent. It's very bright, so bright in fact that it is even possible to see it in full daylight if you know where to look, but be careful here, it can often be quite close to the Sun so check its position carefully before you attempt this.

Jupiter

Jupiter is easily bright enough to be seen in quite bright twilight so no need to wait until after dark to go hunting for this wonder of the Solar System. It is often one of the first 'stars' to come out in the twilight and you will notice that it has a slightly yellowish tinge. Again, with a 'GoTo' telescope it is possible to see Jupiter in broad daylight.

Comets

Most comets which grace our skies are quite faint, requiring a telescope to be seen at all. However, there are occasionally comets which are very bright and can be seen with the naked eye or binoculars at least in the twilight. We may have one such comet to view later this year. Comet ISON is due to pass by the Sun in November and if it survives the gravitational tug of our star, it could put on quite a show.

Iridium flares

The Iridium satellite constellation consists of a network of telecommunications satellites that orbit the Earth and because of the unique shape of their reflective antennae they frequently catch the sunlight and focus it on a small area of the Earth for a few minutes. Because of this effect they can become one of the brightest objects in the sky for those few moments, an effect known as an Iridium flare. They are predictable and **www.heavens-above.com** will let you know when you might see one.

The Sun

Only ever look at the Sun if you have proper filters for your telescope. Look for sunspots and 'granulation' if you have a white light filter. If you don't have a filter you can project the Sun on to a piece of card using a small refractor telescope, but be careful here, too. Make sure the finder scope is capped off and use a piece of card around the tube to cast a shadow; otherwise you won't see the Sun's image.

Mars

Mars is much harder to see than Venus as it is much fainter, but it is possible to see it in twilight soon after sunset or shortly before dawn. It is possible to pick it up in a telescope in daylight but in order to do this you'll either need a 'GoTo' computerised telescope or an equatorially mounted telescope with good setting circles and an ephemeris or chart showing you the position of Mars on the day you are looking.

Stars

There are several stars which can be seen in fairly bright twilight, but it is possible to see one or two of the very brightest stars during the day when the Sun is still low in the sky. You'll need a telescope to spot them, but one to look out for is the star Sirius which can be found in the summer in the late afternoon low down in the south.

The ISS

The International Space Station orbits the Earth several times a day and depending on where it is in its orbit it can be possible to see it from your location. Its solar power panels are highly reflective and catch the sunlight, bright enough to be seen in twilight. If you would like to know when it might be visible for you, visit the website **www.heavens-above.com**. It looks like a steadily moving 'star' travelling west to east.

Atmospheric phenomena

The Sun and Moon, in conjunction with our atmosphere, can produce fascinating lighting effects. Sundogs are one such effect. These can be seen as a small arc of a rainbow either side of the Sun in a hazy or lightly clouded sky. They are caused by ice crystals high up in our atmosphere refracting the sunlight. Crepuscular rays are shafts of sunlight penetrating through the clouds in a very dramatic way. They are parallel rays of light emerging from the Sun, which is hidden by clouds.

Safety first!

The Sun is incredibly bright and can easily damage a human eye if you look directly at it and will certainly destroy eyesight if concentrated through binoculars, telescope or even a camera lens even for an instant. Only use proper solar filters to view the Sun and then only in strict accordance with the manufacturer's instructions.

©NASA

Learn to view the Sun

By looking at the Sun, our nearest star, you can see amazing processes going on all the time, but remember, you need to be very, very careful…

It's sometimes hard to remember that when you see all those tiny twinkling points of light up in the night sky, that each one of them is a raging nuclear inferno. To appreciate this for yourself, you only need look at the Sun. Of course it's so powerful, you need to take great care as it is very easy to blind yourself. If you are in the slightest bit doubtful about what you are doing, then don't do it. But if you are careful and follow the guidelines given here, you will find that observing the Sun is both fun and an endless source of fascination.

The Sun is constantly changing and darker areas called 'sunspots' move across its disc over the course of a few days. They come and go in a cycle of roughly 11 years. Very occasionally you might see a brighter region on the disc. These are known as 'faculae' and are associated with flares where the Sun blows out very hot material into space.

The safest way to see the surface of the Sun or the 'photosphere', to give it its correct name, is to project the disc using a small telescope and two cardboard squares. The first square fitted around the telescope tube casts a shadow on the second so you can see the projected disc of the Sun clearly. You point the scope at the Sun by watching the shadow cast by the 'scope; when the shadow is smallest is when the telescope should be pointing in the right direction. Never attempt to look through the telescope! Focus the telescope in the usual way to get a sharp image of any sunspots. The best time to view the Sun is early to mid-morning or late afternoon. The heat of midday can spoil the view, making the atmosphere turbulent and causing images to wobble.

"You can get special solar filters, but only buy these from reputable dealers"

You can get special solar filters to use with your telescope, but only buy these from reputable dealers. These fit over the front aperture of your telescope and are made from either specially coated glass or from a special metallised film called 'astro-solar film'. This looks a little like aluminium foil, but is designed to block out dangerous radiation such as ultraviolet. Always check such filters before each and every use. Hold them up to a light bulb and check for any scuffs or pinholes which could let sunlight through. If these are present, discard the filter. If you find your telescope supplied with a small filter which is supposed to fit on to the eyepiece, do not use it! These are very dangerous as they can shatter in the heat thereby exposing your eye to the full force of the Sun's energy.

There is a new type of filter available now called a 'hydrogen-alpha filter' often coming fitted into special telescopes designed for solar viewing. These are amazing instruments which will show you otherwise impossible to see features. With such a telescope or filter you can see 'prominences', huge fountains of material standing out from the surface of the Sun and also 'filaments', which look like dark lines etched on the disc. These are in fact prominences seen from above. The disc of the Sun looks mottled through this type of filter as well. Here you are looking at 'cells' of material thousands of miles across, bubbling up from the lower layers of our star. All in all, the Sun is an amazing, dynamic object and well worth your time as long as you're careful. After all, it's astronomy in the warm!

01 Get prepared

First of all you will need to get a sheet of white card or poster board on to which we are going to project the Sun's image.

02 Cast a shadow

You will also need another piece of card around the telescope tube to cast a shadow so you can see the projected image.

03 Beware of overheating

The best telescope to use to view the Sun is a small inexpensive refractor. However, beware of heat building up in the telescope tube.

04 Use a low-power eyepiece

Use a low power eyepiece to get the best results. Again, check regularly to make sure that it is not getting too hot.

05 Focus your telescope

You will need to focus the telescope so that you get a sharp, clear image of sunspots and other features on the Sun's surface.

06 Enjoy the results

The telescope will reflect light from the Sun on to your sheet of white card or poster board, giving you a fascinating and safe view of our star.

What's in the sky?

©Hubble

"Our guides will show you what to look for – and where to look – throughout the year"

December-January

If you are lucky enough to get that longed-for telescope, here are a few of the amazing sights you'll be able to see after dark…

Auriga Clusters (M36, M37 & M38)

Viewable time: Nearly all night

These three star clusters lay on a rough diagonal line passing through the southern part of the Auriga constellation. Although they are all classified as open clusters, they are each different from one another. The clusters are between 3,500 and 4,500 light years away from us and can be found nestling in the faint band of light which stretches across the sky, known as the Milky Way, which is part of a spiral arm of our own galaxy.

Andromeda Galaxy

Viewable time: Early to mid-evening

The Andromeda Galaxy is the furthest object which can be seen with the naked eye from a dark sky site. Binoculars will show it as an elongated, misty patch. With a telescope, the central bulge of the galaxy will seem quite bright. The Andromeda Galaxy lays 2.5 million light years away from us. Because it is so faint, though, it takes long-exposure photographs to show it up well. It can be quite tricky to find, so the chart should help you pin it down.

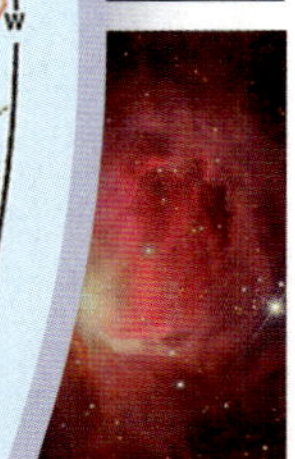

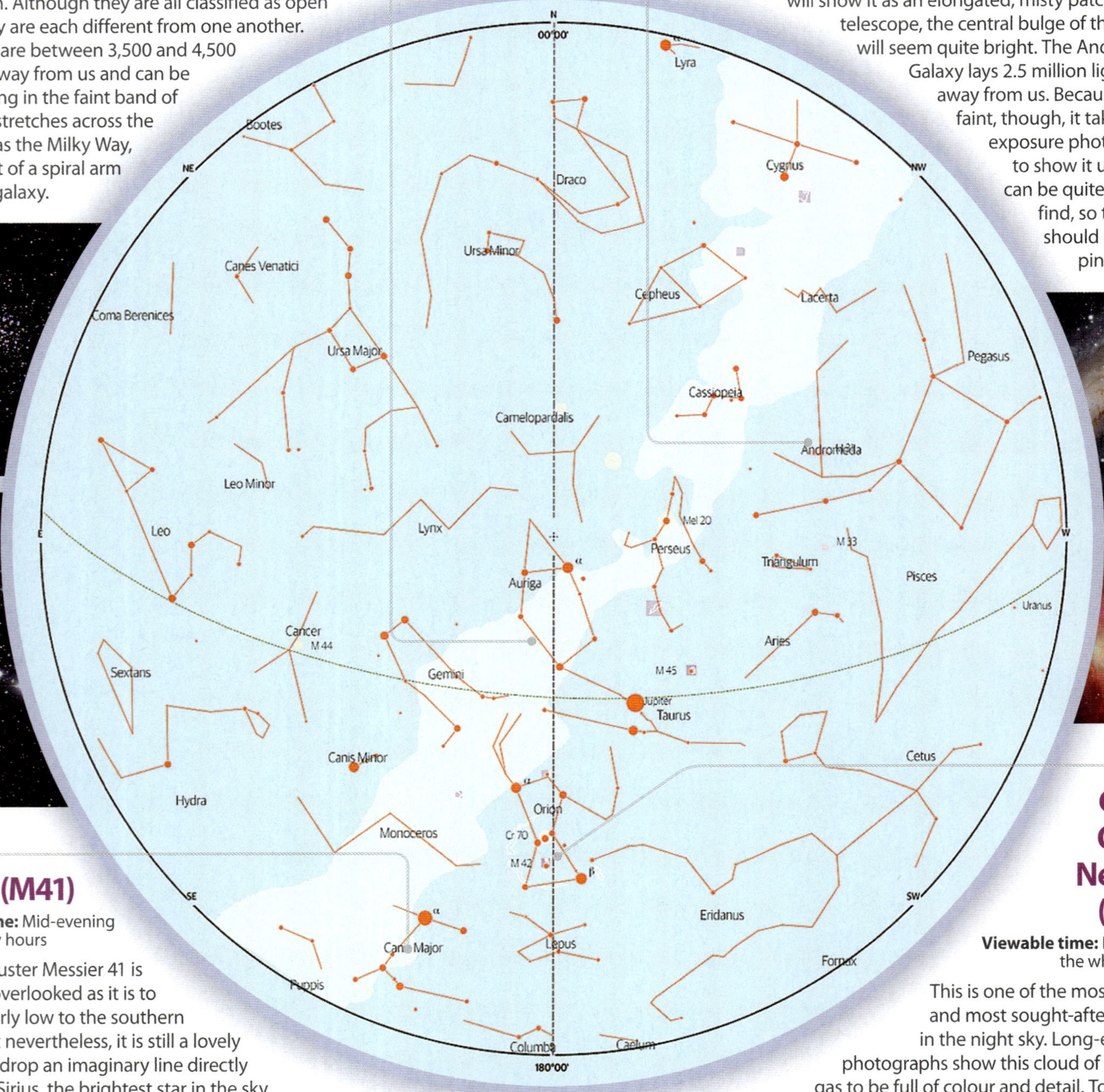

NORTHERN HEMISPHERE

Open cluster (M41)

Viewable time: Mid-evening until the early hours

The open cluster Messier 41 is frequently overlooked as it is to be found fairly low to the southern horizon, but nevertheless, it is still a lovely sight. If you drop an imaginary line directly south from Sirius, the brightest star in the sky, binoculars will easily pick up the small group of stars which creates this beautiful cluster. It looks like an irregular patch of light, but a telescope will show it to be full of stars.

The Great Orion Nebula (M42)

Viewable time: Practically the whole night

This is one of the most viewed and most sought-after objects in the night sky. Long-exposure photographs show this cloud of dust and gas to be full of colour and detail. To the eye, the nebula has a mysterious hazy look with a greenish or greyish colour showing tantalising wisps and tendrils of material. It is part of a much larger region of nebulosity that surrounds almost the entire constellation.

LARGE MAGELLANIC CLOUD

ETA CARINAE

Eta Carinae and the Keyhole Nebula (NGC 3372)

Viewable time: During the hours of darkness

Scan up from the horizon after dark along the Milky Way and soon after the constellation of the Southern Cross you'll notice a bright knot of light. This region is full of nebulosity and brighter and darker patches. The star Eta Carinae is buried in the nebula from which it takes its name. The nebula is expected to explode as a supernova in the future. On viewing, you will notice a dark hole in the brighter nebula which is known as the Keyhole for obvious reasons.

Canopus

Viewable time: During the hours of darkness

Canopus is the second brightest star in the night sky and can be found high in the south through the winter months. It is quite dazzling in binoculars or a telescope, being outshone only by Sirius. It is the brightest star in the constellation of Carina the Keel, originally part of the huge constellation of Argo Navis, which was meant to represent the ship of Jason and his Argonauts. It is a variable star, although it only varies in brightness just a little. It lays 310 light years away and is the brightest star within 700 light years of Earth.

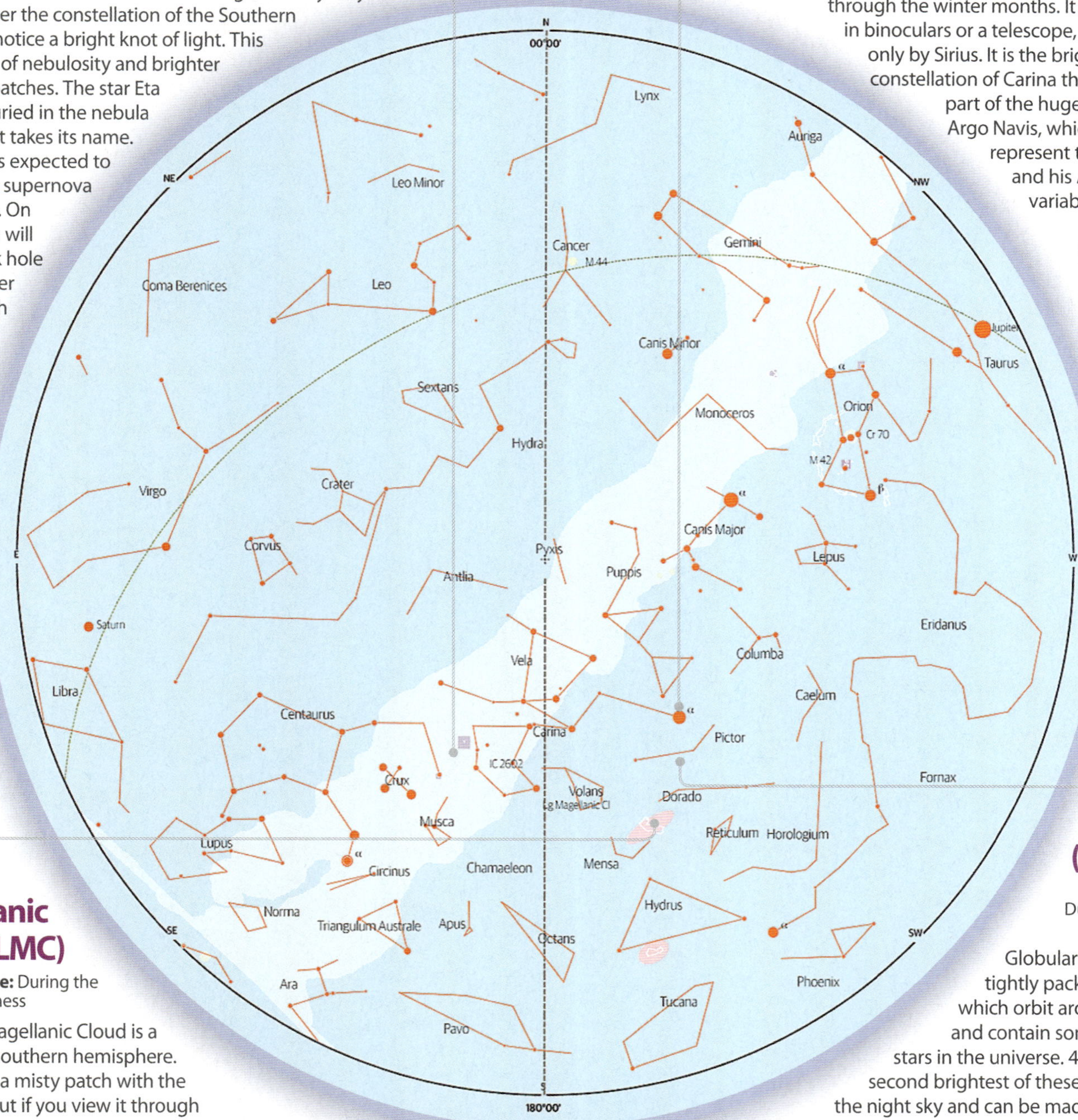

SOUTHERN HEMISPHERE

The Large Magellanic Cloud (LMC)

Viewable time: During the hours of darkness

The Large Magellanic Cloud is a sight of the southern hemisphere. It's visible as a misty patch with the naked eye, but if you view it through binoculars or a small telescope, you'll be greeted with an incredible view. Scan through this area and you will see clouds of misty light interspersed with bright patches and darker channels mixed in with stunning star clusters. What you are looking at is a satellite galaxy of our own Milky Way.

47 Tucanae (NGC 104)

Viewable time: During the hours of darkness

Globular star clusters are tightly packed balls of stars which orbit around our galaxy and contain some of the oldest stars in the universe. 47 Tucanae is the second brightest of these in the whole of the night sky and can be made out as a fuzzy patch of light with the naked eye. Through binoculars, though, the view is simply breathtaking! It is 16,700 light years from Earth and spans an area of space 120 light years across. It lies not far from the Small Magellanic Cloud, a smaller sibling of the LMC.

January-February

From fascinating open clusters to beautiful nebulas, start your new year's viewing with this selection of fantastic night sky sights

Open cluster M67

Viewable time: All through the hours of darkness

Messier 67 is a faint but fascinating open cluster of stars in the constellation of Cancer the Crab. It shows up as a misty patch in binoculars, but a telescope will resolve most of the stars. What is especially interesting about this object is that it contains over 100 stars similar to that of our Sun and of around the same age. The M67 star cluster lies between 2,600 and 2,900 light years away, making it one of the nearest old open star clusters to us.

©2MASS

©2MASS

The Crab Nebula (M1)

Viewable time: Nearly all night

The Crab Nebula is the first object in the French astronomer Charles Messier's catalogue. The Crab Nebula is a supernova remnant, the remains of a star which blew itself apart and was seen by people in 1054 AD even in the daylight as it was so bright. It is quite dim now and can be tricky to find, but if you have a telescope of around three-inch aperture, see if you can spot this misty patch of light.

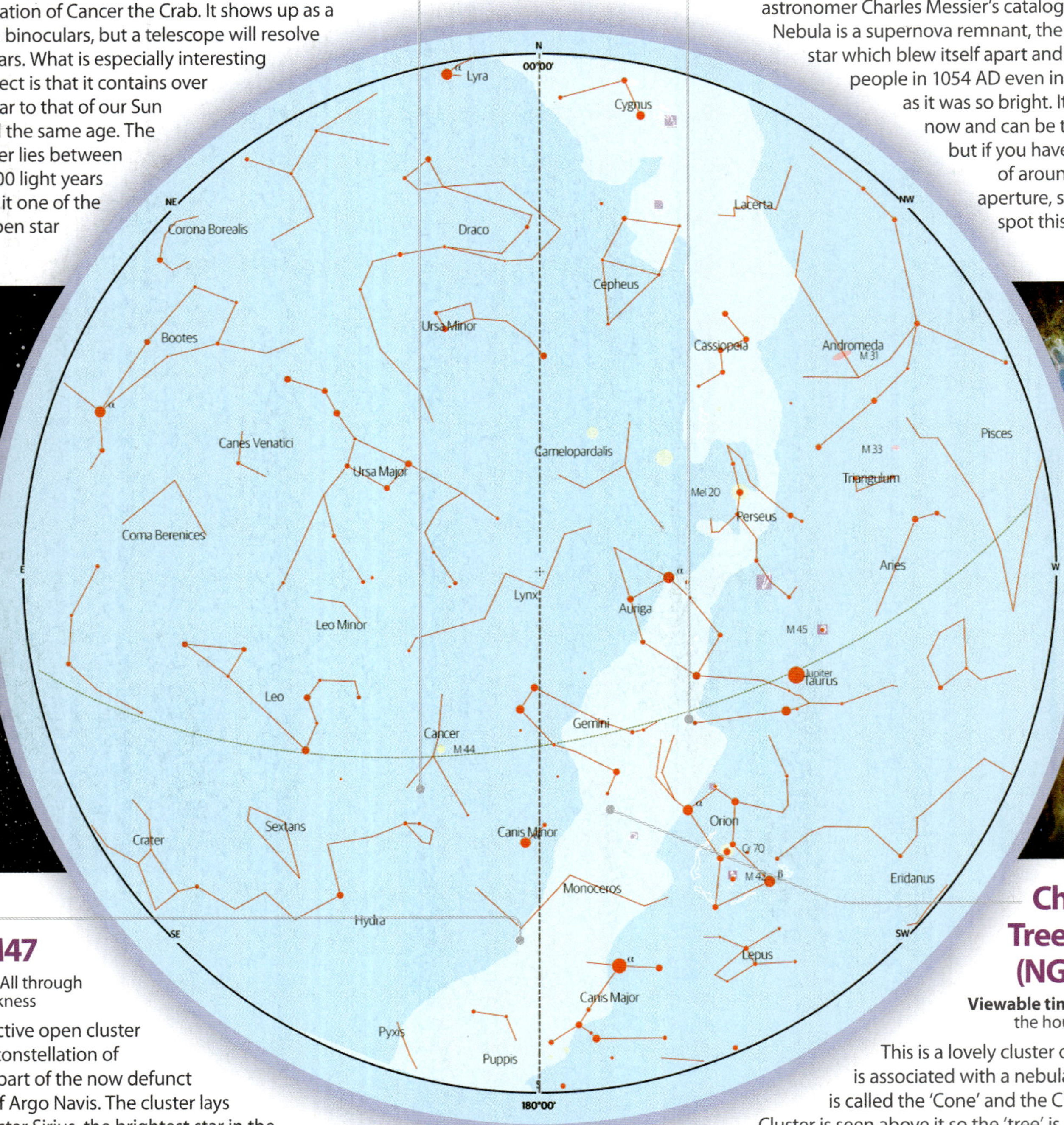

NORTHERN HEMISPHERE

Open cluster M47

Viewable time: All through the hours of darkness

This is an attractive open cluster of stars in the constellation of Puppis. This is part of the now defunct constellation of Argo Navis. The cluster lays quite near the star Sirius, the brightest star in the sky, and contains around 50 stars. It shows up well in binoculars or a small telescope at low magnification. It is thought that the cluster is about 78 million years old and is around 1,600 light years distance.

Christmas Tree Cluster (NGC 2264)

Viewable time: All through the hours of darkness

This is a lovely cluster of stars which is associated with a nebula. The nebula is called the 'Cone' and the Christmas Tree Cluster is seen above it so the 'tree' is upside down in most pictures. The star cluster is quite bright, but the Cone nebula is much harder to see. You'll be able to see the cluster in binoculars and it looks great in small telescopes at low power.

Jewel Box cluster (NGC 4755)

Viewable time: From mid-evening though the night

This is arguably one of the finest star clusters in the southern skies. It lays in the constellation of Crux (the Southern Cross), the iconic star pattern which appears on the flags of Australia and New Zealand. It is one of the youngest star clusters at only 14 million years and has around 100 stars. It is visible with the naked eye and looks magnificent in binoculars or a telescope. The bright orange star is Kappa Crucis and is a very large red supergiant.

©ESO

SOUTHERN HEMISPHERE

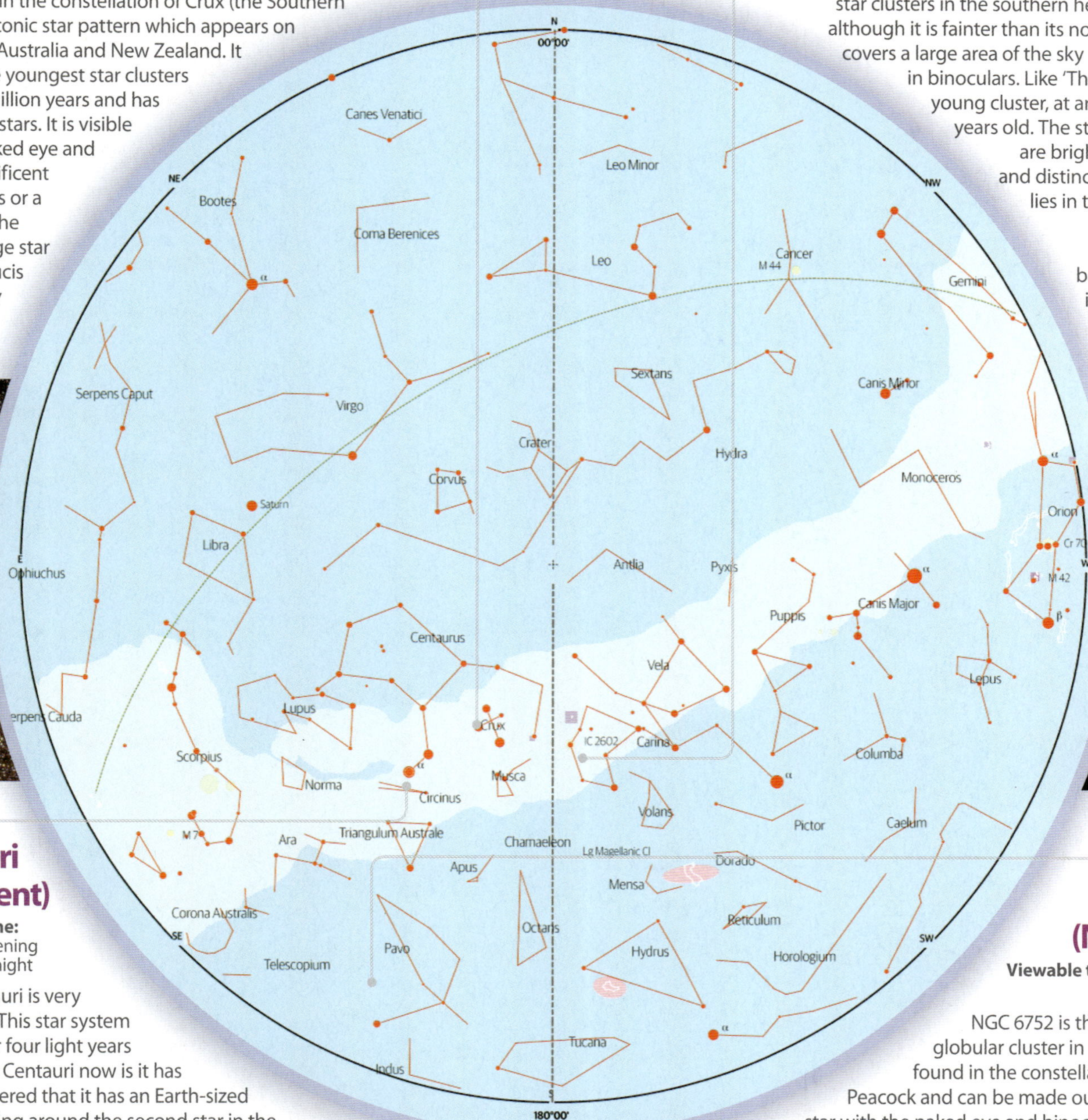

Southern Pleiades (IC 2602)

Viewable time: All through the hours of darkness

The Southern Pleiades is one of the brightest star clusters in the southern hemisphere skies, although it is fainter than its northern cousin. It covers a large area of the sky and is best seen in binoculars. Like 'The Pleiades' it is a young cluster, at around 50 million years old. The stars in the group are bright blue in colour and distinctive. The cluster lies in the constellation of Carina and is nestled in the band of light that is the Milky Way, part of the spiral arm of our own galaxy.

Alpha Centauri (Rigil Kent)

Viewable time: From mid-evening through the night

Alpha Centauri is very interesting. This star system lies just over four light years away. Alpha Centauri now is it has been discovered that it has an Earth-sized planet orbiting around the second star in the system, making it the closest planet outside of our own Solar System. Alpha Centauri appears as just one star to the naked eye and is among the brightest stars in the entire sky.

Pavo globular cluster (NGC 6752)

Viewable time: Late evening to early morning

NGC 6752 is the third brightest globular cluster in the sky. It can be found in the constellation of Pavo the Peacock and can be made out as a faint fuzzy star with the naked eye and binoculars will show it as a misty patch. It looks magnificent in a small telescope, which will resolve many of the outer stars in the cluster. It lays 13,000 light years away.

©ESO

February-March

The cold, dark night skies of February are starting to show us the first hints of spring…

Galaxies M81 and M82

Viewable time: All through the hours of darkness

M81 and M82 are two very different galaxies which lie quite close together in the sky. M81 is a glorious tightly wound spiral galaxy laying about 12 million light years away. The spiral structure is difficult to make out in a small telescope, but the bright core is obvious. M82, at a similar distance to M81, is an irregular, 'starburst' galaxy, which means that stars are being born in M82 at a rate ten times faster than in our own Milky Way galaxy.

Kemble's Cascade

Viewable time: After dark until early morning

This beautiful chain of stars is not a star cluster in the true sense, but an asterism, a pattern of unrelated stars which isn't a proper constellation. Lying in the rather faint constellation of Camelopardalis, you need binoculars or a small telescope to see it. It looks rather like a line of colourful stars, almost as if they were falling over a cliff and tumbling towards a lovely open cluster known as NGC 1502, which appears as a small bright knot of stars.

©Kelsey Kaemingk

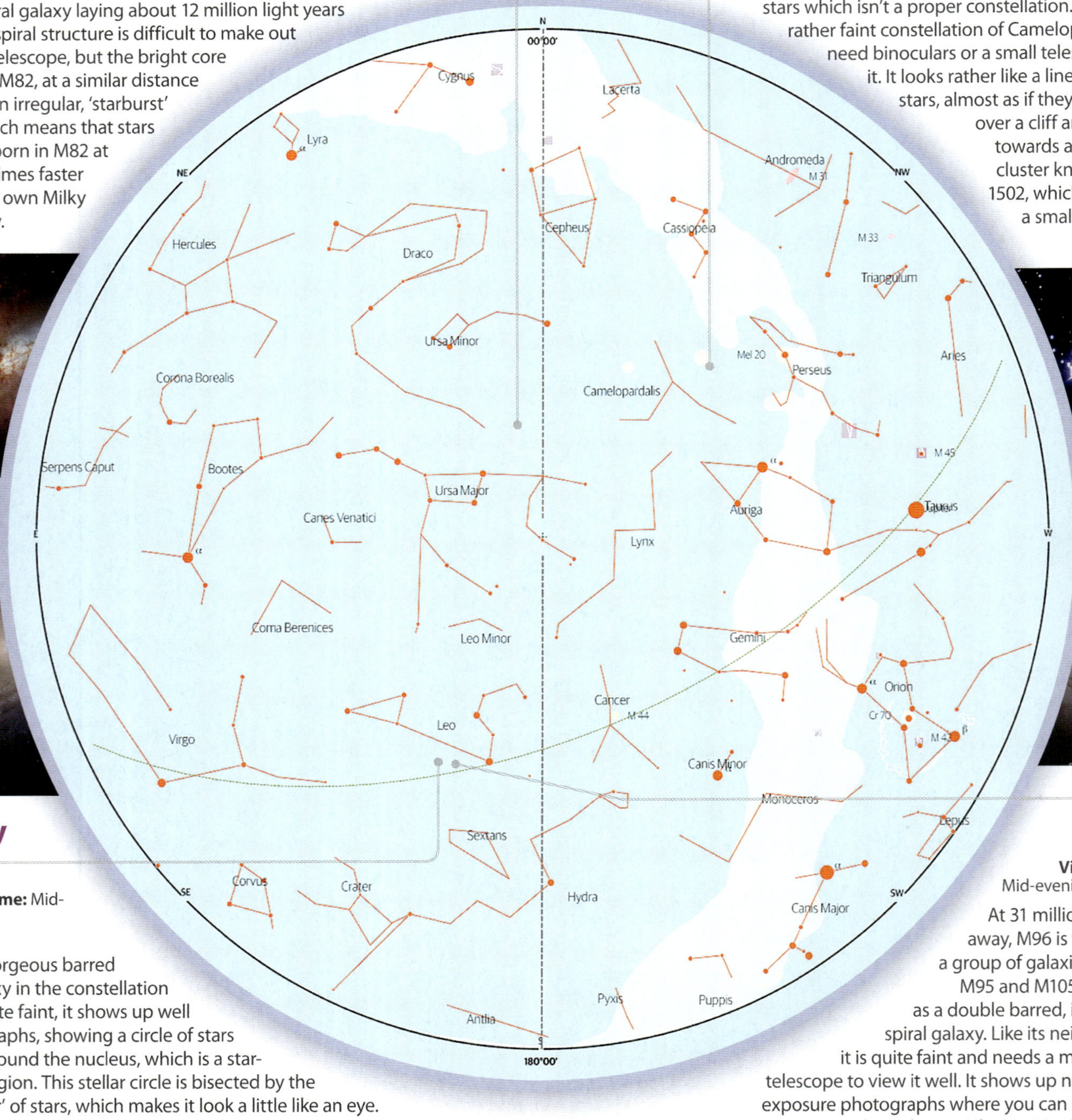

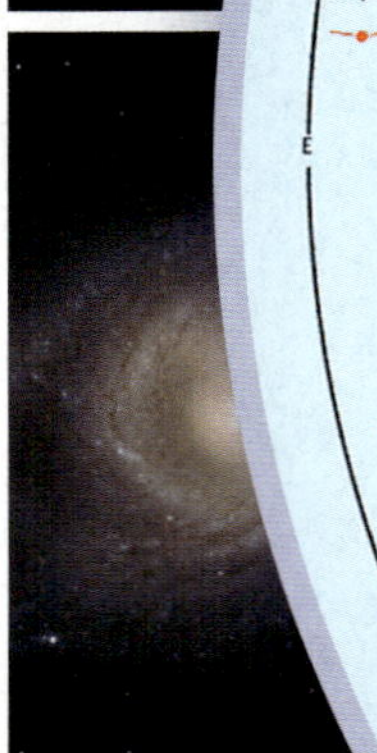

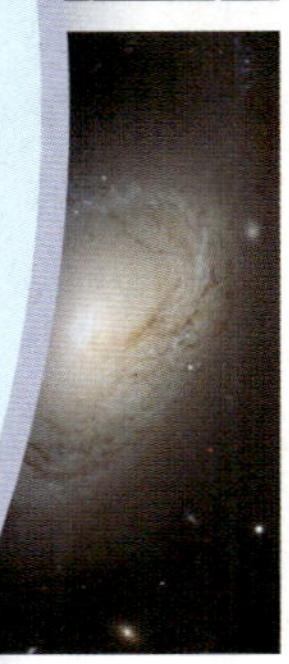

Galaxy M95

Viewable time: Mid-evening until dawn

M95 is a gorgeous barred spiral galaxy in the constellation of Leo. Quite faint, it shows up well in photographs, showing a circle of stars in a ring around the nucleus, which is a star-forming region. This stellar circle is bisected by the central 'bar' of stars, which makes it look a little like an eye. It was home to a supernova, which was seen to blow itself to pieces in March 2012. It is part of a group of galaxies, centred on the brighter galaxy M96.

NORTHERN HEMISPHERE

Galaxy M96

Viewable time: Mid-evening until dawn

At 31 million light years away, M96 is the centre of a group of galaxies, including M95 and M105. It is classed as a double barred, intermediate spiral galaxy. Like its neighbour M95 it is quite faint and needs a medium-sized telescope to view it well. It shows up nicely in long-exposure photographs where you can see its rather asymmetrical spiral arms. Like M95, it played host to a supernova explosion in 1998. This galaxy is thought to contain a supermassive black hole.

Globular Cluster Omega Centauri

Viewable time: Mid-evening until dawn

Omega Centauri is the brightest globular cluster in our skies and is easily visible with the naked eye as a fuzzy star. It is the biggest known globular cluster to be orbiting our Milky Way galaxy and was listed in Ptolemy's catalogue 2,000 years ago as a star.

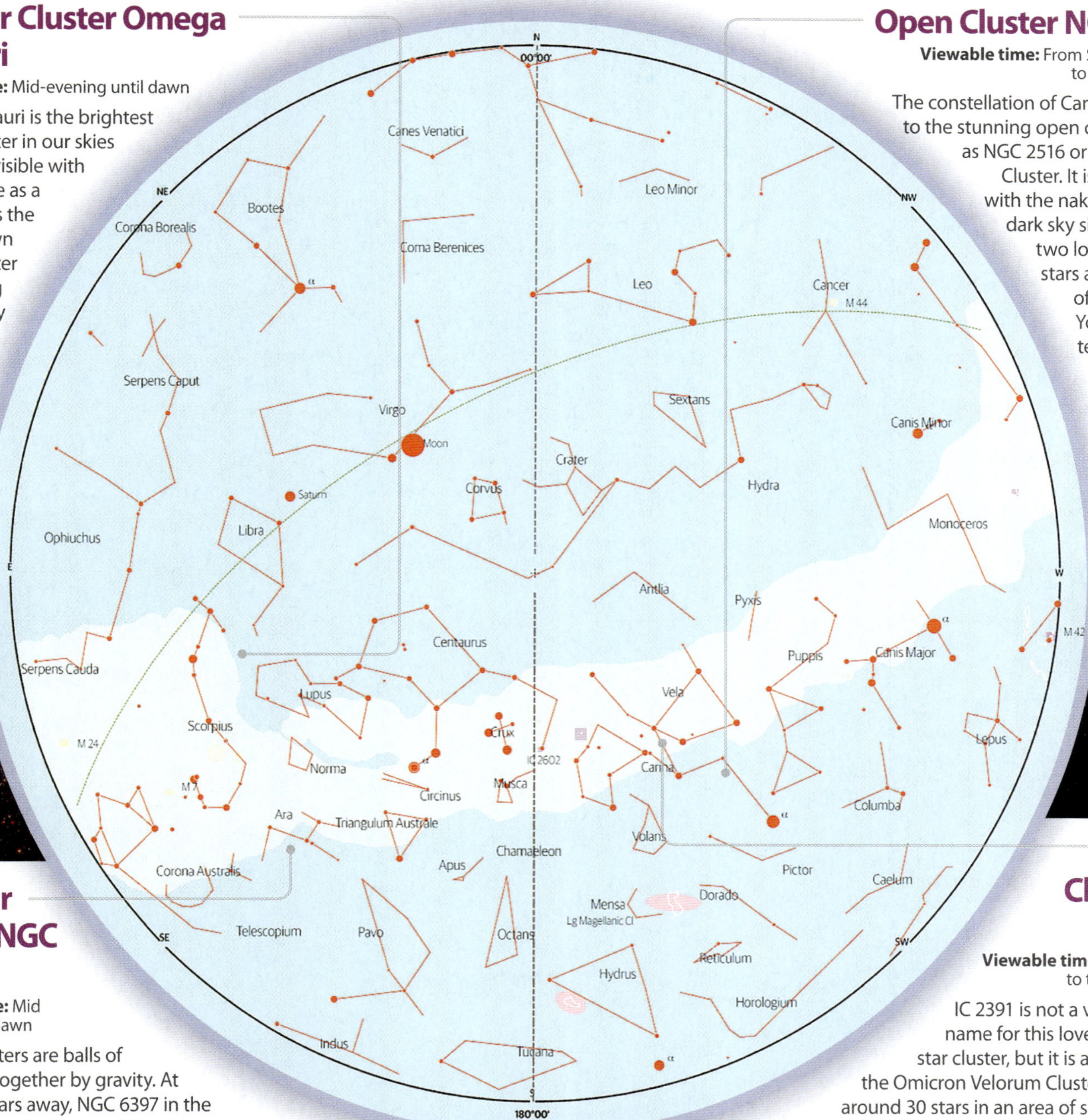

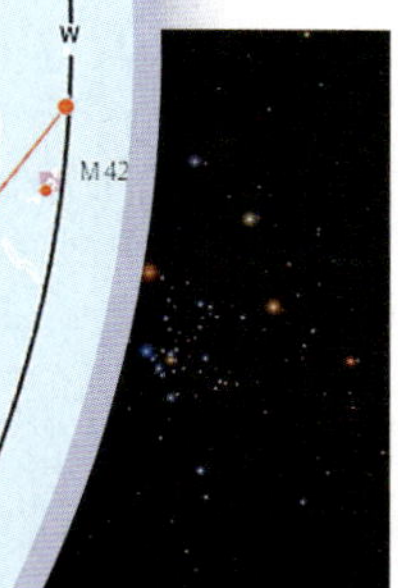

Open Cluster NGC 2516

Viewable time: From Sunset through to the early hours

The constellation of Carina plays host to the stunning open cluster known as NGC 2516 or the Diamond Cluster. It is easily visible with the naked eye from a dark sky site. It contains two lovely red giant stars and three sets of double stars. You will need a telescope to to detect these: It lies 1,300 light years away from Earth and is 135 million years old.

Globular Cluster NGC 6397

Viewable time: Mid evening until dawn

Globular clusters are balls of stars bound together by gravity. At 7,200 light years away, NGC 6397 in the constellation of Ara is one of the nearest to us. It can be seen with the naked eye and shows up well in binoculars and small telescopes. It contains around 400,000 stars and has undergone a 'core collapse', which means the centre of the cluster has contracted to a dense agglomeration.

Open Cluster IC 2391

Viewable time: After Sunset to the early hours

IC 2391 is not a very arresting name for this lovely naked eye star cluster, but it is also known as the Omicron Velorum Cluster. It contains around 30 stars in an area of sky just a little larger than the full Moon and it lies in a region of the Milky Way which was once part of the largest constellation called Argo Navis, the ship of Jason and the Argonauts, that has now been broken up into more manageable parts. The cluster lies around 500 light years from Earth.

SOUTHERN HEMISPHERE

What's in the sky?

March-April

See what the Spring skies are beginning to offer…

The Whirlpool Galaxy (M51)

Viewable time: All through the hours of darkness

Otherwise known as the Whirlpool Galaxy, M51 is possibly one of the most famous galaxies after the Andromeda and Milky Way galaxies. The reason for this is the beautiful photograph taken by the Hubble Space Telescope. As you can see in the picture, the larger galaxy is pulling material from the smaller – an act of celestial vandalism.

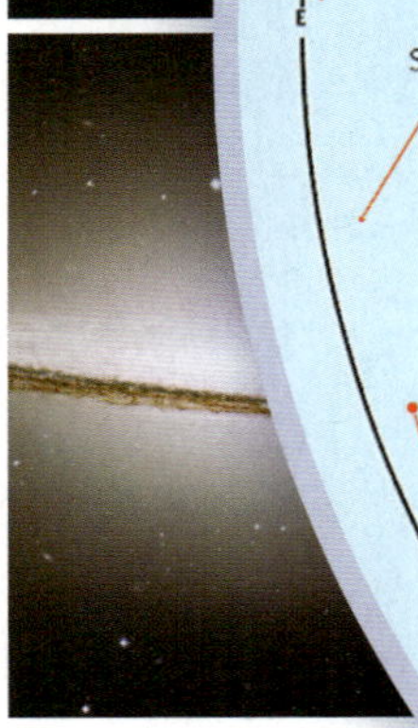

The Beehive Cluster (M44)

Viewable time: After sunset through to the early hours

This lovely cluster, which looks like a swarm of bees around a hive, was recorded by ancient Chinese astronomers. It is full of red giant and white dwarf stars and is around 550 light years away. It also goes by the name of Praesepe, the Latin word for 'manger'. It is also known by its catalogue number of Messier 44.

©2MASS

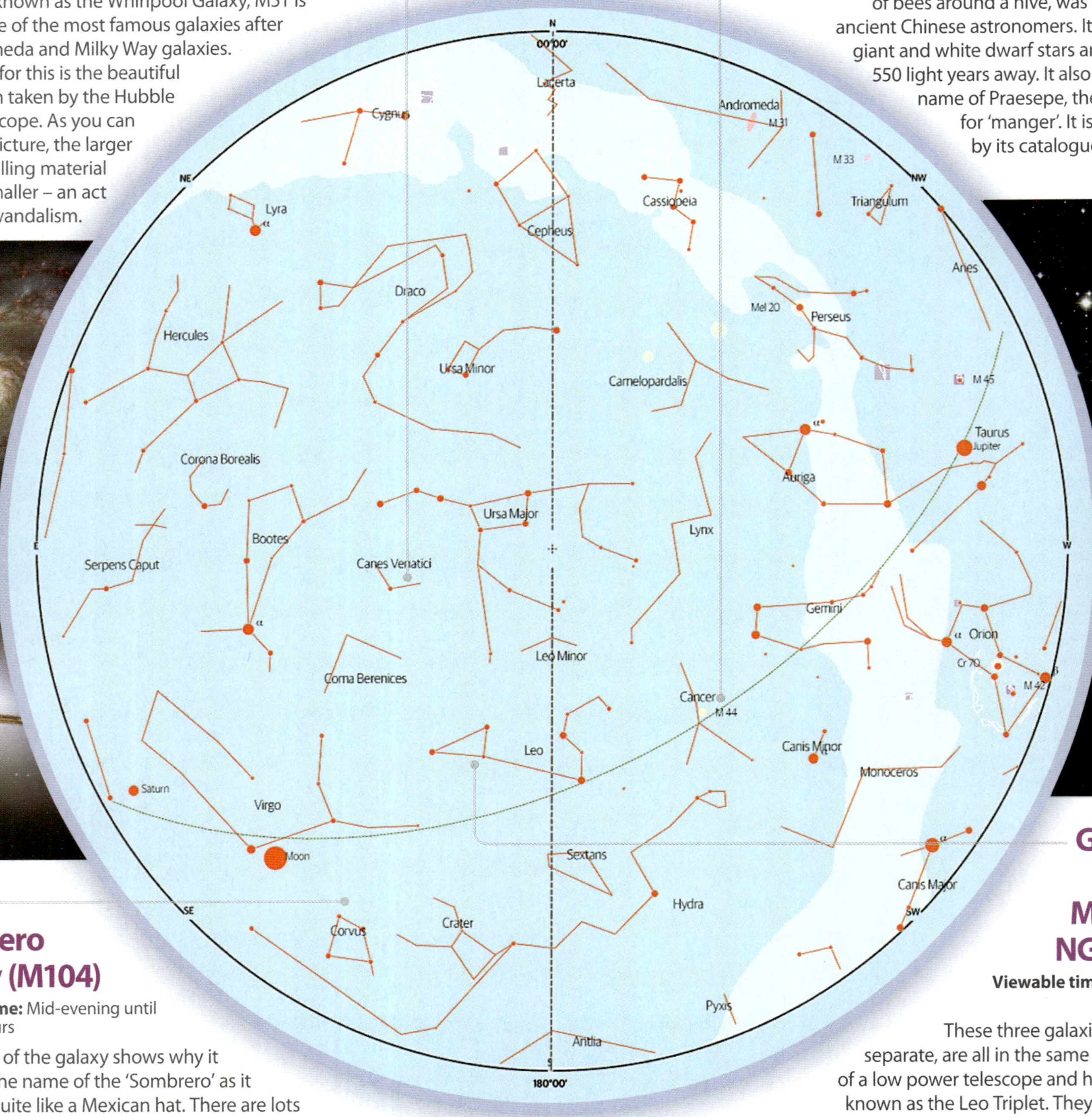

NORTHERN HEMISPHERE

The Sombrero Galaxy (M104)

Viewable time: Mid-evening until the early hours

The picture of the galaxy shows why it picked up the name of the 'Sombrero' as it does look quite like a Mexican hat. There are lots of features that make this an interesting galaxy, including its bright nucleus and large central bulge and more specifically the dark dust lane running around the edge of this beautiful object.

Galaxies M65, M66 and NGC 3628

Viewable time: Almost the whole night

These three galaxies, although separate, are all in the same field of view of a low power telescope and have become known as the Leo Triplet. They are all spiral galaxies but each is tilted at a different angle. M65 and M66 are at oblique angles so we can see the spiral structure, whereas NGC 3628 is edge on to us.

©ESO

Omega Centauri

Viewable time: All through the night

There are few sights in the heavens to match Omega Centauri. It's the brightest and largest known globular cluster associated with our galaxy. Easily visible with the naked eye, the view of this object through binoculars or a small telescope is magnificent. It's around the size of the full Moon, about 15,800 light years from Earth.

The Coal Sack

Viewable time: All through the hours of darkness

The Coal Sack is a dark patch in the bright band of the Milky Way, the river of light which we see stretching across the night sky. It's part of one of the spiral arms of our galaxy. It is a dense region of gas and dust which is obscuring the light from the stars behind it. It's the largest such 'dark' nebula in the night sky. It's visible with the naked eye on a clear dark night.

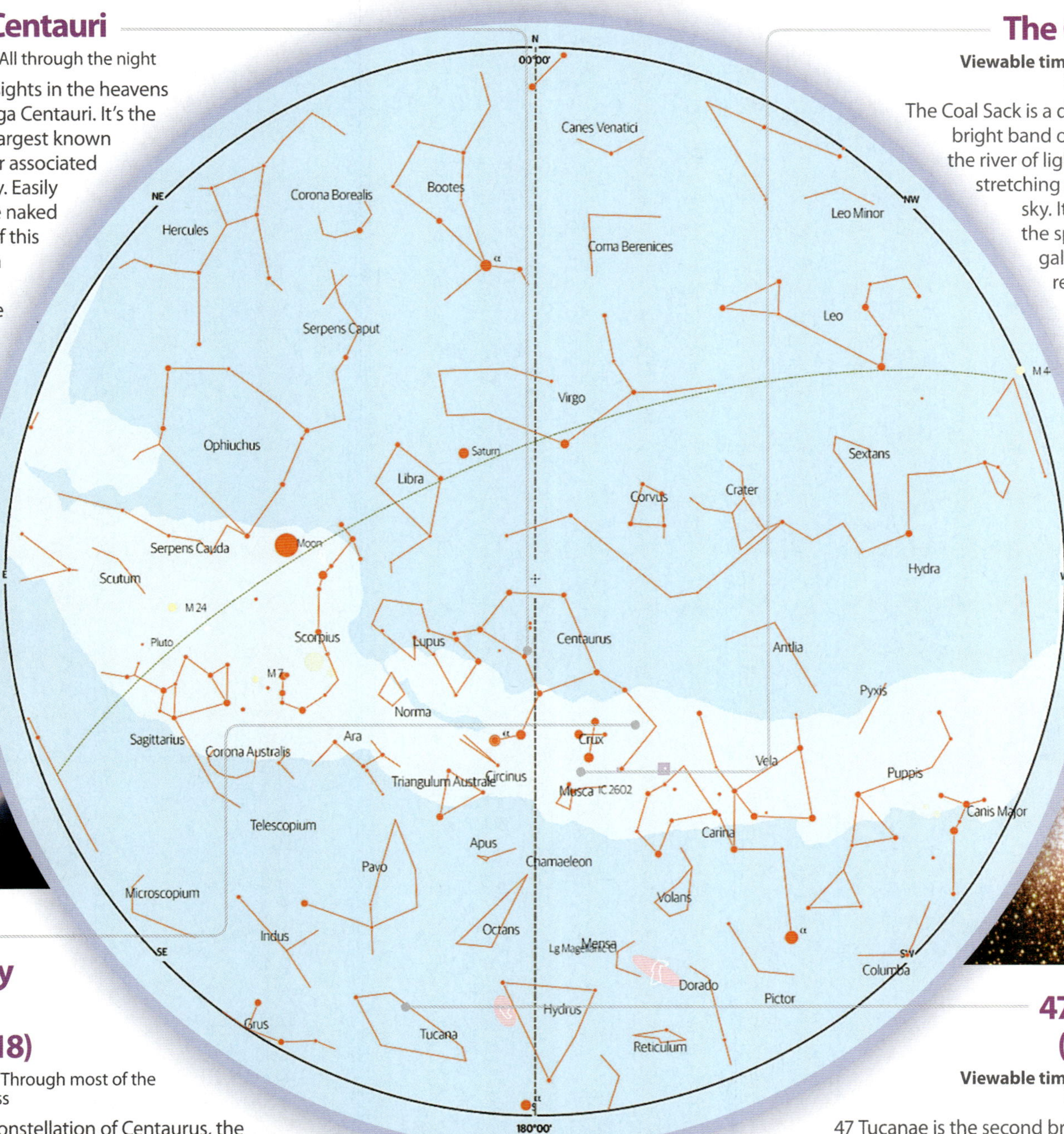

SOUTHERN HEMISPHERE

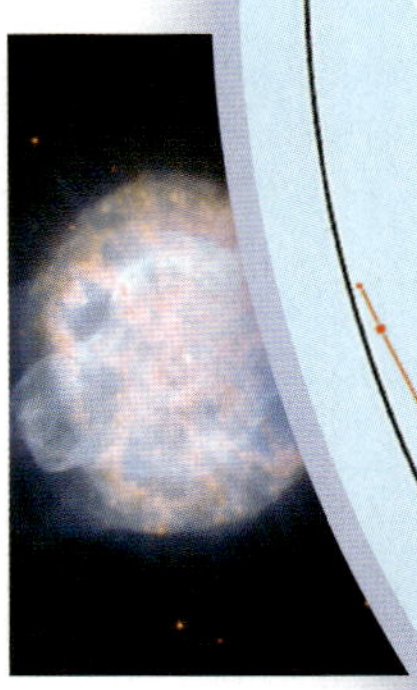

Blue Planetary Nebula (NGC 3918)

Viewable time: Through most of the hours of darkness

Found in the constellation of Centaurus, the Blue Planetary Nebula, which is also known as The Southerner, is easily visible in a small telescope and, as the name suggests, has a bluish tinge making it look a little like Neptune. Interestingly, the faint central star at the heart of the nebula is invisible to visual observers.

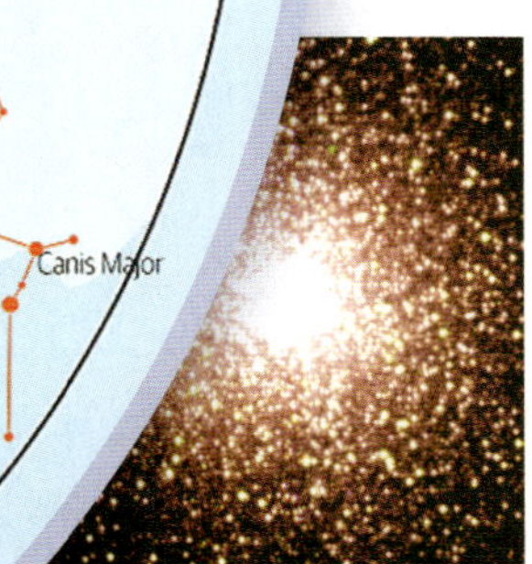

47 Tucanae (NGC 104)

Viewable time: All through the hours of darkness

47 Tucanae is the second brightest globular cluster after Omega Centauri. It can be seen with the naked eye and appears roughly the size of the full Moon. It is a magnificent sight in binoculars or a small telescope. Globular clusters are enigmatic objects, as they contain some of the oldest stars in the known universe.

April-May

The constellations of spring are now on show with a myriad of deep-sky delights to be seen

Globular Cluster M3

Viewable time: All through the hours of darkness

One of the finest globular star clusters in the northern hemisphere, you'll need binoculars or a small telescope to spot M3. Globular star clusters orbit the Milky Way and this one is around 33,900 light years away and is thought to be around 8 billion years old. It contains about 500,000 stars. It lies on an imaginary line halfway between the stars Arcturus in Boötes and Cor Caroli or 'Charles's Heart', the brightest star in Canes Venatici.

Black Eye Galaxy M64

Viewable time: All through the hours of darkness

Discovered in 1779 by Edward Pigott, this galaxy is unusual due to its dark dust lane which makes it look as if it has a black eye. It's thought that this galaxy is the result of a merger of two star systems as the dark dust in the outer region is rotating in the opposite direction to the stars and dust in the inner. It's thought that this occurred over a billion years ago. It lies at a distance of around 24 million light years.

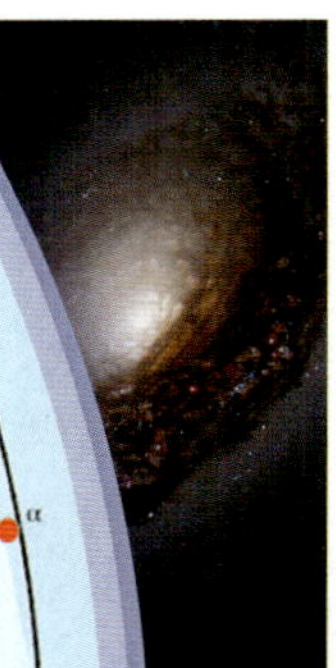

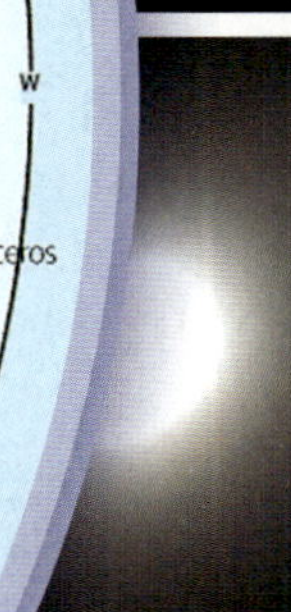

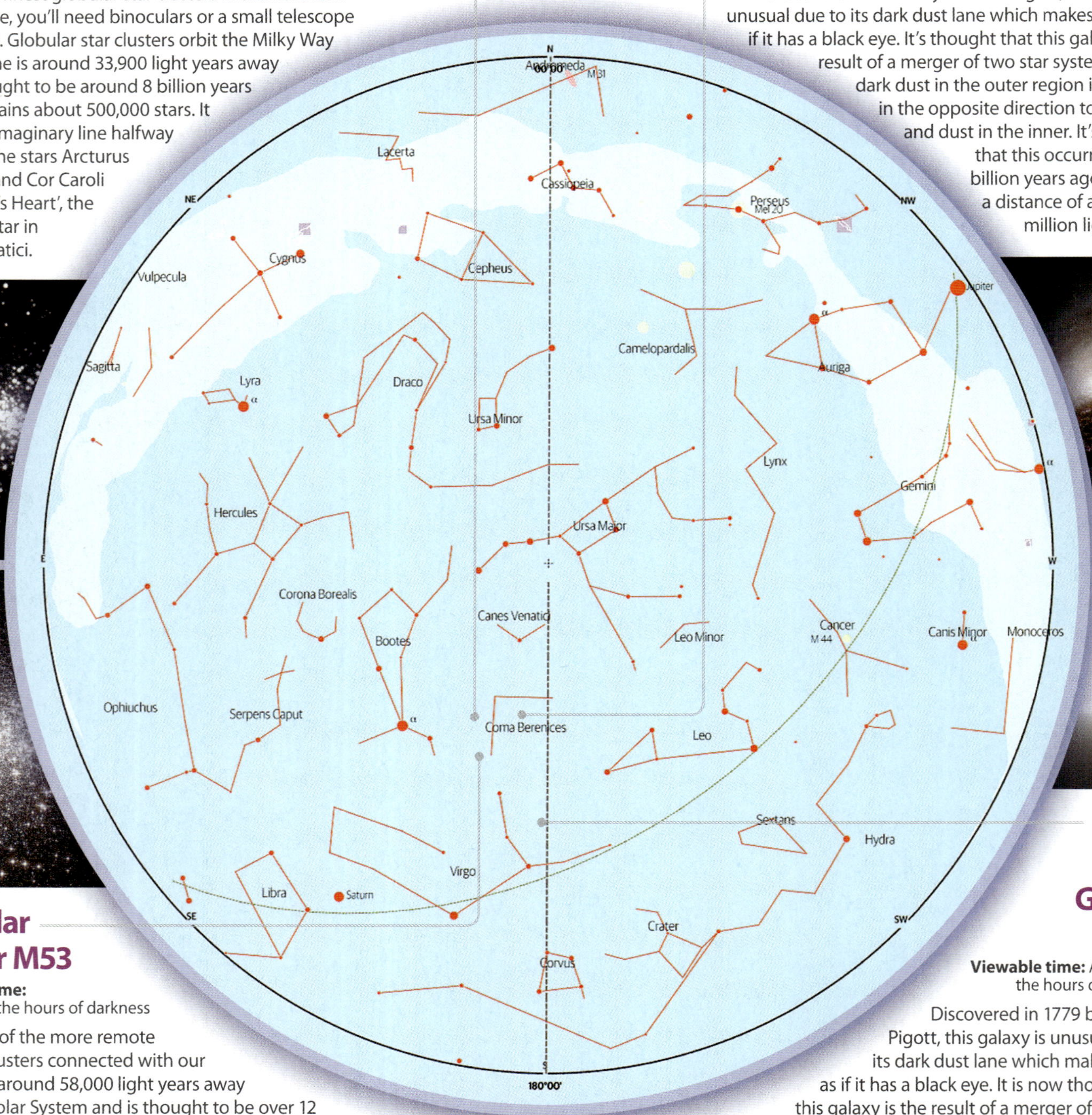

NORTHERN HEMISPHERE

Globular Cluster M53

Viewable time:
All through the hours of darkness

This is one of the more remote globular clusters connected with our galaxy. It's around 58,000 light years away from our Solar System and is thought to be over 12 billion years old! Again, like many others, this globular cluster contains around half a billion stars. It will show up in binoculars as a small misty patch of light; a small telescope will reveal its true nature though.

Black Eye Galaxy M64

Viewable time: All through the hours of darkness

Discovered in 1779 by Edward Pigott, this galaxy is unusual due to its dark dust lane which makes it look as if it has a black eye. It is now thought that this galaxy is the result of a merger of two such star systems as the dark dust in the outer region is rotating in the opposite direction to the stars and dust in the inner. It is also thought that this merger occurred over a billion years ago. It lies at a distance of around 24 million light years.

Open Star Cluster NGC 6231

Viewable time: After dark until the early hours

A bright and attractive star cluster, NGC 6231 lies relatively close to us at a distance of just 5,900 light years. It's also only 3.2 million years old. It was discovered by Giovanni Batista Hodierna prior to 1654 who listed it in his catalogue of deep sky objects. It can be easily seen in binoculars and shows up well in a small telescope.

Globular Cluster NGC 5986

Viewable time: All through the hours of darkness

NGC 5986 is another very ancient city of stars. This globular cluster, a tight ball of stars orbiting our galaxy, contains stars as old as 12 billion years! That makes them some of the oldest stars in the known universe. Although you'll need a telescope to see this object well, binoculars will show it as a small misty patch with a granular look.

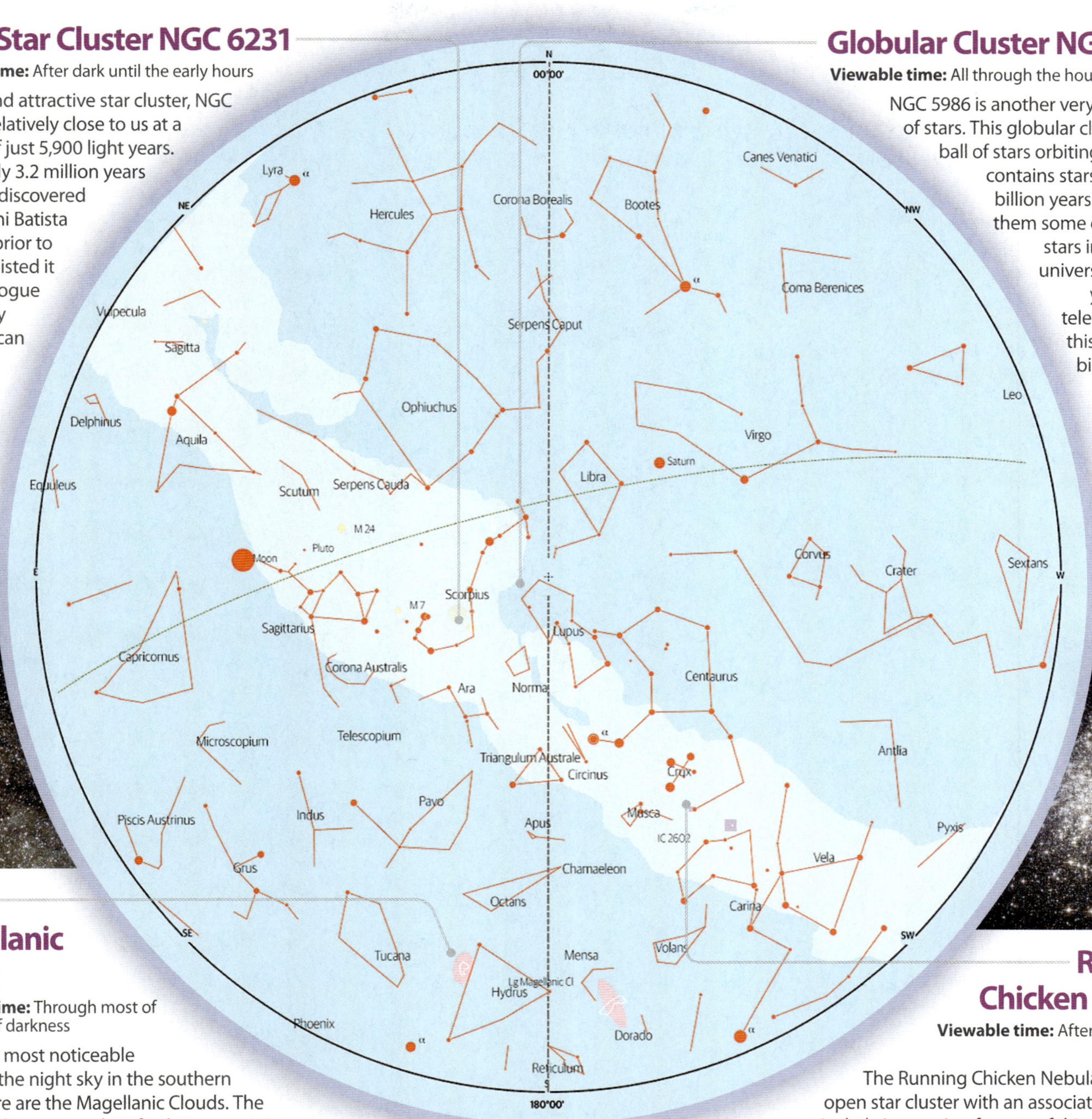

Small Magellanic Cloud

Viewable time: Through most of the hours of darkness

Two of the most noticeable objects in the night sky in the southern hemisphere are the Magellanic Clouds. The smaller of the two is a dwarf galaxy containing many hundreds of millions of stars. It is one of the nearest neighbours to our own Milky Way Galaxy, lying around 200,000 light years away and is one of the most distant objects to be seen with the naked eye.

SOUTHERN HEMISPHERE

Running Chicken Nebula

Viewable time: After dark until the early hours

The Running Chicken Nebula is in fact an open star cluster with an associated nebula. A particularly interesting feature of this nebula is the inclusion of a type of object called Bok globules. These are dark patches in the nebula which are known to be star-forming regions. However, there has, unusually, been no such star formation detected within this nebula.

May-June

The constellations of late spring bring us a range of wonders to enjoy on balmy evenings…

Globular Cluster M5

Viewable time: All through the hours of darkness

If you live far away from artificial lights, you might be able spot Messier 5 with your unaided eye. Charles Messier in fact thought it was a nebula, but this is one of the oldest globular star clusters known, at around 13 billion years old. It lies in the constellation of Serpens. Binoculars will show it as a small fuzzy star; a small telescope will start to show its true nature and a medium to large telescope should be able to resolve many of the outer stars. It is also one of the larger globular clusters at some 165 light years in diameter. It is 24,500 light years away from Earth.

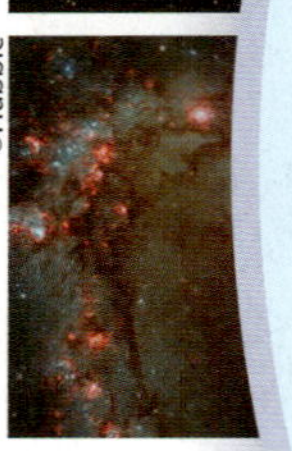

©Hubble

Sunflower Galaxy M63

Viewable time: All through the hours of darkness

One of the prettiest spiral galaxies in the night sky is arguably M63, or the Sunflower Galaxy. It sits in the constellation of Canes Venatici and was discovered by French astronomer Pierre Méchain in 1779 and then catalogued by Charles Messier. It consists of a central disc surrounded by several short spiral arms. It belongs to the M51 Group of galaxies which also includes the Whirlpool Galaxy. In 1971, a star blew itself apart in this galaxy as a supernova explosion. You can see M63 as a faint smudge of light in binoculars, but it looks better in a medium-sized telescope.

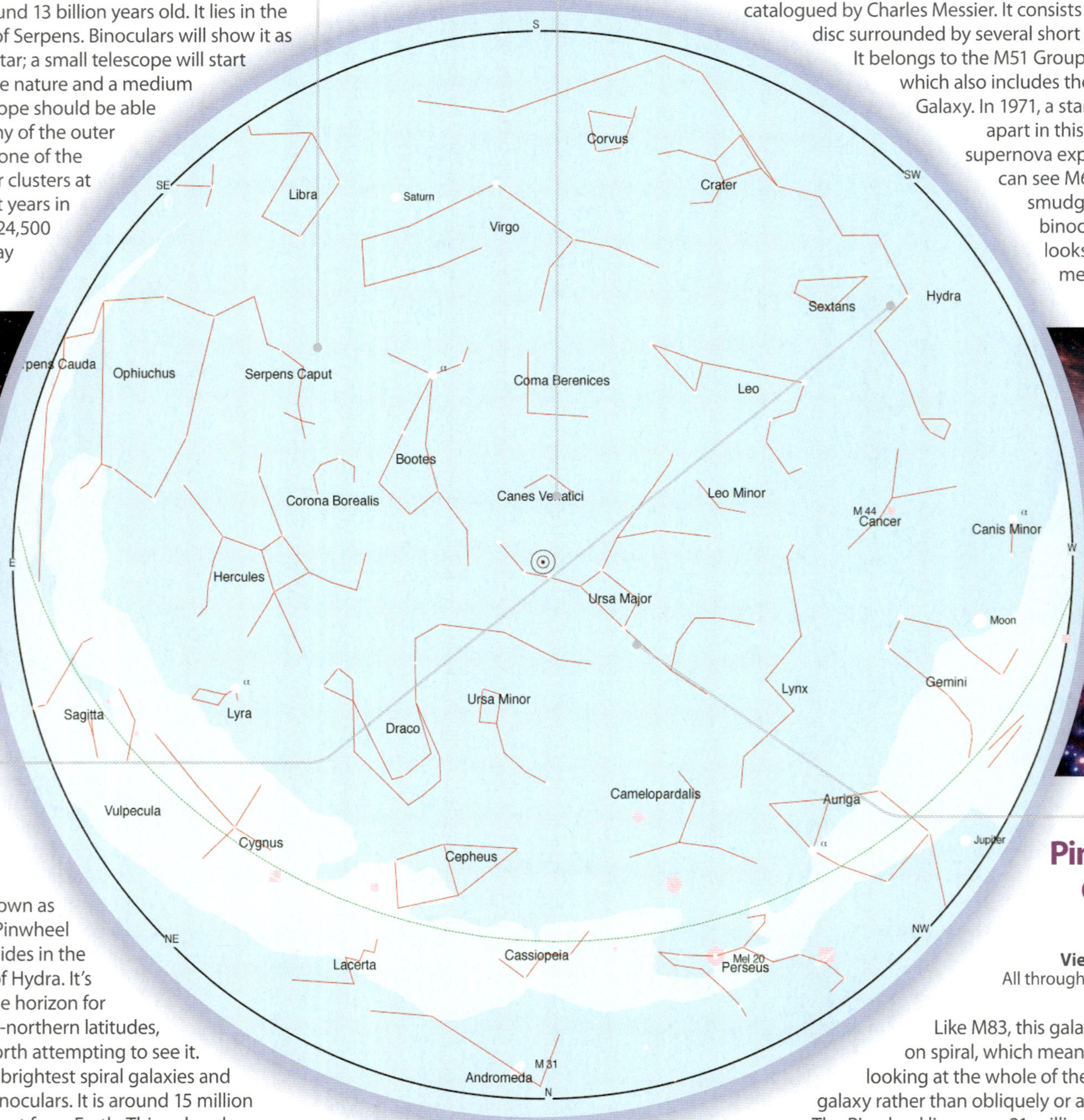

NORTHERN HEMISPHERE

Galaxy M83

Viewable time: All through the hours of darkness

M83 is also sometimes known as the Southern Pinwheel Galaxy and resides in the constellation of Hydra. It's quite low to the horizon for viewers in mid-northern latitudes, but it's well worth attempting to see it. It is one of the brightest spiral galaxies and shows up in binoculars. It is around 15 million light years distant from Earth. This galaxy has a central 'bar' of stars similar, it is thought, to the Milky Way. It is also a face-on spiral galaxy, so we can see its structure quite easily.

The Pinwheel Galaxy M101

Viewable time: All through the hours of darkness

Like M83, this galaxy is a face-on spiral, which means that we're looking at the whole of the disc of the galaxy rather than obliquely or at one edge. The Pinwheel lies some 21 million light years away from us in the constellation of Ursa Major. It is 70 per cent larger than the Milky Way at 170,000 light years in diameter.

Globular Cluster M4

Viewable time: All through the hours of darkness

This globular star cluster is easy to spot, being only 1.3 degrees west of the bright star Antares in Scorpius. Binoculars will show it as a fuzzy blob of light and a small telescope will start to pick out some of the outer stars. A larger telescope will resolve the object as a tight, granular ball of stars. M4 is around 7,200 light years away.

Globular Cluster M62

Viewable time: All through the hours of darkness

Sitting on the borders of the constellations of Scorpius and Ophiuchus, M62 is another globular cluster of stars that's associated with our galaxy. This cluster resides about 22,500 light years away from Earth, and it is thought to be around 11.8 billion years old. It is dimmer than its neighbour M4.

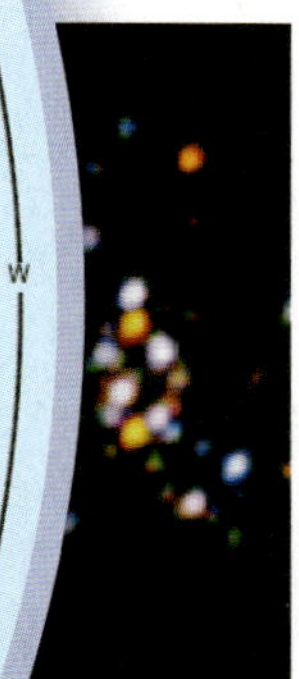

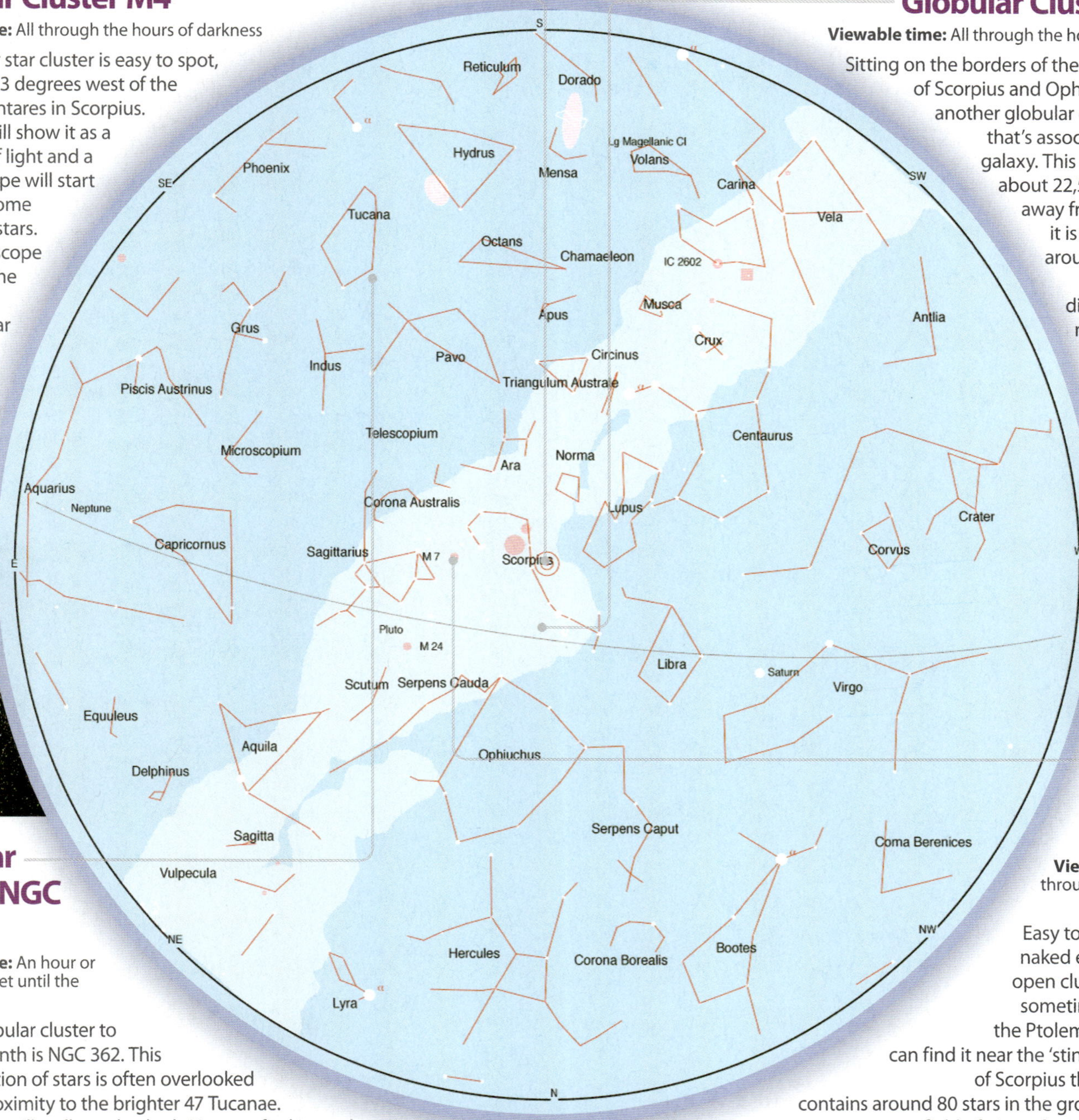

Globular Cluster NGC 362

Viewable time: An hour or two after sunset until the early hours

Another globular cluster to view this month is NGC 362. This conglomeration of stars is often overlooked due to its proximity to the brighter 47 Tucanae. However, it is still well worth a look. You can find it south of 47 Tuc and, like its neighbour, it sits on the border of the Small Magellanic Cloud. It will show up as a round smudge in your binoculars.

Open Cluster M7

Viewable time: All through the hours of darkness

Easy to spot with the naked eye, this lovely open cluster of stars is sometimes known as the Ptolemy Cluster. You can find it near the 'stinger' in the tail of Scorpius the Scorpion. It contains around 80 stars in the group and spans a field of view of 1.3 degrees. M7 is around 980 light years distant, which equates to an actual diameter of 25 light years. It is thought to be about 200 million years old.

June

The constellations of summer mean that we may have to stay up late but it's well worth it…

Globular Cluster M92

Viewable time: All through the hours of darkness

It may be often overlooked due to its brighter neighbour M13, but M92 is the other globular star cluster in the Hercules constellation and is still one of the brightest in the night sky. It lies a little further away than M13 at 26,700 light years distance. It is one of the oldest objects in the universe at around 13 billion years of age. The cluster is easily visible in binoculars, but a small telescope will begin to resolve many of its outlying stars.

Globular Cluster M13

Viewable time: All through the hours of darkness

Messier 13 is the brightest globular cluster viewable from the northern hemisphere. Just visible with the naked eye from a dark sky site as a small misty patch of light, in binoculars it looks like a fuzzy ball of light and with a small telescope you can start to resolve many of the outer stars in the cluster. It contains around 300,000 stars and lies around 25,000 light years away from us. The cluster is about 145 light years in diameter.

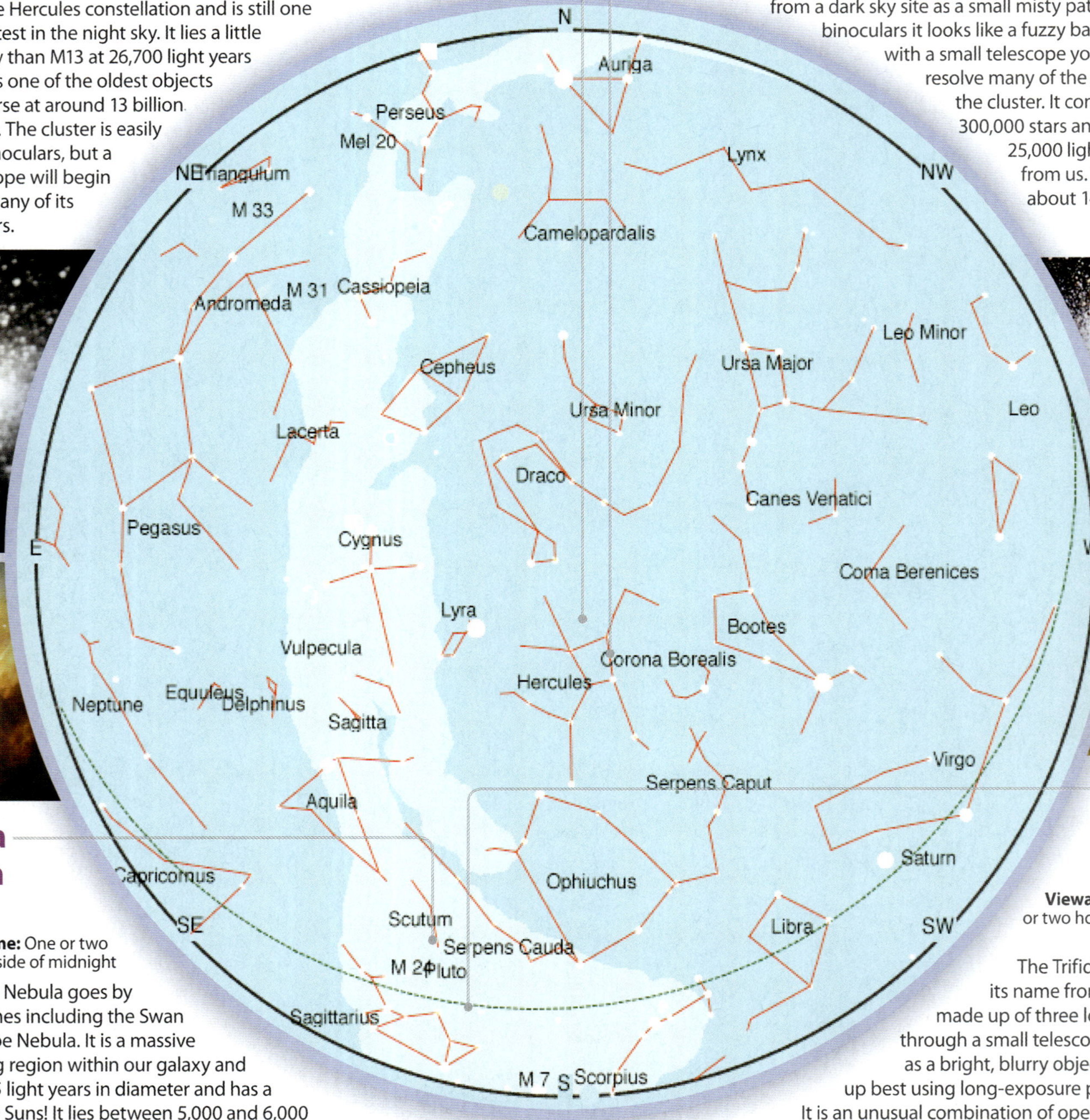

NORTHERN HEMISPHERE

Omega Nebula M17

Viewable time: One or two hours either side of midnight

The Omega Nebula goes by various names including the Swan or Horseshoe Nebula. It is a massive star-forming region within our galaxy and is around 15 light years in diameter and has a mass of 800 Suns! It lies between 5,000 and 6,000 light years from Earth. Through a small telescope it, like M20, seems to be a bright, blurry object that looks quite like the Greek letter omega from where it gets its name.

Trifid Nebula M20

Viewable time: One or two hours either side of midnight

The Trifid Nebula gets its name from the fact it's made up of three lobes. Viewed through a small telescope it appears as a bright, blurry object and shows up best using long-exposure photography. It is an unusual combination of open star cluster, emission and reflection nebulas and a dark nebula. It is 5,200 light years away from us and is host to a stellar nursery where new stars are being formed. The Hubble Space Telescope famously imaged this object in 1997.

Globular Cluster NGC 2808

Viewable time: All through the hours of darkness

This cluster lying at a distance of 31,300 light years is one of the most massive associated with the Milky Way. It contains over 1 million stars and is thought to be 12.5 billion years old. It lies within the boundary of the constellation of Carina and is easily visible in binoculars. Telescopes will resolve many of the stars in the cluster. Imaged by the Hubble Space Telescope in 2005 and 2006.

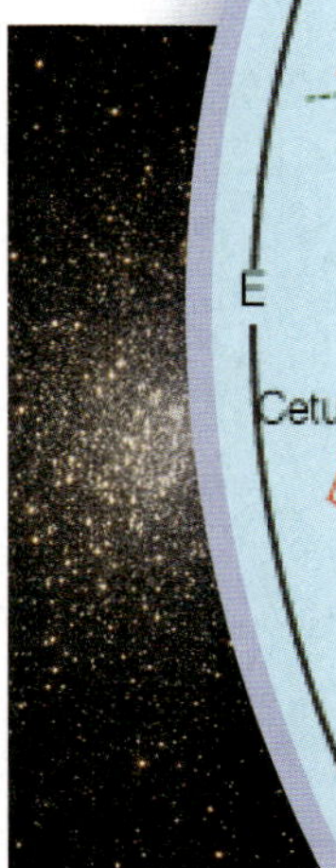

Open Cluster NGC 6025

Viewable time: All through the hours of darkness

Just visible to the naked eye as a faint misty patch of light, this is a lovely open cluster that shows up well in binoculars or a small telescope. It lies 2,700 light years away and was discovered by Abbe Lacaille in 1752 when he went to South Africa to observe the southern skies. There are around 30 stars easily visible in the cluster although it is thought that there may be as many as 78 altogether in the group.

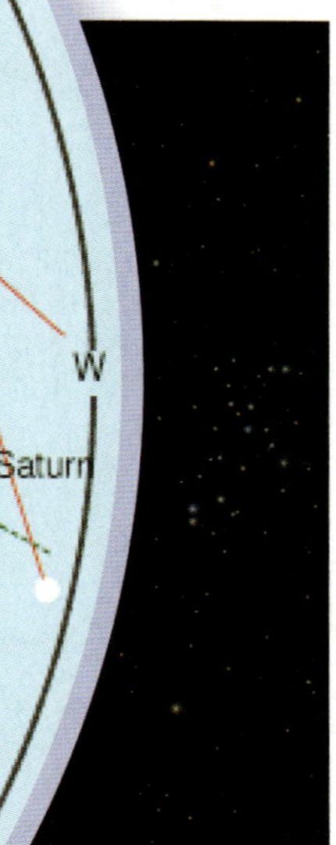

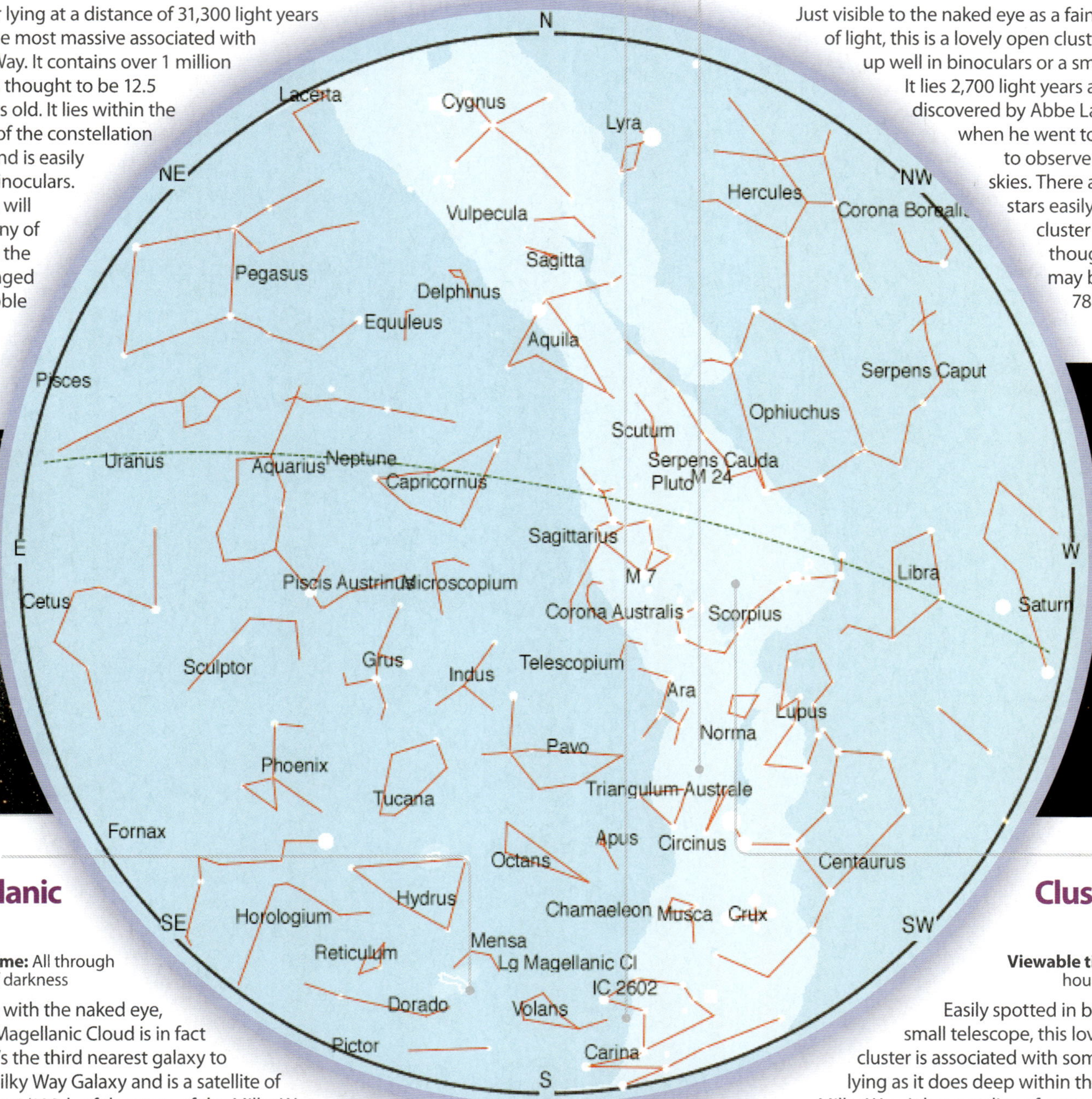

SOUTHERN HEMISPHERE

Large Magellanic Cloud

Viewable time: All through the hours of darkness

Easily seen with the naked eye, the Large Magellanic Cloud is in fact a galaxy. It's the third nearest galaxy to our own Milky Way Galaxy and is a satellite of it. It is about 1/100th of the mass of the Milky Way and it has probably been distorted through gravitational interactions with it. The Large Magellanic Cloud has a diameter of around 14,000 light years and lies around 163,000 light years from us. It is a member of the 'Local Group' of galaxies.

Open Cluster NGC 6281

Viewable time: Up to two hours before dawn

Easily spotted in binoculars or a small telescope, this lovely open star cluster is associated with some nebulosity, lying as it does deep within the band of the Milky Way. It has a radius of some 26 light years and has 55 known members in the group. It resides around 1,600 light years away. It was missed from both the Messier and Caldwell catalogues, but listed by John Herschel who described it as "curiously large".

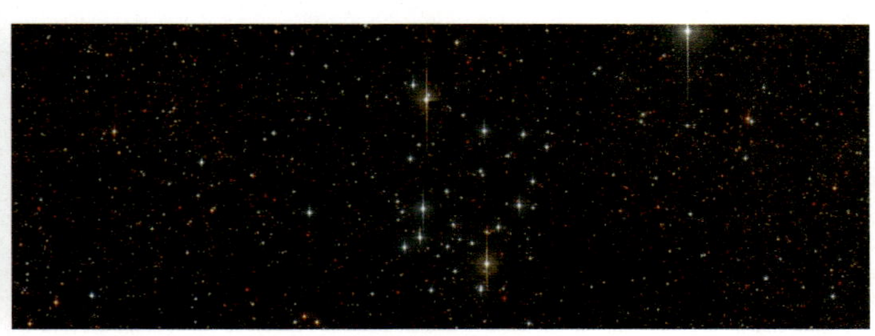

What's in the sky?

July

The summer offers some fantastic night-sky sights. Here are some of this month's must-sees

Deneb

Viewable time: All night

The star Deneb or Alpha Cygni is interesting because it's so bright. In fact it is slightly fainter than nearby Vega in Lyra the Lyre, but whereas Vega lies just over 25 light years from us, Deneb is around 2,600 light years away! So in order to appear almost as bright as Vega, it must be colossally bright. If Deneb was around 25 light years from us, it would drown out practically all the other stars in the sky.

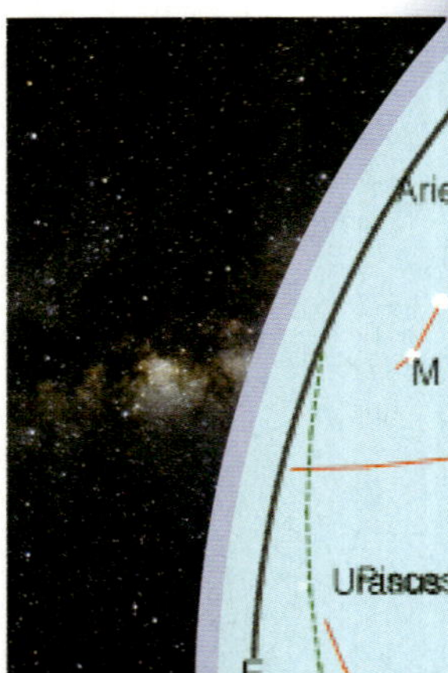

Planetary Nebula M57

Viewable time: All through the hours of darkness.

Otherwise known as the Ring Nebula for obvious reasons once you see it through a telescope, M57 is one of the brightest planetary nebulas in the sky. The term planetary nebula is a misnomer as these objects have nothing to do with planets. They are bubbles of gases which are puffed off the outer shell of a star similar to our Sun as it collapses into a white dwarf star. This will happen to the Sun in around 4 billion years' time.

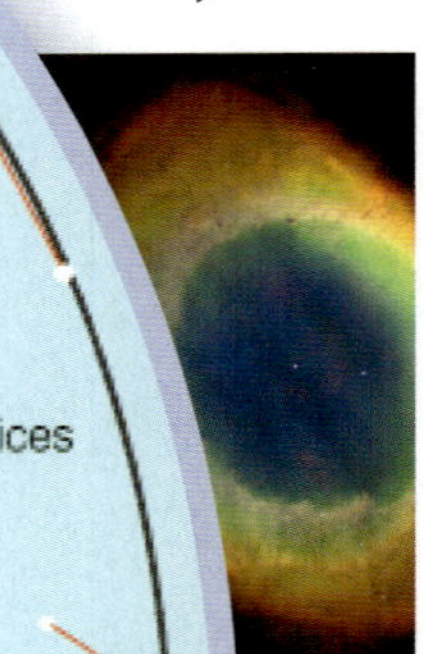

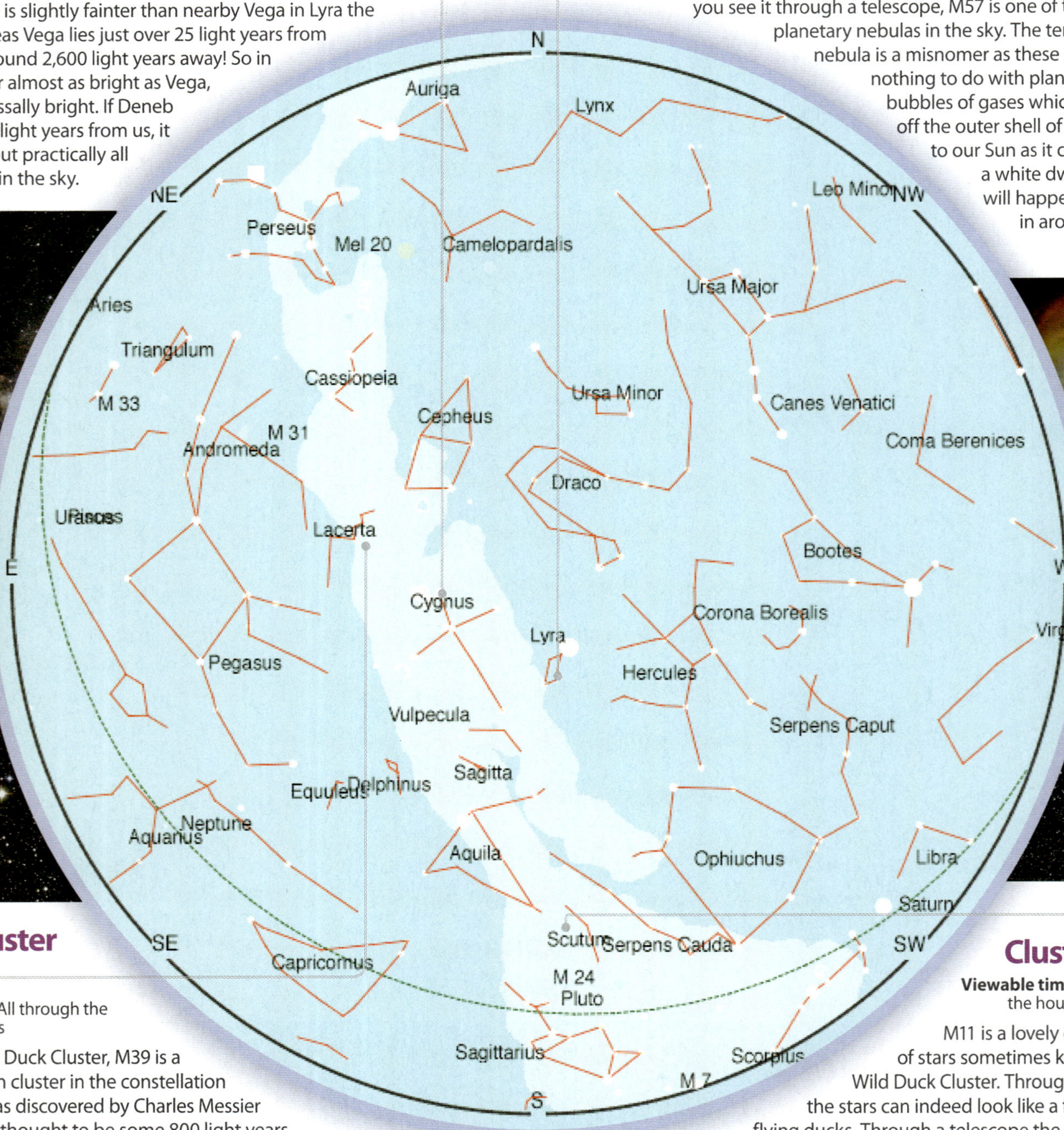

NORTHERN HEMISPHERE

Open Cluster M39

Viewable time: All through the hours of darkness

Unlike the Wild Duck Cluster, M39 is a very loose open cluster in the constellation of Cygnus. It was discovered by Charles Messier in 1764 and it's thought to be some 800 light years away from us. Its age is uncertain, probably being between 200 and 300 million years. Through a small telescope it looks like a collection of bright stars in the field of view of a low-power eyepiece. It shows up quite well in binoculars, too.

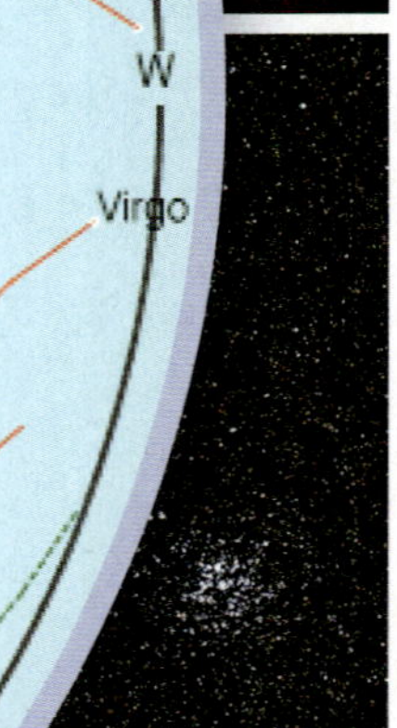

Open Cluster M11

Viewable time: All through the hours of darkness

M11 is a lovely open cluster of stars sometimes known as the Wild Duck Cluster. Through binoculars the stars can indeed look like a formation of flying ducks. Through a telescope the stars appear compact, almost like a globular cluster. This is in fact one of the richest and most compact star clusters known. It contains approximately 2,900 stars and is thought to be 220 million years old. It lies in the constellation of Scutum the Shield.

Formalhaut

Viewable time: All through the hours of darkness

The brightest star in the constellation of Piscis Austrinus is fascinating because it is known to have a 'protoplanetary disc' and at least one planet in orbit around it. It is the third brightest known star to have a planetary system. Formalhaut is nearly twice as massive as the Sun and younger, being at the most 400 million years in age. It is 25 light years away from Earth. Its name comes from Arabic and means 'mouth of the southern fish'.

SOUTHERN HEMISPHERE

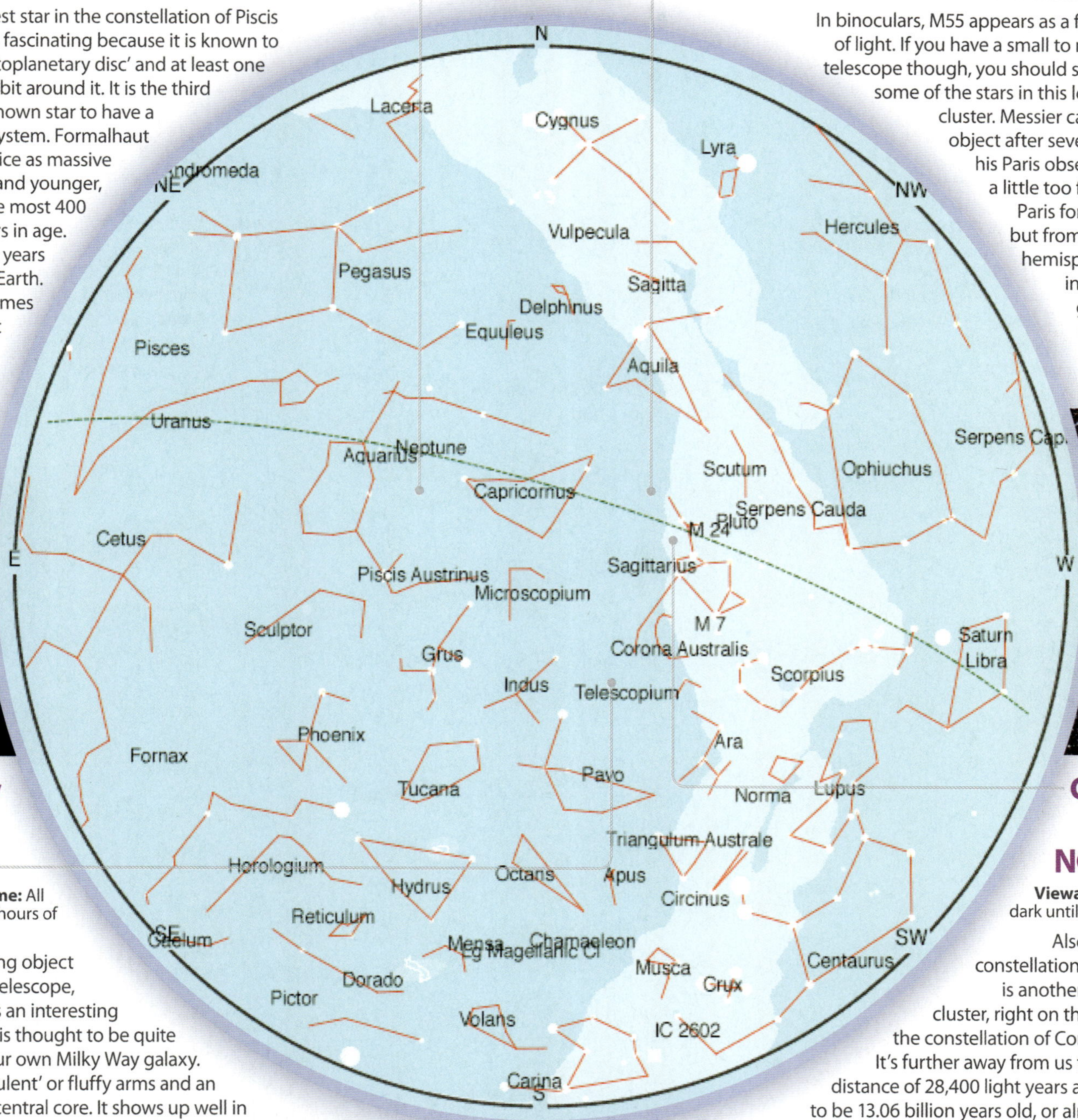

Globular Cluster M55

Viewable time: After dark until the early hours

In binoculars, M55 appears as a faint fuzzy ball of light. If you have a small to medium-sized telescope though, you should start to resolve some of the stars in this lovely globular cluster. Messier catalogued this object after several goes from his Paris observatory. It lies a little too far south from Paris for easy viewing but from the southern hemisphere it is high in the sky and a great target. It resides 17,600 light years from Earth.

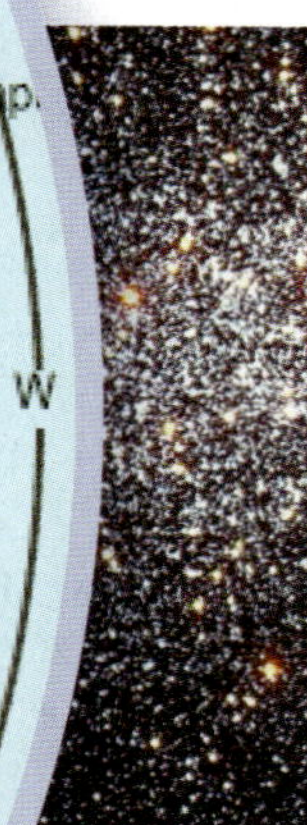

Galaxy NGC 6744

Viewable time: All through the hours of darkness

A challenging object for a small telescope, NGC 6744 is an interesting galaxy as it is thought to be quite similar to our own Milky Way galaxy. It has 'flocculent' or fluffy arms and an elongated central core. It shows up well in long-exposure astrophotography and is thought to lie around 31 million light years from us. It is quite difficult to spot in small telescopes, due to its low surface brightness.

Globular Cluster NGC 6723

Viewable time: After dark until the early hours

Also found in the constellation of Sagittarius is another fine globular cluster, right on the border with the constellation of Corona Australis. It's further away from us than M55, at a distance of 28,400 light years and is thought to be 13.06 billion years old, or almost as old as the known universe! It is bright enough to show up in binoculars as a faint smudge of light and looks better through a small to medium-sized telescope.

August-September

Late Summer/Autumn night skies are full of riches and wonders. Here are just a few of the best…

The Andromeda Galaxy

Viewable time: From an hour or two after dark until dawn

Messier 31, better known as the Andromeda Galaxy, is the most famous galaxy in the night sky. Visible to the naked eye as a faint smudge of light, binoculars will show the bright central core and a small telescope will give you an impression of just how large this object is. It lies 2.5 million light years from us and contains around 1 trillion stars, twice that of the Milky Way Galaxy.

Open Cluster M39

Viewable time: After dark and through to the early hours

This loose, open cluster of stars lies not far from the star Deneb in Cygnus (the Swan). It's one of the nearer star clusters to us at around 800 light years away. It is thought to be between 200 and 300 million years old. There are about 30 stars in this group and all contained in a volume of space about seven light years across. It's just visible to the naked eye from a dark sky site and binoculars will show it up well.

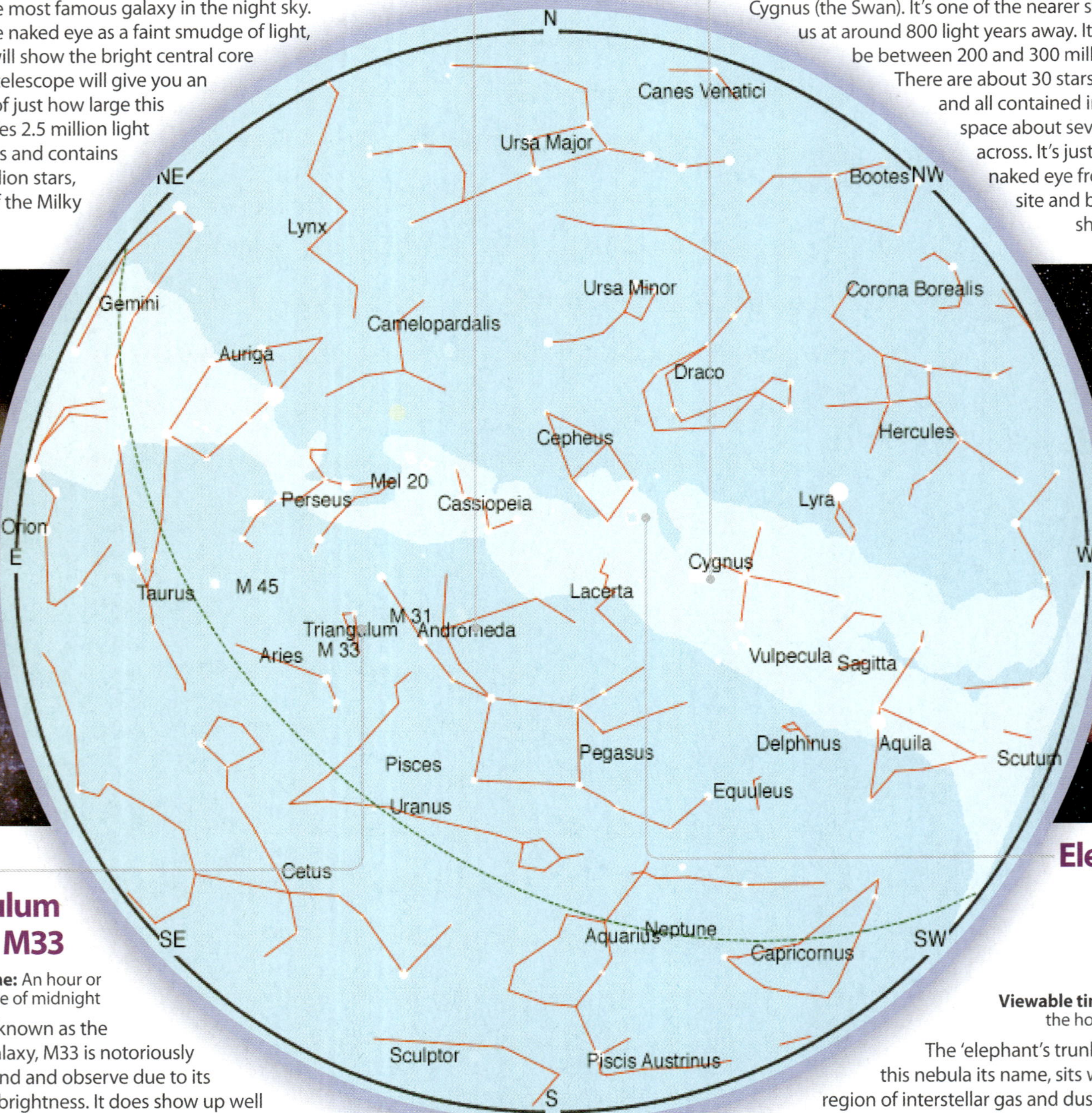

NORTHERN HEMISPHERE

The Triangulum Galaxy M33

Viewable time: An hour or two either side of midnight

Sometimes known as the Pinwheel Galaxy, M33 is notoriously difficult to find and observe due to its low surface brightness. It does show up well in long-exposure images, though. Through a small telescope you can pick it up as a faint, misty patch of light. It lies about three million light years away and is the third-largest member of the 'Local Group' of galaxies, which includes the Andromeda Galaxy and our own Milky Way Galaxy.

Elephant's Trunk Nebula IC 1396

Viewable time: All through the hours of darkness

The 'elephant's trunk' which gives this nebula its name, sits within a larger region of interstellar gas and dust. It's found in the constellation of Cepheus and lies 2,400 light years away. This dense area of gas is illuminated by a very bright and massive star. It is a star-forming region as it contains several very young, hot stars. The nebula is not visible to the naked eye, but shows up well in long-exposure images.

Globular Cluster
NGC 1261

Viewable time: All through the hours of darkness

Globular clusters are tight balls of stars which orbit around the plane of the Milky Way. NGC 1261 is a faint example at eighth magnitude, but is visible in binoculars and small telescopes. It lies in the constellation of Horologium and in a barren part of the sky for deep-sky objects accessible to amateur instruments. It's thought this cluster is around 12 billion years old, making the stars some of the oldest in the universe.

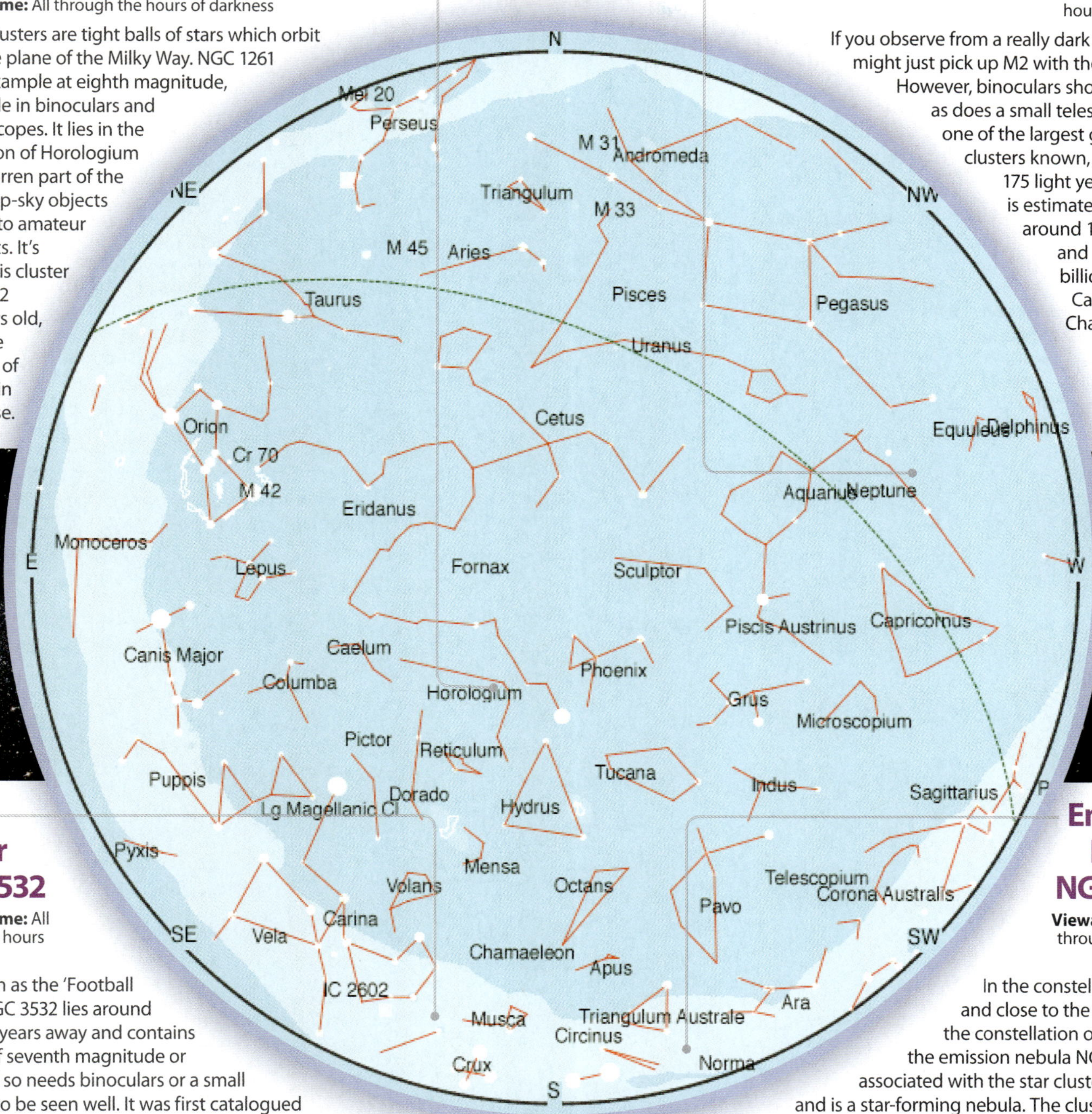

Globular Cluster M2

Viewable time: All through the hours of darkness

If you observe from a really dark sky site, you might just pick up M2 with the naked eye. However, binoculars show it up well, as does a small telescope. This is one of the largest globular star clusters known, being some 175 light years across. It is estimated to contain around 150,000 stars and is around 13 billion years old. Catalogued by Charles Messier in 1760, this cluster lies 33,000 light years away.

Open Cluster NGC 3532

Viewable time: All through the hours of darkness

Also known as the 'Football Cluster', NGC 3532 lies around 1,320 light years away and contains 150 stars of seventh magnitude or fainter and so needs binoculars or a small telescope to be seen well. It was first catalogued by Nicolas Lacaille in 1755 and was the first object to be observed by the Hubble Space Telescope in 1990. John Herschel considered it one of the finest irregular clusters in the night sky.

Emission Nebula NGC 6188

Viewable time: All through the hours of darkness

In the constellation of Ara and close to the border with the constellation of Norma lies the emission nebula NGC 6188. It is associated with the star cluster NGC 6193 and is a star-forming nebula. The cluster is visible to the naked eye, but the nebula only shows up in long-exposure astrophotography. It occupies a region of space around 600 light years across and can be found 4,000 light years away from Earth.

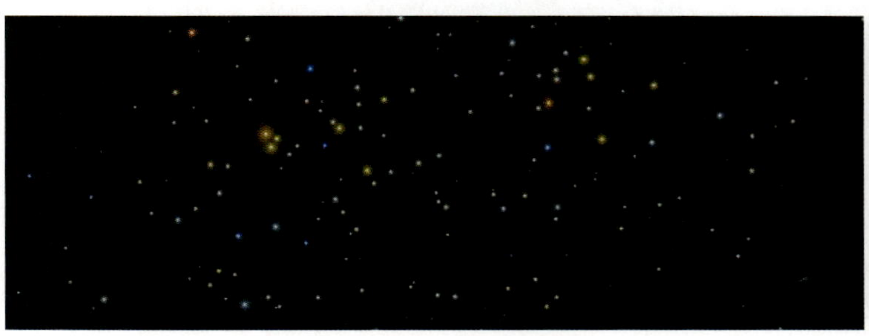

©ESO

September-October

The skies are darker for longer now, so there's more time to view those lovely deep-sky objects…

Star Cluster NGC 752

Viewable time: From an hour or two after dark until dawn

This star cluster was originally discovered by Caroline Herschel in 1783 and catalogued in 1786. It lies in the constellation of Andromeda and is just detectable with the naked eye from a very dark sky site. A telescope will show around 60 stars in the cluster but they are all quite faint. Long-exposure photography will show this group in its true glory. It's thought these stars are around 1,300 light years from Earth.

Galaxy M74

Viewable time: An hour or so after dark and through to the early hours

Messier 74 is a face-on spiral galaxy lying around 32 million light years away from us. You'll need a moderate-sized telescope to see it well as it is quite faint. You can see the spiral arms in long-exposure photographs. It can be found in the constellation Pisces near the star Eta Piscium, it played host to a recent bright supernova and for a brief period was brighter than the rest of the entire galaxy.

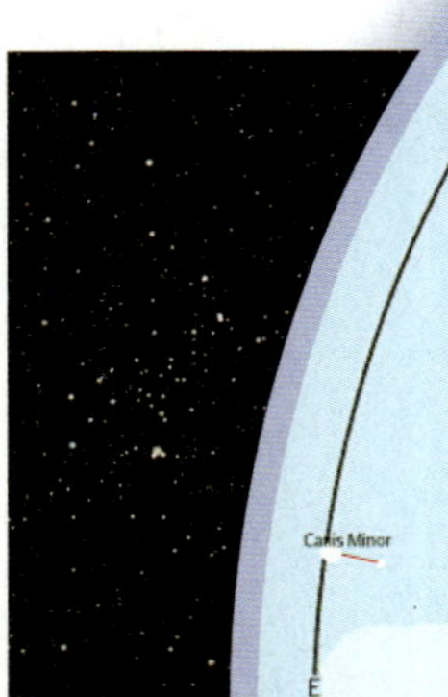

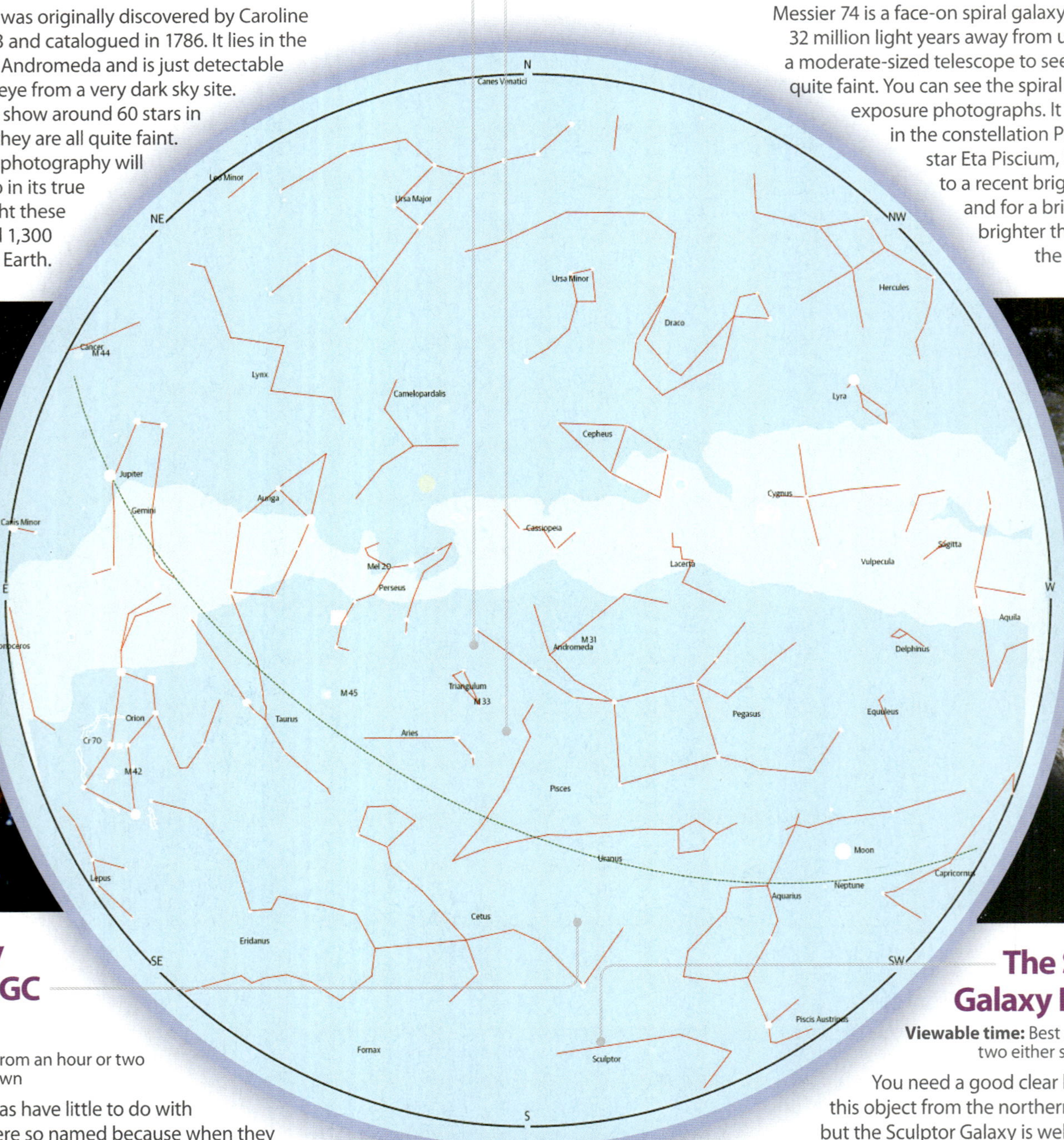

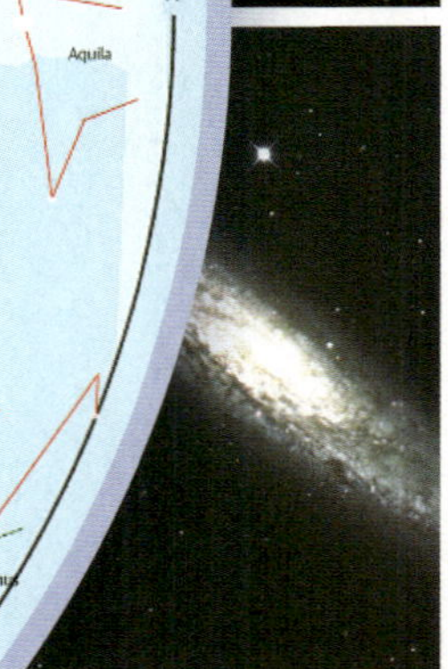

Planetary Nebula NGC 246

Viewable time: From an hour or two after dark until dawn

Planetary nebulas have little to do with planets, they were so named because when they were discovered it was thought they looked a little like ghostly planets. NGC 246 is named the Skull Nebula and the Pac-Man Nebula. It's the remains of a star that has ejected its outer layers of gas, which then formed a bubble surrounding it and is expanding into space.

The Sculptor Galaxy NGC 253

Viewable time: Best seen an hour or two either side of midnight

You need a good clear horizon to see this object from the northern hemisphere, but the Sculptor Galaxy is well worth a look through a telescope. It's sometimes known as the Silver Coin and is an intermediate spiral galaxy approximately 13 million light years away. You will need a large aperture telescope to see its spiral structure, but it shows up well in long-exposure photographs.

NORTHERN HEMISPHERE

GALAXY NGC 1300

GLOBULAR CLUSTER NGC 1851

NGC 2070 STAR CLUSTER WITH NEBULOSITY

Globular Cluster M79

Viewable time: From an hour or two after dark until dawn

M79 is an attractive globular cluster of stars in the Lepus constellation. It shows up as a misty patch of light in binoculars, while a small telescope will start to resolve some of its stars. It's 42,000 light years away and is believed to be one of just a handful of clusters that have been captured by our own Milky Way Galaxy rather than being a native to it.

Galaxy NGC 1300

Viewable time: All through the hours of darkness

About 70 million light years away lies the barred spiral galaxy NGC 1300. The Hubble Space Telescope took an amazing picture of this galaxy clearly showing the spiral arms, the 'bar' and the dust and gas within it. It's110,000 light years across and was discovered in 1835 by John Herschel. You'll need quite a large telescope to see it well, but binoculars will show it as a faint smudge of light.

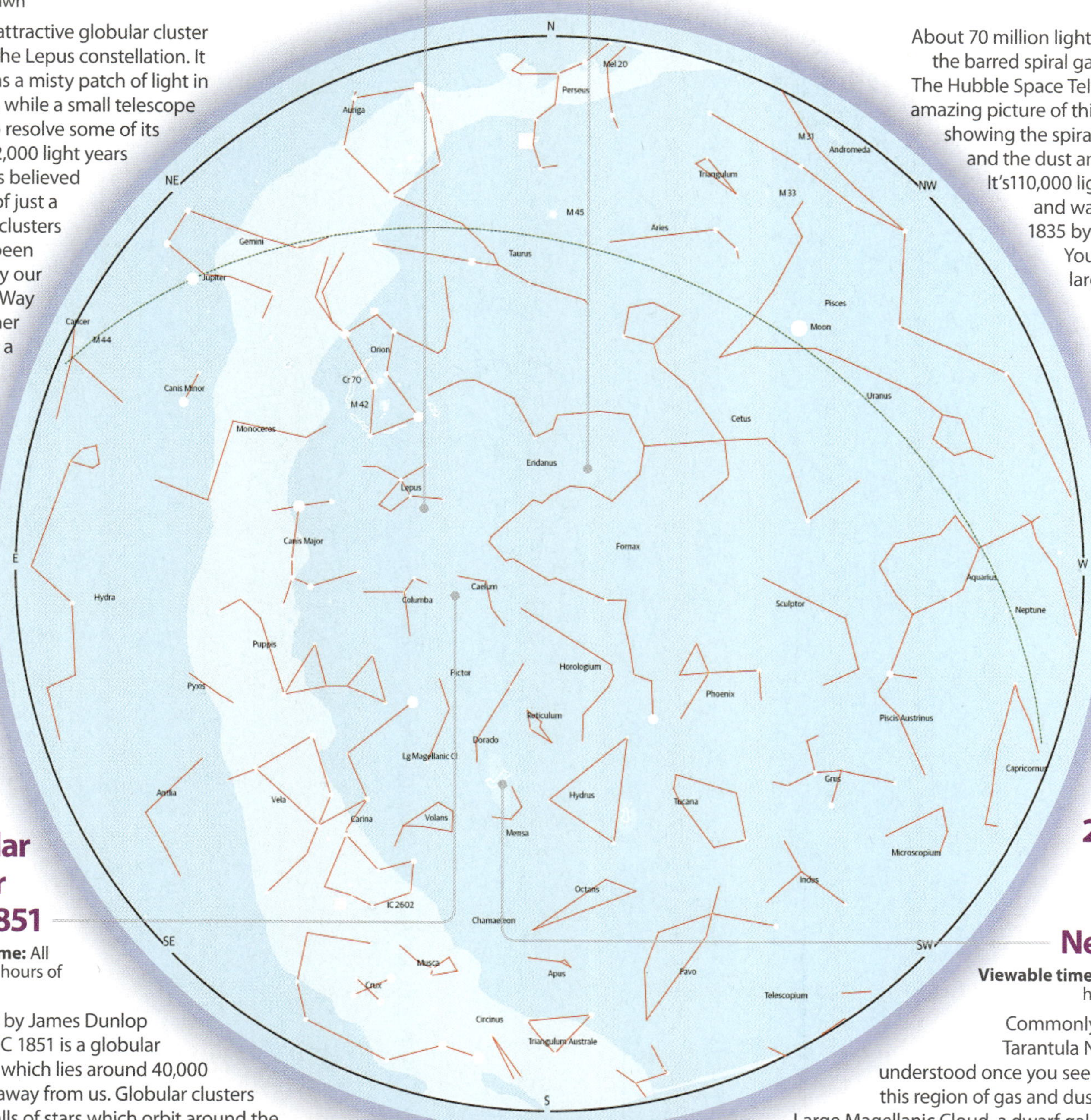

SOUTHERN HEMISPHERE

Globular Cluster NGC 1851

Viewable time: All through the hours of darkness

Discovered by James Dunlop in 1826, NGC 1851 is a globular star cluster which lies around 40,000 light years away from us. Globular clusters are tight balls of stars which orbit around the plane of our galaxy, the Milky Way. Easily visible in binoculars and small telescopes, this cluster can be found in the constellation of Columba. Long-exposure photographs show the structure of the cluster well. It is thought to be around 10 billion years old.

NGC 2070 Star Cluster with Nebulosity

Viewable time: All through the hours of darkness

Commonly known as the Tarantula Nebula, a name understood once you see a photograph, this region of gas and dust resides in the Large Magellanic Cloud, a dwarf galaxy interacting with our own Milky Way Galaxy. Also known as 30 Doradus, this cloud of gas and dust glows brightly, receiving its energy from the cluster, and must be very active because it is easily visible despite lying around 160,000 light years away from us.

October-November

October and November offer some of the most spectacular night sky sights. Here are eight of the best for you to discover

Andromeda Galaxy (M31)

Viewable time: Around midnight

Our nearest neighbouring galaxy is ideally positioned high in the north for northern hemisphere observers in the autumn. We can clearly see its central 'bulge' in binoculars or a small telescope. With a large telescope, M31's major dust lane can be seen. To find this monster, first locate Beta Andromedae (Mirach). From here, sweep to Mu Andromedae and then continue for the same distance again.

Veil Nebula

Viewable time: Before midnight

The Veil Nebula glows as it collides with interstellar gas and dust, and is clearly visible in binoculars and telescopes. Start from Epsilon Cygni and sweep approximately four degrees south to the star 52 Cygni. This bright star appears connected to the Western Veil – nicknamed the Witch's Broom – which appears like a silver blade. The larger Eastern Veil is just a couple of degrees to the east.

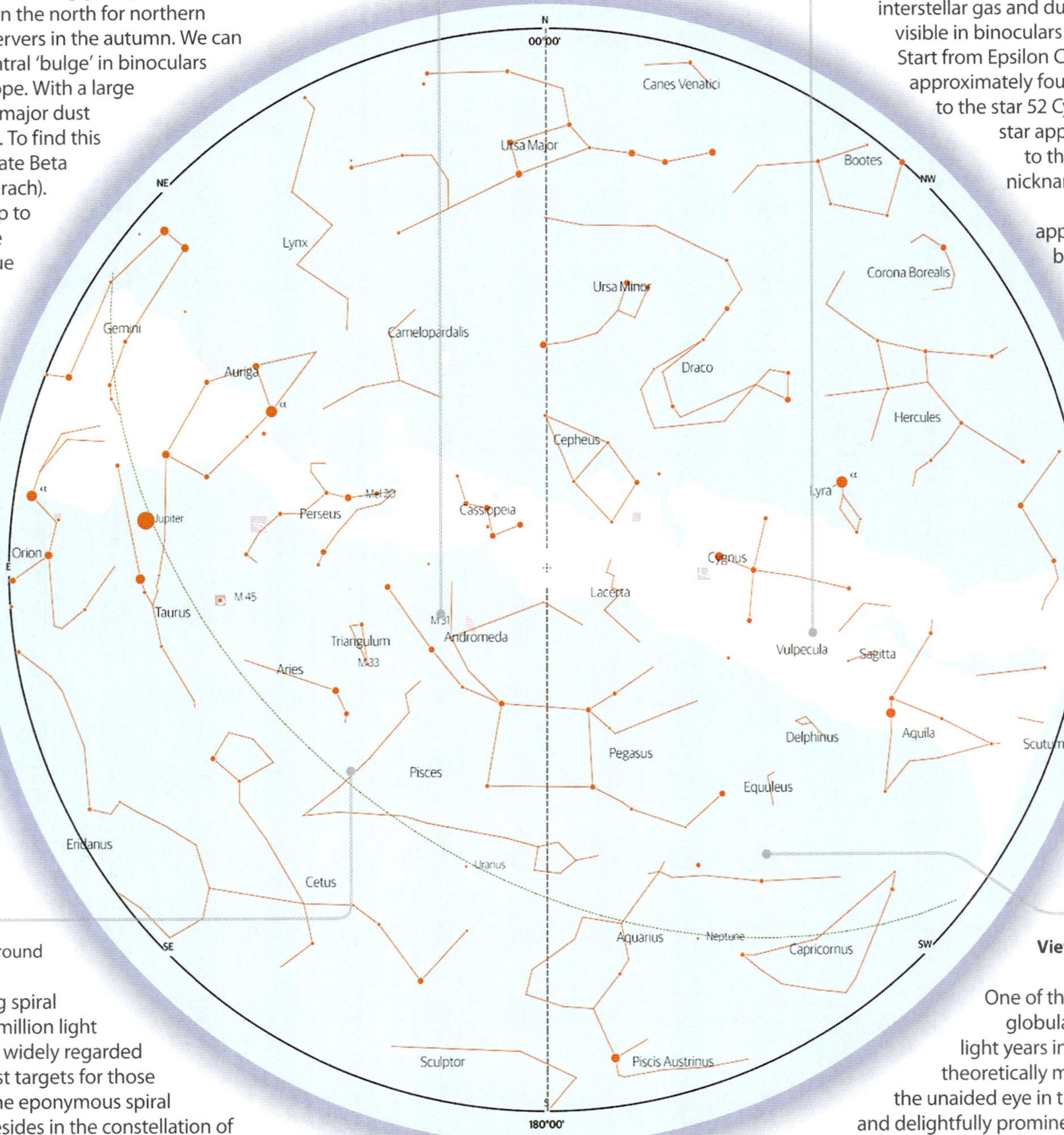

M74

Viewable time: Around midnight

M74 is a stunning spiral galaxy some 32 million light years distant. It's widely regarded as one of the best targets for those wishing to see the eponymous spiral structure. M74 resides in the constellation of Pisces (the fishes), but it's helpful to use the two brightest stars in the neighbouring Aries (the golden ram). From Hamal (Alpha) sweep to Sheratan (Beta) and continue for about twice the distance to Eta Piscium. M74 lies about one degree south of this line.

NORTHERN HEMISPHERE

M2

Viewable time: After sunset

One of the largest known globular clusters at 175 light years in diameter, M2 is theoretically manageable with the unaided eye in the darkest skies, and delightfully prominent in binoculars and small telescopes. M2 occupies the fairly complex constellation of Aquarius (the Water Bearer) but its unmistakable non-stellar appearance makes it a snap to find. Simply find the double star Beta Aquarii (Sadalsuud) and from here sweep about five degrees northward.

The Orionids

Viewable time:
October, before dawn

This meteor shower is a regular occurrence and this year it will be best viewed just before dawn. If you trace the meteors backwards you will find that they seem to originate from the club of the constellation Orion (the hunter).

M79

Viewable time: After midnight

Over 40,000 light years from Earth, the globular cluster M79 is a curious object. Research within the last decades supports the idea that it may have been gently persuaded by the gravitational pull of the Milky Way galaxy, to leave its home – the Canis Major dwarf galaxy. Therefore, it's unusually placed for a globular, in Lepus. Find Beta Lepus (Nihal) and sweep about four degrees southward at low power to see this treat.

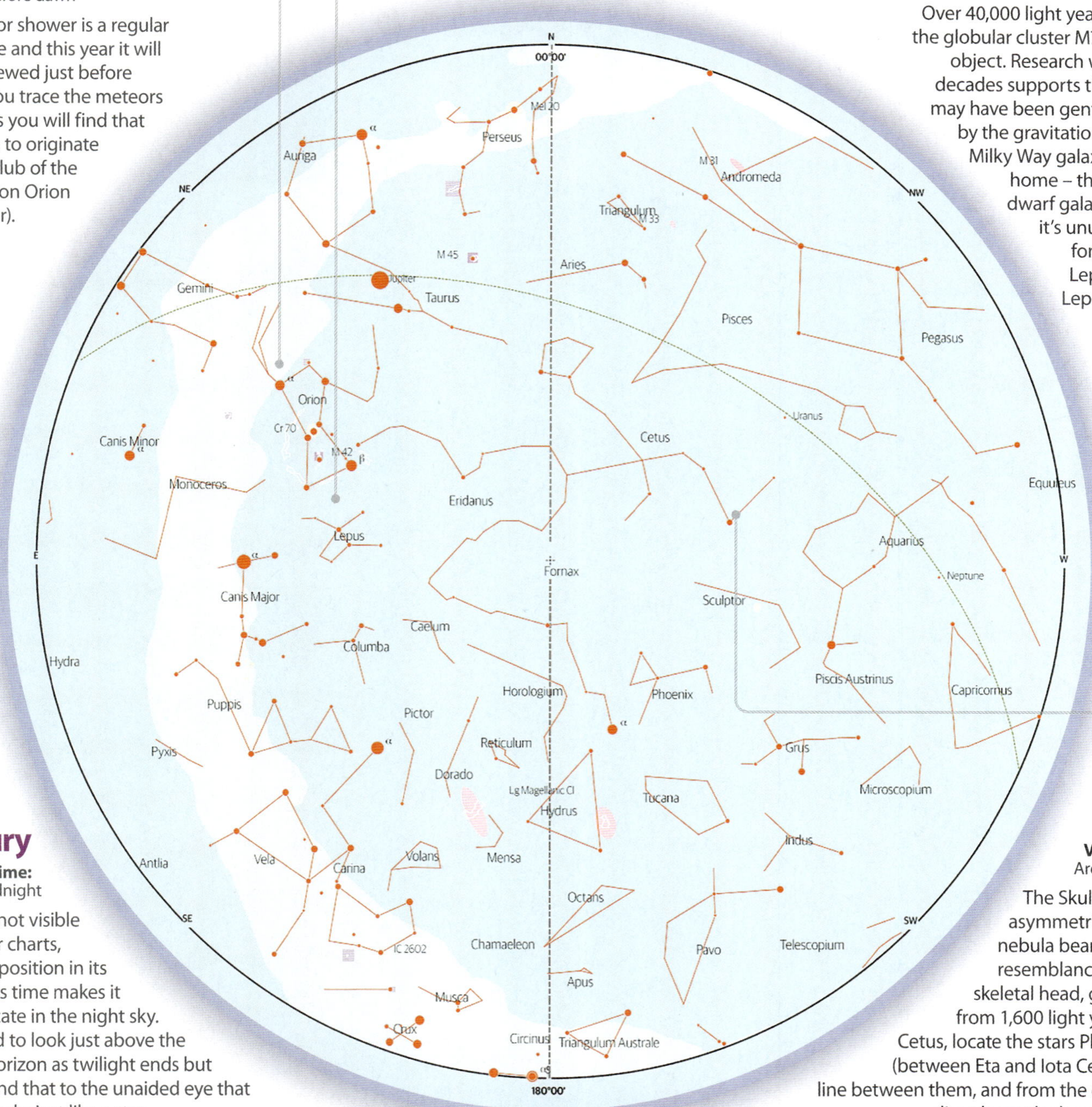

Mercury

Viewable time:
Around midnight

Although not visible on our star charts, Mercury's position in its orbit at this time makes it easy to locate in the night sky. You'll need to look just above the western horizon as twilight ends but bear in mind that to the unaided eye that Mercury looks just like a star.

Skull Nebula (NGC 246)

Viewable time:
Around midnight

The Skull Nebula is an asymmetrical planetary nebula bearing a striking resemblance to a ghastly skeletal head, grinning at us from 1,600 light years away. In Cetus, locate the stars Phi-1 and Phi-2 (between Eta and Iota Ceti). Bisect the line between them, and from the centre sweep directly south about one degree.

SOUTHERN HEMISPHERE

What's in the sky?

November-December

Whether you're using the naked eye, binoculars or a telescope, there's plenty to see. Here are some of the season's highlights…

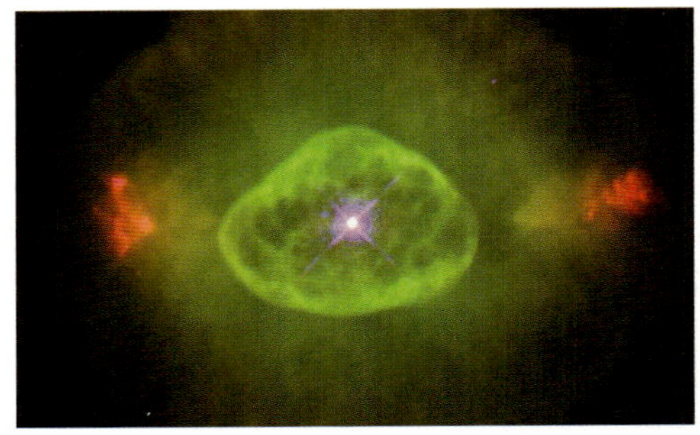

NGC 663

Viewable time: After dark and all night

This young cluster of a few hundred stars sparkles in the constellation of Cassiopeia like a jewel in a crown. It's found between the stars Ruchbach and Segin, and it's a compelling sight via your binoculars or a small telescope. Train a large telescope on it and prepare to be absorbed by a rich, uniformly bright field of lights like a swarm of fireflies.

Blinking Nebula (NGC 6826)

Viewable time: After dark and all night

Why does this little nebula blink when seen through a telescope? It's an illusion caused by the bright central star overwhelming the pale gas and dust around it. You can find it in the feathers of the swan near the star Theta Cygni.

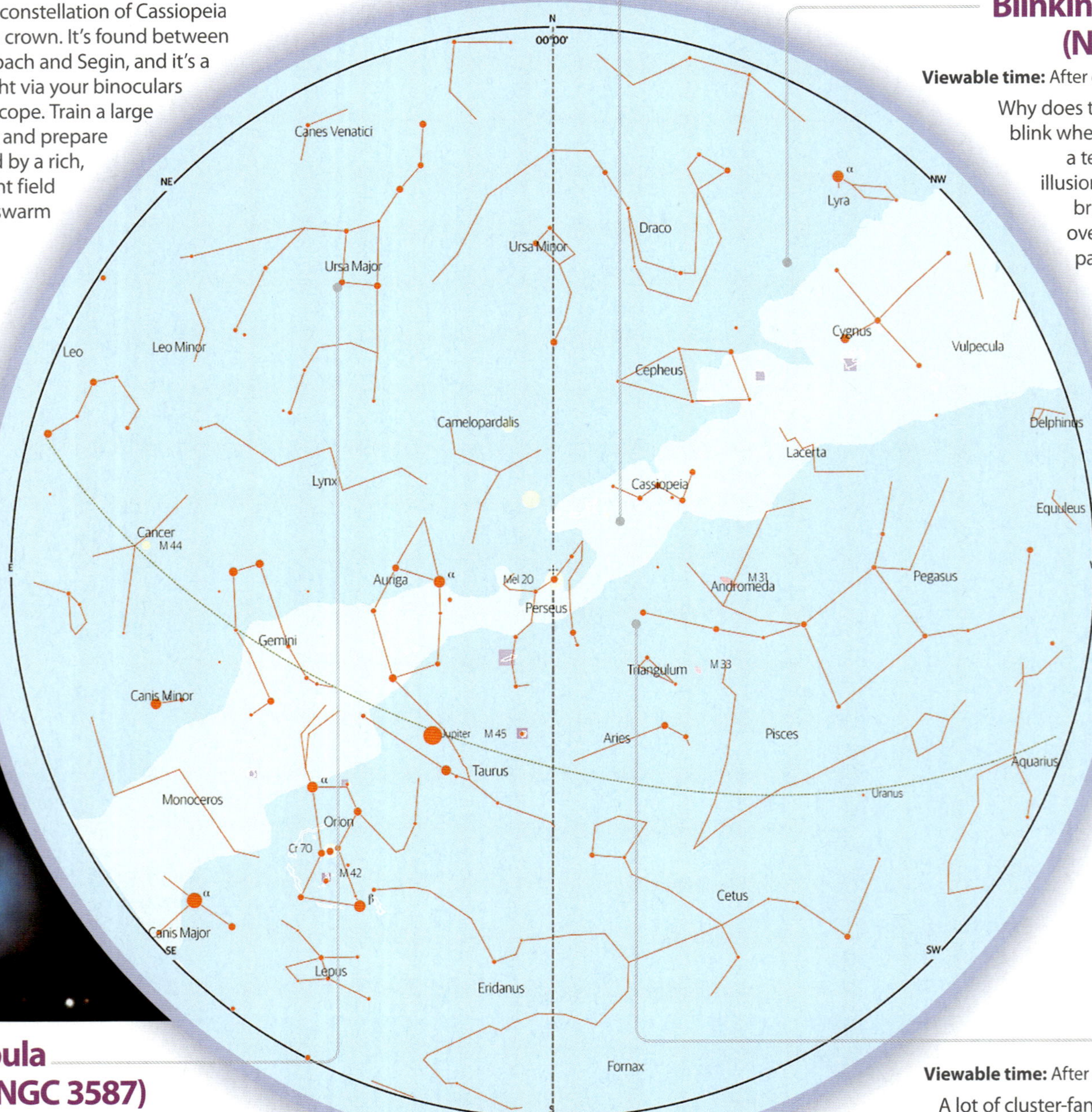

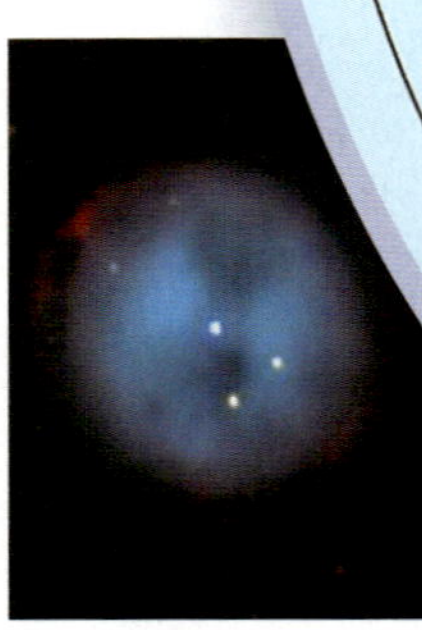

Owl Nebula (M97 or NGC 3587)

Viewable time: After dark and all night

You'll need a large telescope to understand the name, but even a small telescope will reveal a hint of this popular planetary nebula in Ursa Major. Its big eyes gaze at us from over 2,500 light years away, but studies show it's been watching for less than 6,000 years. This is a young nebula. It sits within a couple of degrees from Merak.

NORTHERN HEMISPHERE

NGC 752

Viewable time: After dark and all night

A lot of cluster-fans refer to this as Hodierna's cluster, because we think Giovanni Hodierna was the first to discover it back in the 17th century. Then for over 100 years it was lost or forgotten, only to be rediscovered by none other than Caroline Herschel in 1783. Look for it in Andromeda, around five degrees south-west of the star Almaak in the direction of Triangulum.

Regor (Gamma Velorum)

Viewable time: After dark and all night

Famously named by Apollo astronaut Gus Grissom for his friend Roger, this beautiful system of at least six stars appears as a tiny open cluster at the eyepiece, and its most prominent pair are readily split with just binoculars. Regor is the star adjoining Vela to Carina, the great ship once known as Jason's Argo Navis.

M41

Viewable time: An hour or so after dark

One of the greatest open clusters of all, and another discovered by Hodierna, M41 glitters in the constellation of Canis Major about four degrees south of Sirius, the brightest star in the whole sky. Even though they vary wildly in apparent brightness, a significant number of the cluster's 100 or so stars can be teased out with a rich-field telescope.

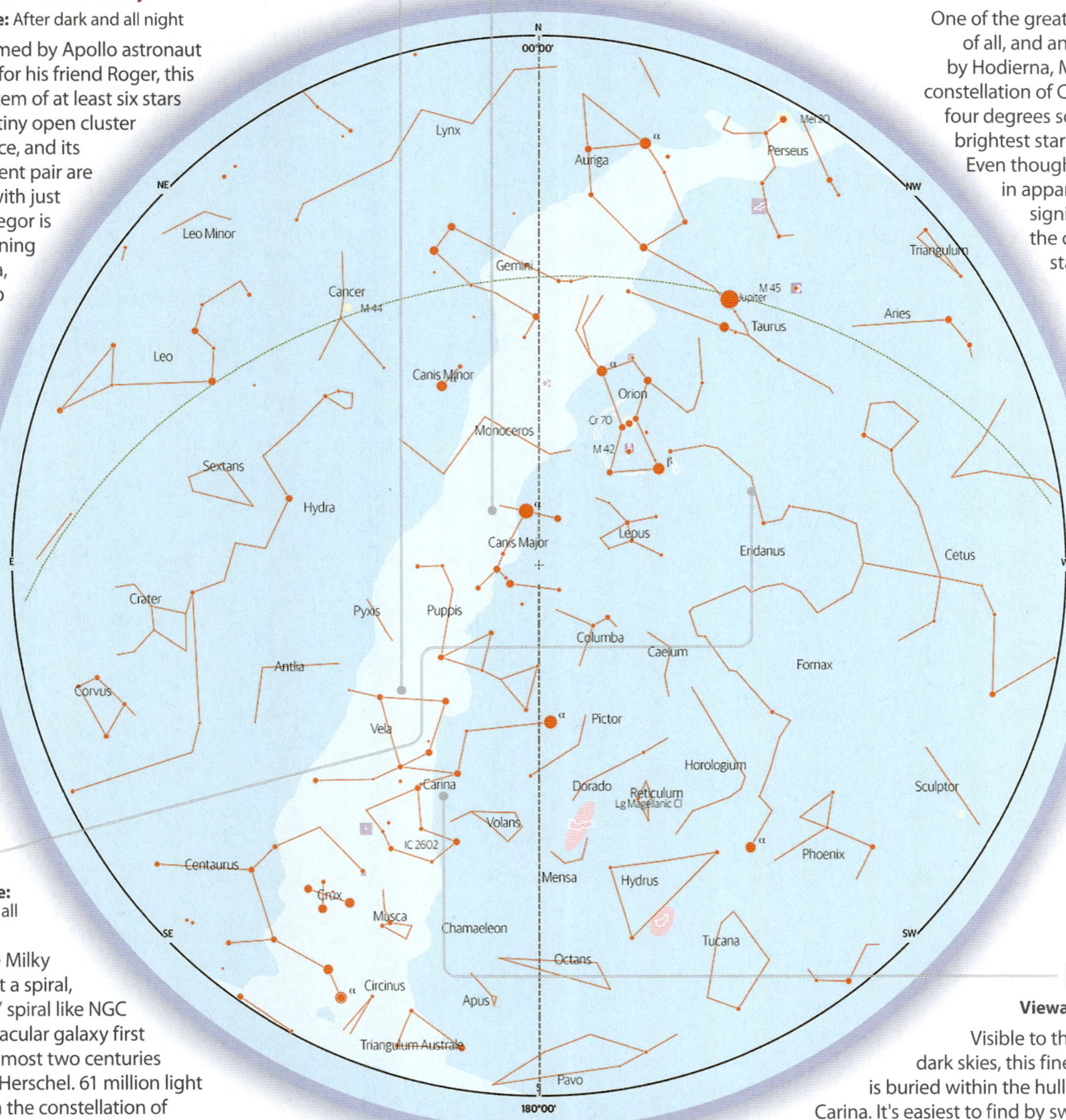

SOUTHERN HEMISPHERE

NGC 1300

Viewable time: After dark and all night

We know the Milky Way's not just a spiral, but a 'barred' spiral like NGC 1300, a spectacular galaxy first discovered almost two centuries ago by John Herschel. 61 million light years away in the constellation of Eridanus (the river), NGC 1300 is also similar in size to our home galaxy, and can be seen with a large telescope. Look just over two degrees north of 16 Eridani.

NGC 2808

Viewable time: All night

Visible to the unaided eye in dark skies, this fine globular cluster is buried within the hull of the great ship Carina. It's easiest to find by sweeping a couple of degrees north-east from the star Alpha in the neighbouring constellation of Volans (the flying fish). In binoculars or a telescope, some of its 1 million stars can be individually resolved.

December

As the year comes to an end, many of us will celebrate another year of accomplishments. Why not celebrate the wonder of the sky, too?

Bode's Nebulae (M81 & M82)

Viewable time: All night

This pair of galaxies is an awesome sight. M81 is a near face-on spiral, whereas M82 appears like a cosmic cigar. The two are physically interacting and are close enough together to be nicely framed with good detail. Locate them by sweeping about ten degrees northwest of Dubhe.

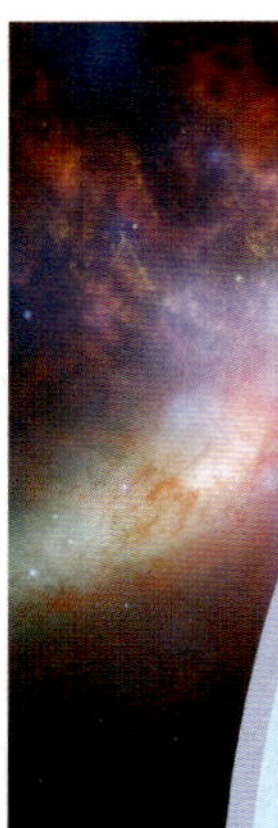

Auriga Clusters (M36, M37 & M38)

Viewable time: All night

Auriga hosts many star clusters, but the greatest must be the three catalogued by Charles Messier. Found in the southern half of the constellation, the trio are individually very interesting, but just unmissable when framed together at low power. Open clusters are common in the plane of the galaxy, where Auriga lies, and remind us that the Milky Way is a spiral.

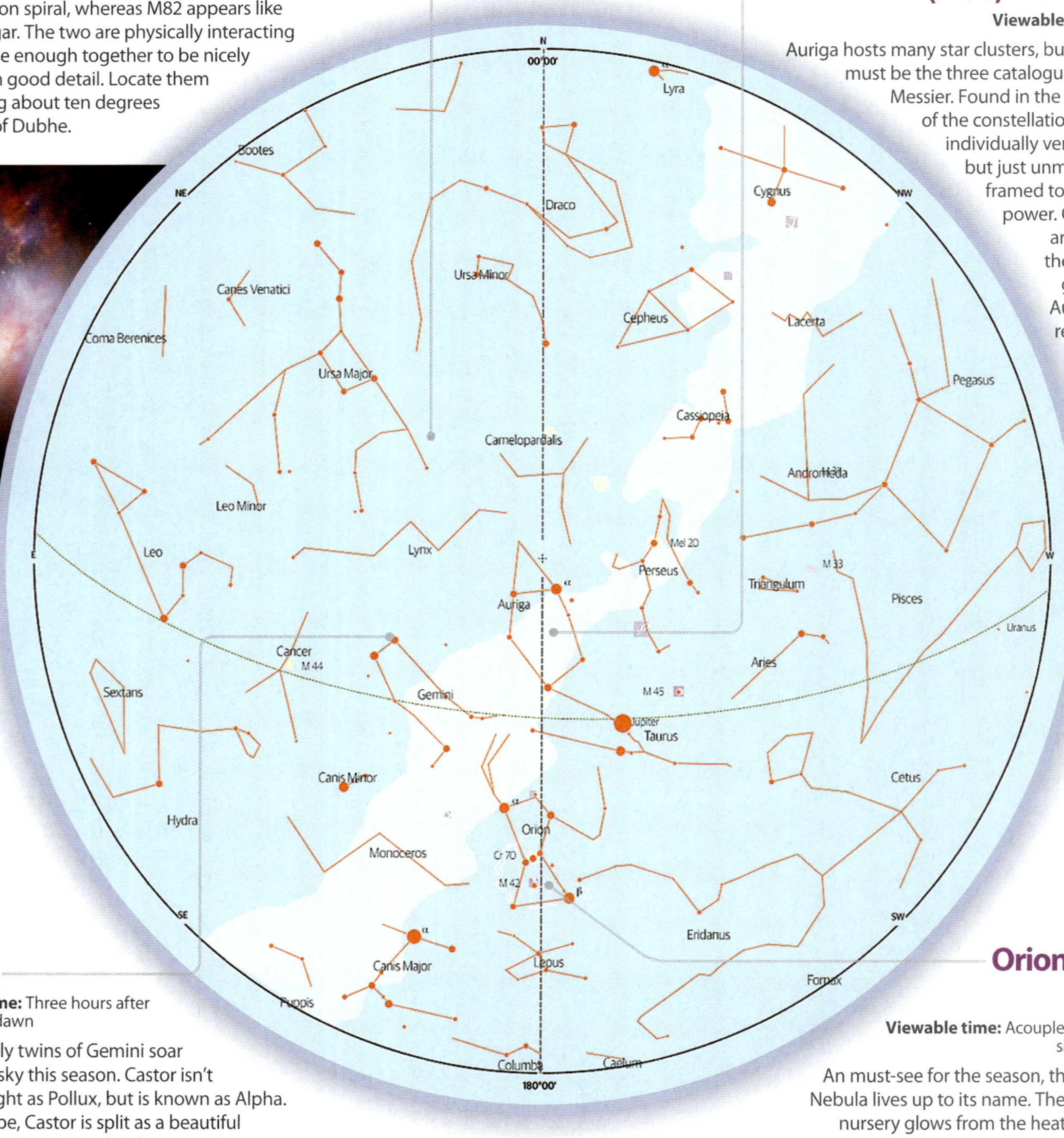

NORTHERN HEMISPHERE

Castor

Viewable time: Three hours after sunset until dawn

The heavenly twins of Gemini soar high in the sky this season. Castor isn't quite as bright as Pollux, but is known as Alpha. In a telescope, Castor is split as a beautiful close binary star, and each is known to be a spectroscopic binary. The two visible stars orbit each other about once every 470 years.

Orion Nebula (M42)

Viewable time: Acouple of hours either side of midnight

An must-see for the season, the Great Orion Nebula lives up to its name. The young stellar nursery glows from the heat produced by powerful infant stars at its core. In binoculars or a telescope, it 'sa distinct 'bow' shape, and can be found in the middle of Orion's sword.

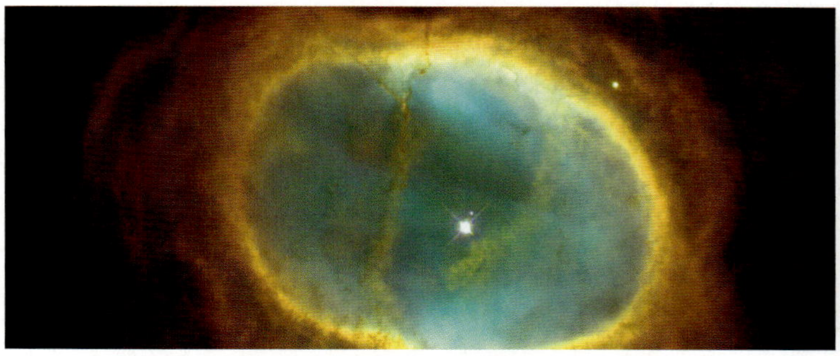

Eight-Burst Nebula (NGC 3132)

Viewable time: All night

Sitting in the constellation Vela, the Sail, the Eight-Burst Nebula is a fine sight in a larger telescope at high power. The dim central star at the centre is really a double, with the fainter of the two being the white dwarf responsible for the nebulosity, sometimes also known as the Southern Ring Nebula. Find it just northwest of the star q Velorum.

M47 (NGC 2422)

Viewable time: All night

The frequently overlooked constellation of Puppis (the Poop Deck) actually runs through the Milky Way, and contains a large number of open clusters. One of the finest is M47, lying some 1,600 light years distant. It harbours around 50-100 stars, and can be found by sweeping about five degrees east-northeast of Sirius. With binoculars you may also spot M46 in the same field.

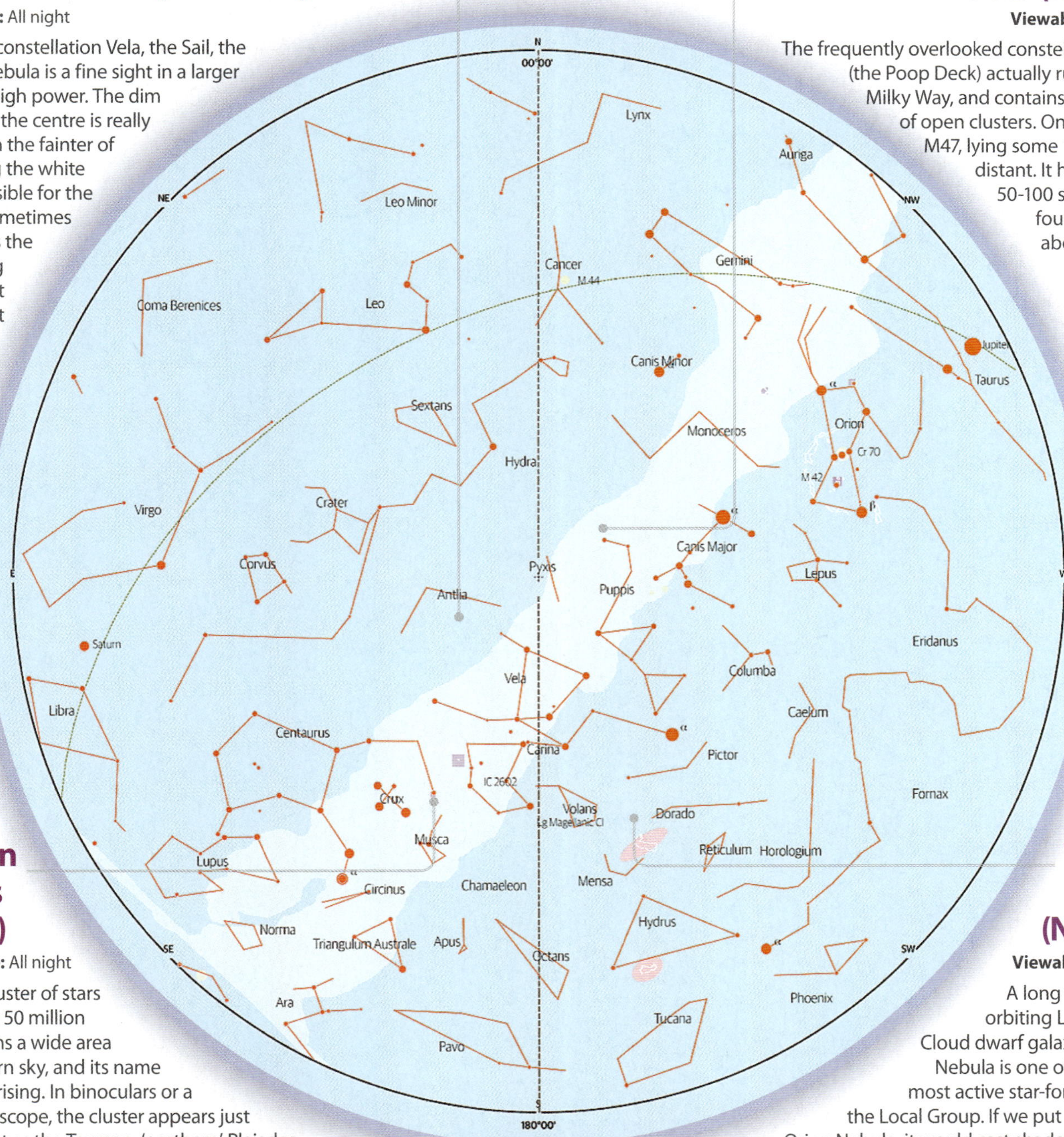

SOUTHERN HEMISPHERE

Southern Pleaides (IC 2602)

Viewable time: All night

This young cluster of stars no more than 50 million years old spans a wide area of the southern sky, and its name is hardly surprising. In binoculars or a widefield telescope, the cluster appears just as magnificent as the Taurean, 'northern' Pleiades. It too can also be seen with the unaided eye, and can be found simply by locating Theta Carinae, which the cluster surrounds.

Tarantula Nebula (NGC 2070)

Viewable time: All night

A long way away in the orbiting Large Magellanic Cloud dwarf galaxy, the Tarantula Nebula is one of the largest and most active star-forming regions in the Local Group. If we put it in place of the Orion Nebula, it would cast shadows at night. This colossal cloud looks remarkable in telescopes, showing plenty of detail and structure. Try finding it first with the unaided eye!

What to observe

©NASA

©NASA

"From planets and stars to moons and meteors, there's an almost endless list of objects waiting to be seen"

©ESO

102 Great lunar sights

114 Amazing star clusters

©NASA

118 The Big Dipper

©Alamy

View planets through a telescope

We've all seen hi-res illustrations of what the planets of our galaxy look like up close, but what do they look like through a telescope?

You'll need the right conditions to get the most-impressive views of the planets

Would you like to see another world with your own eyes? You probably already have! While they don't have futuristic alien civilisations, five of the seven planets of our Solar System (those other than Earth) are visible to the naked eye, appearing as bright, untwinkling and fast moving objects in the night sky. These five planets are Mercury, Venus, Mars, Jupiter and Saturn, with the latter four having an unmistakable yellow or orange tint as they shine alongside the other stars. Uranus and Neptune can be seen with binoculars, but by far the best way to see them all, save for having your own interplanetary spacecraft, is with a telescope. These pictures will help to give you some idea of what to look for and what to expect, though photos do not really convey the deeply personal, subjective experience of visual astronomy. Those beautiful pictures of the cosmos from space telescopes such as Hubble and probes like Voyager, comprising huge exposure times and post-processing, dazzling depth and astonishing colour; they're immeasurably inspiring to be sure.

To the eye, however, the view is quite different. Details are much more subtle at the eyepiece, and your view depends upon which telescope you're using, and more importantly, upon how favourable the atmospheric conditions are. Don't lose heart though, because to see the other planets – worlds as real as ours – with your own eyes, is an unforgettable experience.

"Your view depends upon which telescope you use and the atmospheric conditions"

Mercury

Telescope: Astro-Physics Stowaway f5

In close-up, the smallest planet in our Solar System looks strikingly similar to the dark-side of our Moon, albeit almost twice as large. Unfortunately, we never get such a close-up from Earth, but large aperture instruments at high power will show Mercury's phases at the eyepiece. Make sure the Sun has set completely before trying to observe Mercury, as it will be obscured in its glare due to its proximity. It does rotate – however a Mercurian day lasts 1.5 Mercurian years, about 132 days!

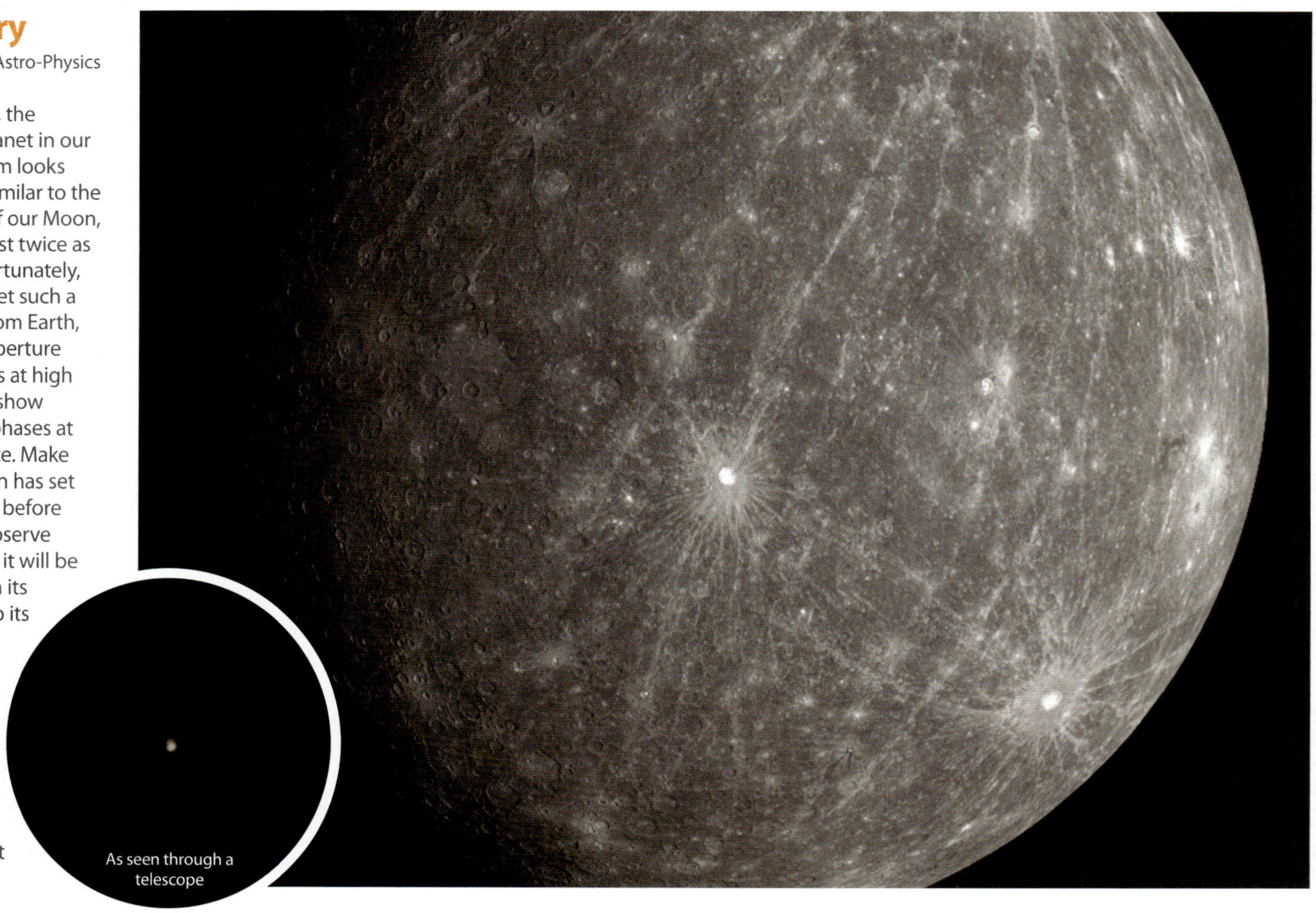
As seen through a telescope

Venus

Telescope: Astro-Physics Stowaway f5

Since the launch of the International Space Station, Venus is the third brightest object in the sky. Though peaceful in appearance, it is not the kind of place you'd want to go on holiday, with ridiculously high pressures, clouds of sulphuric acid, and a surface temperature of 735°K. Fortunately, we can stay at home and enjoy its beautiful set of 'moon-like' phases through a telescope, retracing the landmark observations of Galileo, which would provide strong evidence that the planets revolved around the Sun.

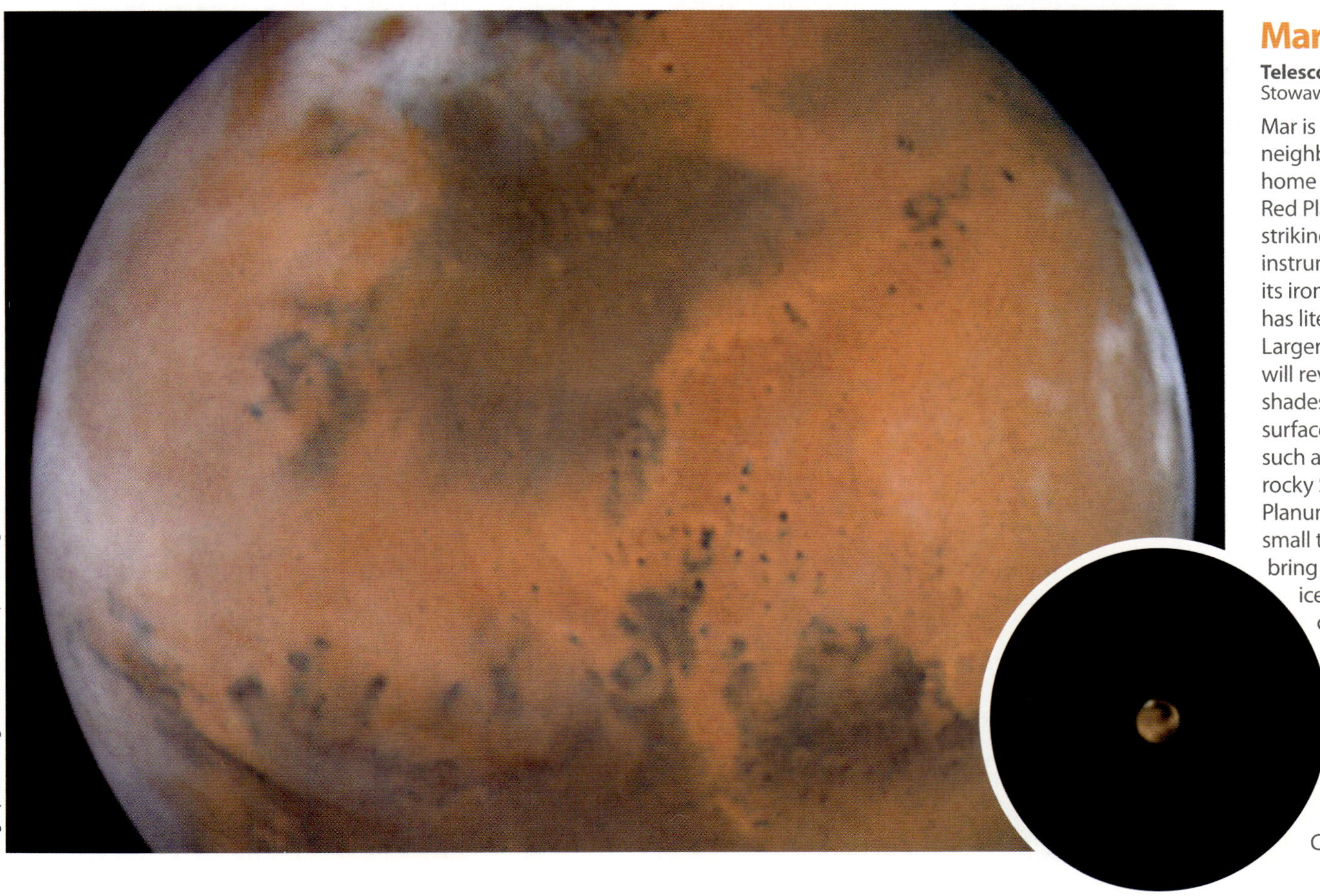

Larger planet images ©NASA; Circled planet images ©Tom Kerss

Mars

Telescope: Astro-Physics Stowaway f5

Mar is our closest neighbour and current home of Curiosity. The Red Planet shows a striking colour in any instrument thanks to its iron-rich soil that has literally rusted. Larger apertures will reveal the subtle shades of the major surface features, such as the dark and rocky Syrtis Major Planum, and even small telescopes can bring out the brilliant ice-covered polar caps. Mars looks small, though, so you'll need steady skies, and unfortunately, you won't see Curiosity either.

What to observe

Jupiter

Telescope: Astro-Physics Stowaway f5

Jupiter is the largest planet in the Solar System, and despite being around 11 times wider than the Earth, it rotates once every ten hours! Hurricane winds craft intricate, swirling cloud formations in its upper atmosphere. You can see these different coloured layers of cloud that surround it through a reasonably powerful telescope, as well as the famous Red Spot super-hurricane. Also visible are the four stunning Galilean moons, Io, Europa, Ganymede, Callisto, each larger than our own Moon. Sadly, Jupiter's rings are too faint to observe though.

Saturn

Telescope: Celestron C6

With the naked eye, you can sometimes mistake Mars for Saturn, however once you point a telescope at it, this changes. As almost everyone's favourite planet – the 'wow' factor of Saturn's gorgeous rings lights up the faces of many first-time planet-gazers. It's hardly surprising! The rings gradually tilt to and fro, periodically revealing the Cassini Division, a major gap. Saturn hosts many moons. The largest, Titan, is clearly visible in small telescopes. Some of the cloud layers will be a touch fuzzier than Jupiter's, as they are not as pronounced anyway.

Larger planet images ©NASA; Circled planet images ©Tom Kerss

Uranus

Telescope: Meade LX200 12″

One of the two planets in the solar system that are not visible to the naked eye. At first believed to be a star, and later a comet, Uranus became the first planet to be discovered using a telescope, with William Herschel taking the credit. Uranus is known to observers for its distinct greenish hue, and clouds have been spotted on rare occasions. Its moons, while large, are not nearly large enough to be easily noticed – however there are 27 of them.

Planetary alignment

There are optimal times to see all seven planets as they make their way across the sky. Mercury, Mars, Saturn and indeed Uranus are best seen in the morning sky, while Venus shows up in the evening and Jupiter at dawn. There's not much preference to seeing Neptune other than pointing your telescope towards it.

Pluto is not on this list as it was recently, and controversially, reclassified as a dwarf planet due to the discovery of Eris. Eris is a Kuiper Belt object larger than Pluto, and would have been the tenth planet if the IAU had not stepped in to finally set down rules for what makes a planet. Eris and Pluto were both classified as dwarf planets after this ruling Pluto is also extremely difficult to find, and its size makes it even harder to make out any detail – you'll need professional telescopes to see it as any more than a faint light.

■ This image of Pluto was taken by the Hubble telescope, and puts into perspective how difficult it is to view

Neptune

Telescope: Meade LX200 12″

The farthest outlying planet in the solar system, Neptune is a remote, cold world. It's roughly the same size as Uranus, however it's 50 per cent more distant than its light-blue cousin. Despite its size, almost four times wider than the Earth, it was not seen until 1846, and has only just completed one orbit since its discovery! It's great to see the gorgeous blue colour, while knowing you are looking over 4.2 billion kilometres (2.6 billion miles) away.

Ten sights to see on Saturn

Saturn is probably the most beautiful and eye-catching of all the planets of the Solar System. Here's what it can look like through a telescope

If you are an early riser you will be able to see the planet Saturn shining low in the south-east before dawn. It's quite bright and has a slightly yellow hue. If you ever get the chance to look at it through a telescope the first thing you'll notice is the rings. They are stunning and at the moment look quite 'open' to us. Even a fairly small telescope should show them well. If you can drag your eye away from the rings, though, take time to look at the planet itself. You might be able to see that the disc looks a little uneven. This is because Saturn has cloud belts not unlike Jupiter, although they are not as pronounced. Then remind yourself that you are looking at an object which lies nearly a billion miles from us and is over nine times the diameter of Earth!

Titan

The Cassini Division

Other moons

The Ringed Planet

Spokes
Size: Variable – can be up to several thousand kilometres.
Type: Radial features in the main rings.
Appearance: The 'spokes' in the rings look like darker markings pointing away from the planet and rotate as Saturn spins on its axis. They come and go and it's thought they're connected with Saturn's magnetic field. They were first discovered by the Voyager probes and cannot easily be seen with Earth-based telescopes.

The cloud belts
Size: The whole planet.
Type: Mostly ammonia ice.
Appearance: Although much fainter and broader than the cloud belts of Jupiter, Saturn's clouds take on a yellowish-brown hue and are visible through moderate-sized amateur telescopes. They encircle the planet from the equator to the poles and sometimes spring surprises… Spots and swirls have been seen and photographed in these amazing frozen clouds.

Shadow transits
Size: Several hundred kilometres.
Type: Shadows cast by the moons falling on the disc of Saturn.
Appearance: These can only be seen when the rings are edge-on to us here on Earth. Because of this they are fairly rare events, but fascinating to watch when they do occur.

Aurora
Size: Variable around the planet's poles.
Appearance: Earth is not the only planet to experience the northern and southern lights. Charged particles from the Sun get caught up in the magnetic field of Saturn and are channelled down towards the top of the planet's atmosphere, causing it to glow in a ring, just as it does on Earth.

The planet's shadow
Size: Over 50,000Kms across.
Appearance: Saturn casts a shadow onto the rings opposite the sunward side of the planet. It is easily seen in amateur telescopes. As the planet moves in its orbit relative to us and changes its angle of tilt over time, this shadow can be more or less pronounced.

Moons
Size: From less than 1Km to 5,151Kms in diameter.
Type: Made mostly from ice, dust and rock.
Appearance: Saturn has over 60 main moons, ranging from the very small to the very large. It is possible to see around six through an amateur telescope, with Titan (the largest) being the most obvious.

The rings
Size: 364,900Kms in diameter.
Type: Various-sized particles made almost entirely of water ice.
Appearance: Although the rings look solid, they are made from lumps of ice varying in particles the size of sand, to many meters across. Due to how the planet orbits the Sun, the rings appear to open and close over a period of around 18 years.

Polar vortex
Size: 1,500Kms in diameter.
Type: A huge hurricane of enormous proportions.
Appearance: A massive storm raging around the north pole has recently been discovered by the Cassini probe. It's a huge vortex blowing in the atmosphere at over 1,100 miles per hour.

Shepherd moons
Size: Up to 136Kms across.
Type: Made from ice and dust orbiting within or just outside of the ring system.
Appearance: Too small to be seen in Earth based telescopes, the 'Shepherd moons' of Saturn's rings sculpt the rings, giving them a hard edge and keeping them in order.

The Cassini Division
Size: 4,700Kms wide.
Type: A thin, sparsely populated ring.
Appearance: A dark ring around the planet that contains much less material than the other more rings. Discovered by the Voyager space probes in 1980 and 1981.

Ten great sights on Jupiter

The largest planet in the Solar System is one of the most exciting places to point your telescope

During different points of the year, Jupiter will be perfectly placed in the evening sky for observers all over the world, depending upon where you live. The mighty planet's disk and four largest natural satellites can be glimpsed using just a pair of binoculars, but with a small telescope and high-power eyepiece, you'll be well on your way to exploring the Jovian system in meticulous detail, from the great swirling storms in Jupiter's cloud tops, to the shadows cast by distant moons. Over 400 years ago, Galileo made history as the first to ever observe Jupiter with a telescope, and you can follow in his footsteps, albeit with a much better instrument. At a distance of more than 390 million miles, it's amazing to appreciate how much detail we can glean when observing the dynamic Jupiter from our own gardens. Here are its top ten sights.

Great red spot

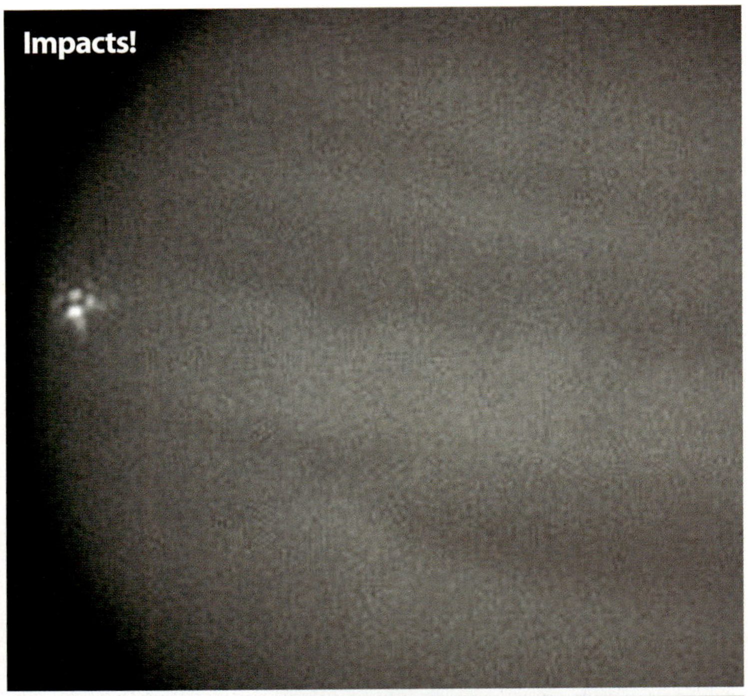
Impacts!

Many moons

Shadow transit

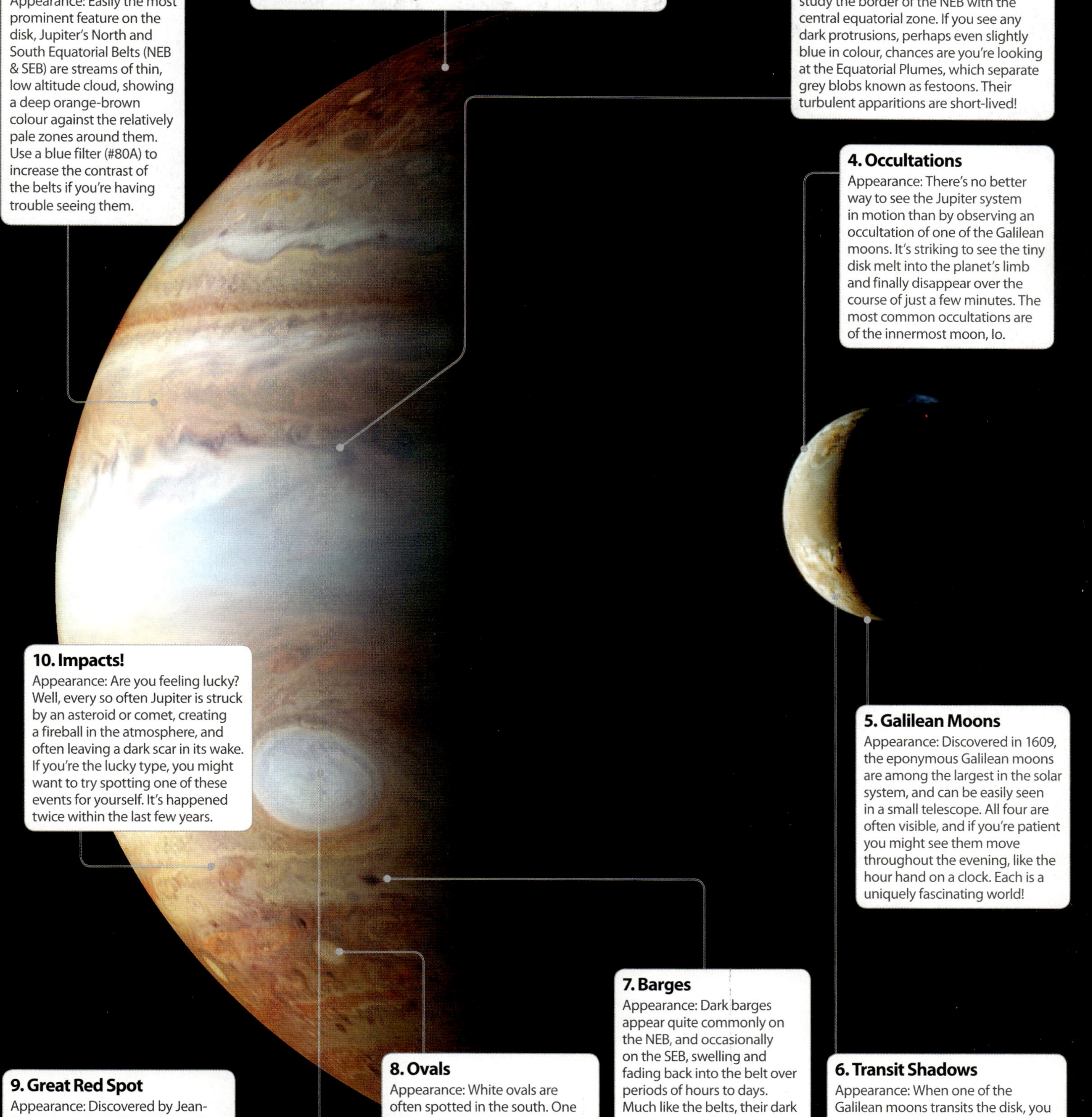

1. Equatorial Belts

Appearance: Easily the most prominent feature on the disk, Jupiter's North and South Equatorial Belts (NEB & SEB) are streams of thin, low altitude cloud, showing a deep orange-brown colour against the relatively pale zones around them. Use a blue filter (#80A) to increase the contrast of the belts if you're having trouble seeing them.

2. Polar Regions

Appearance: Notice the subtle differences in colour, with the South Polar Region appearing slightly darker, and if you like a challenge, hunt for spots at the extreme latitudes. In 2009, the SPR was struck by a sizeable object leaving a dark scar behind.

3. Festoons

Appearance: Whenever you look at Jupiter's equatorial belts, take time to study the border of the NEB with the central equatorial zone. If you see any dark protrusions, perhaps even slightly blue in colour, chances are you're looking at the Equatorial Plumes, which separate grey blobs known as festoons. Their turbulent apparitions are short-lived!

4. Occultations

Appearance: There's no better way to see the Jupiter system in motion than by observing an occultation of one of the Galilean moons. It's striking to see the tiny disk melt into the planet's limb and finally disappear over the course of just a few minutes. The most common occultations are of the innermost moon, Io.

5. Galilean Moons

Appearance: Discovered in 1609, the eponymous Galilean moons are among the largest in the solar system, and can be easily seen in a small telescope. All four are often visible, and if you're patient you might see them move throughout the evening, like the hour hand on a clock. Each is a uniquely fascinating world!

6. Transit Shadows

Appearance: When one of the Galilean moons transits the disk, you can be sure a shadow isn't far from it. In fact, with a small telescope you'll probably glimpse the shadow first! If you see a tiny black spot, look around for the culprit. Transits are an exciting sight for any Jupiter enthusiast!

7. Barges

Appearance: Dark barges appear quite commonly on the NEB, and occasionally on the SEB, swelling and fading back into the belt over periods of hours to days. Much like the belts, their dark appearance is due to low pressure and transparently thin top-layer clouds failing to sufficiently cover them up. Barges are sometimes mistaken for the GRS!

8. Ovals

Appearance: White ovals are often spotted in the south. One collection of ovals, formed in 1939, famously merged into 'Oval BA' in March 2000, a second red spot in the SEB. Unlike cyclonic barges, white ovals are predominantly anticyclonic in nature.

9. Great Red Spot

Appearance: Discovered by Jean-Dominique Cassini in 1655, the Great Red Spot (GRS) is a massive storm that's been raging for over 350 years. It cruises in the SEB, rotating over a period of days, churning the clouds in a tremendous anticyclonic vortex!

10. Impacts!

Appearance: Are you feeling lucky? Well, every so often Jupiter is struck by an asteroid or comet, creating a fireball in the atmosphere, and often leaving a dark scar in its wake. If you're the lucky type, you might want to try spotting one of these events for yourself. It's happened twice within the last few years.

Viewing the Galilean moons

Named after their discoverer Galileo Galilei, the four moons which orbit around Jupiter are easily seen in binoculars and small telescopes

The moons of Jupiter are some of the most fascinating things to observe in the night sky. The reason being is that they change their position from night to night and are relatively easy to see; a pair of 7x50 or 10x50 binoculars will show them well.

First recorded in 1610 by the Italian astronomer Galileo, the moons of Jupiter have proved to be an endless source of fascination for amateur and professional astronomers ever since. Jupiter, we now know, has dozens of moons orbiting around it, but the four largest are the only ones visible using ground-based amateur telescopes.

Among the most interesting things to observe with respect to these moons are the ways they move almost on an hourly basis. They can change their position from two moons each side of the planet to all being in a row on just one side as well as various other combinations. Even more interesting are the occultations and transits. An occultation is where the moons pass behind the planet, so for a short time being obscured to us here on Earth, whereas when they pass in front of the disc of Jupiter, it is known as a transit.

Ganymede
Not only is Ganymede a moon of Jupiter, it is also the largest moon in the Solar System and is slightly larger than the planet Mercury! It also has the largest mass of any planetary satellite, being a little over twice the mass of our own Moon.

Callisto
The third largest moon in the Solar System, Callisto is slightly smaller than Mercury. It's 'tidally locked' to Jupiter, and therefore it always presents the same face to the planet. It's made up from rock and ice and may even contain liquid water.

Europa
The smallest moon of Jupiter, Europa has a very tenuous oxygen atmosphere and it's thought that it may have an ocean of water under its surface ice. It is also thought that this ocean may possibly harbour extraterrestrial life.

Io
Io is the innermost of the four moons. It's being continually kneaded by Jupiter's gravitational pull and so has a molten core. It's the most geologically active object in the Solar System and has active volcanoes producing plumes of sulphur.

Jupiter
Jupiter was one of the first objects that Galileo viewed through his new telescope. When he saw the four moons travelling around Jupiter he realised the Earth could not be at the centre of the Solar System.

Which telescope?

You can spot the four moons in modest binoculars, 7x50 or 10x50 being the best for this, and you'll even be able to watch them weave around the planet night by night. If you have a small telescope where you can increase the magnification depending on which eyepiece you use, you'll see the planet much more clearly and the moons will be more obvious.

Among the most interesting events to observe in the Solar System are the transits, occultations and shadow transits, where you can watch the shadow cast by a moon move across the surface of Jupiter's disc. This can be accompanied by the transit of the moon itself before, during or after the passing of the shadow. In order to see this well, you'll need at least a three-inch aperture (75mm) refractor telescope or a six-inch (150mm) reflector. A reasonable magnification of around 120x or even more is also required, as is a good quality eyepiece. Here, the Plössl design of eyepiece is good as it provides a nice wide and flat field of view with minimal distortions. Bear in mind that the quality of the atmosphere counts here too, so you may have to reduce the power if the air is particularly unstable causing a 'wobbly' image.

Longer focal length telescopes are better for planetary viewing, so this is where refracting telescopes also have an advantage, but again reflectors can also give you splendid views of the giant planet and its moons.

Io

Diameter: 3,642km (2,263 miles)

Io is an amazing little world. Orbiting Jupiter every 1.8 days, it has over 400 active volcanoes which were only discovered during a flyby of Jupiter by the Voyager probes. Like the other three main moons, it was discovered by Galileo in 1610. Sometimes described as looking a little like a pizza, its surface is covered in sulphur and sulphur dioxide. Unlike most other moons in the Solar System it is composed of silicate rock surrounding a molten iron core, the heat being produced by the gravitational squeezing effect of Jupiter. Because of its fairly close proximity to the planet there are strong interactions between Io and Jupiter's magnetic and radiation belts, resulting in the moon being bathed in huge amounts of radiation every day.

Callisto

Diameter: 4,800km (2,985 miles)

The fourth Galilean moon out from Jupiter is Callisto. Because of its greater distance from the giant planet than the other three moons, it doesn't experience the tidal flexing the others do. However, there is still the possibility of subsurface liquid water, although this has yet to be confirmed. It is the second largest moon of Jupiter and the third largest in the Solar System. It is made up from approximately equal amounts of rock and ice and we know that the surface is covered mostly in water ice, carbon dioxide and silicates with some organic compounds, although this isn't the same as having life. It is heavily cratered on the side facing away from Jupiter as can be seen in the picture.

Ganymede

Diameter: 5,268mm (3,273 miles)

Orbiting Jupiter roughly every seven days, Ganymede is also the largest moon in the Solar System. It is the third main moon out from Jupiter and due to its distance from the planet it is tied into a 1:2:4 ratio 'orbital resonance' with two other satellites of Jupiter – Io and Europa. It has a molten iron core and because of this has a magnetosphere. It also has a very thin atmosphere consisting mostly of oxygen. It's heavily cratered due to asteroid impacts over its 4 billion year history, but mostly only on its darker regions, suggesting that the lighter areas are or have been renewed probably due to the action of plate tectonics reshaping the surface, this in turn being due to tidal heating caused by Jupiter's immense gravitational pull.

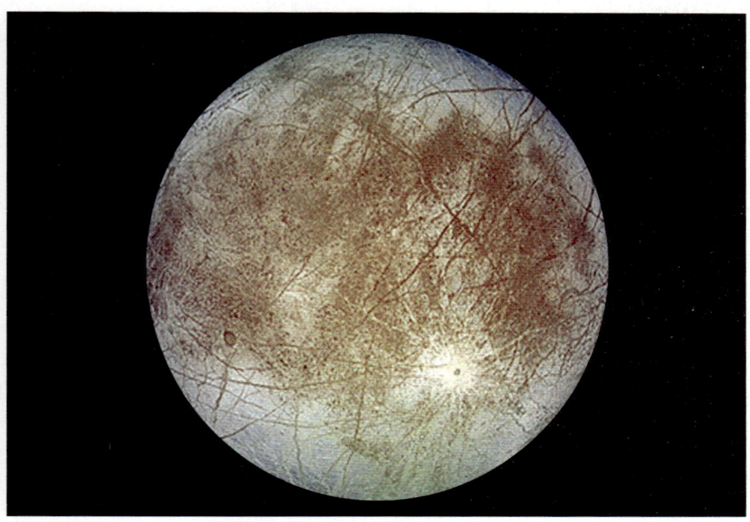

Europa

Diameter: 3,100km (1,900 miles)

The smallest of the four moons, Europa is also the most interesting. Its icy surface seems to be scored with dark lines, but little cratering is evident, suggesting that there may be an ocean of liquid water under the surface, which could be warm enough to sustain life. Europa has a near circular orbit and goes around the planet in just over three and a half days. It is tidally locked to Jupiter, so always shows the same face to the giant planet. The dark streaks in the surface ice are possibly caused by the ice cracking and re-freezing, although the surface of Europa is one of the smoothest in the Solar System. Due to its potential habitability, Europa is now the focus of ideas for missions to explore its ocean in the search for life.

20 great sights on the Moon

Earth's nearest neighbour has always captivated our imagination. Why not take a telescopic tour?

The Moon has accompanied our planet in its orbit for billions of years. Spared from atmospheric erosion, its surface charts a pristine geological (or rather 'selenological') record of Solar System history, from massive scale volcanism to catastrophic, seemingly apocalyptic bombardment from space. The rugged surface catches the light of the Sun, and casts dynamic and intricate shadow patterns throughout the Lunar Month, about 29.5 days. If we look at the Moon from one night to the next, we can see its various craters, mountains and plains illuminated from different angles, giving us a tremendous sense of 3D during the mornings and evenings local to those features. Scanning along the Moon's terminator – the line where day meets night – is arguably the best way to get familiar with this fascinating landscape, but you'll need a telescope for best results. Even a small telescope will produce awe-inspiring images.

"We can see its various craters, mountains and plains"

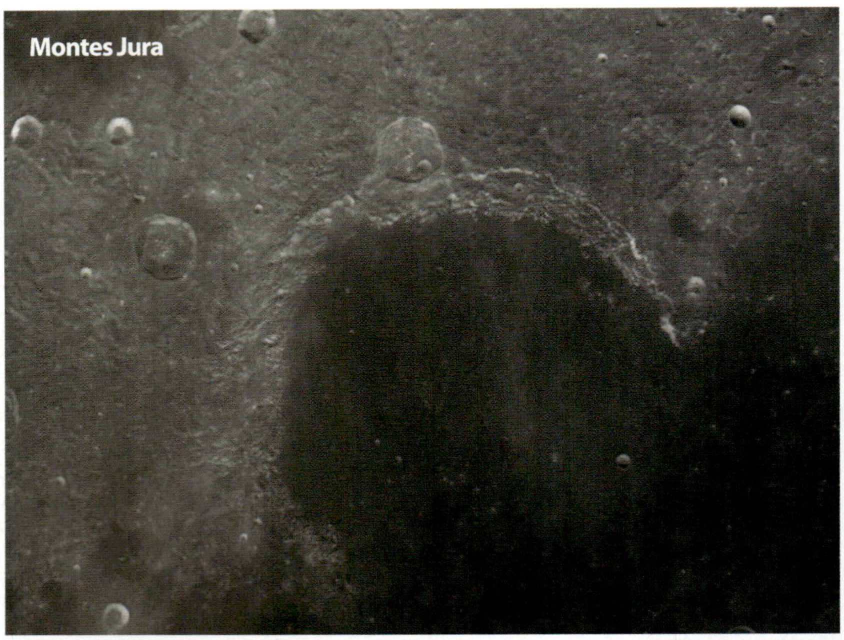
Montes Jura

Montes Apenninus

Tycho

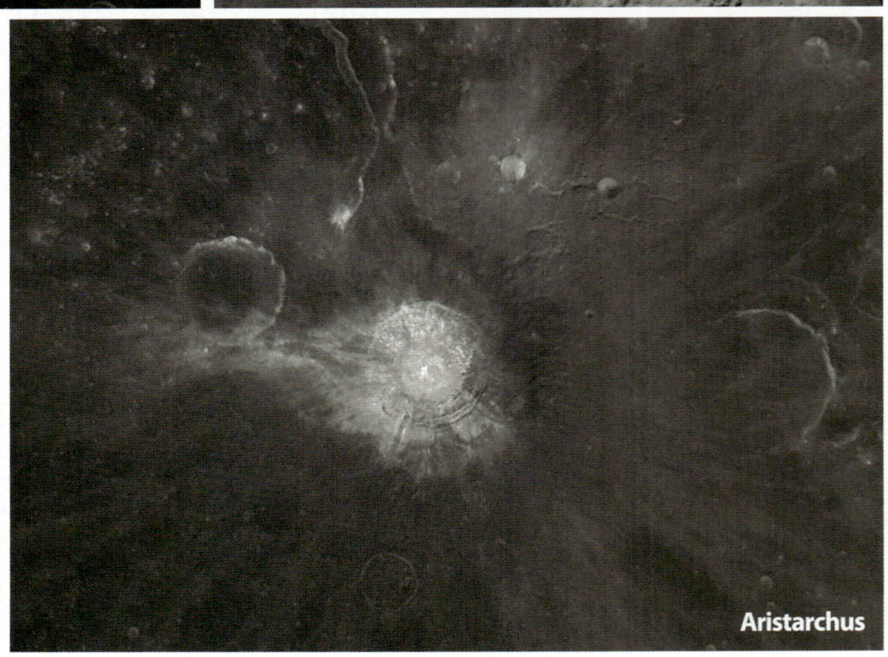
Aristarchus

1. Montes Jura

Size: 420km **Type:** Mountain range

Appearance: If the lunar maria were real seas, and the Moon's mountains covered with lush jungles, the Jura Mountains around the Bay of Rainbows (Sinus Iridium) in the Sea of Showers (Mare Imbrium) would be an idyllic holiday location.

3. Montes Apenninus

Size: 600km **Type**: Mountain range **Appearance:** Only two astronauts – David Scott and James Irwin of Apollo 15 – have stepped foot here. In a telescope with the right sun angle, this mountain range seems to jump off the face of the Moon.

4. Apollo 11 landing site

Size: 870km **Type:** Volcanic basin

Appearance: In a rather unremarkable desert just north of the Hypatia region, Neil Armstrong and Buzz Aldrin took one small step to the surface of the Moon to make history.

2. Plato

Size: 110km **Type:** Impact Crater

Appearance: Plato's flat floor is a sure sign that it filled with lava after the impact that created it some 3.8 billion years ago. Indeed, so smooth is its basin that the low albedo renders it strikingly dark against the surrounding mountains and maria. Can you spot any craterlets in there?

5. Theophilus Cyrillus & Catharina

Size: About 100km each

Type: Impact craters

Appearance: This eye-opening triplet provides a fascinating insight into the gradual erosion of the Moon's surface from tiny meteorite strikes.

10. Aristarchus

Size: 40km

Type: Impact crater

Appearance: The brightest crater on the Moon. Aristarchus is so bright in a telescope it often warrants the use of a Moon Filter for comfortable viewing of this 450 million year old marvel.

6. Clavius

Size: 225km

Type: Impact crater

Appearance: Clavius grazes the lunar south pole, and is fondly observed for its healthy collection of craterlets, the largest of which outclass many of the Moon's standalone craters in size. It's an awesome sight, but it may be better known to most as the home of a human settlement in Arthur C Clarke's *2001: A Space Odyssey.*

9. Copernicus

Size: 93km

Type: Impact crater

Appearance: Copernicus is a beautiful sight. Look out for its distinctive hexagonal shape and the gentle, wrinkly slopes to the crater floor.

8. Rupes Recta

Size: 110km **Type:** Rille

Appearance: Hidden in plain sight in the Sea of Clouds (Mare Nubium) is the Rupes Recta. It's almost invisible at Full Moon, but clearly seen when it casts a shadow. This ridge is really a smooth slope about 2km (1.2 miles) wide and 250m (820ft) tall.

7. Tycho

Size: 86km

Type: Impact crater

Appearance: The depth and definition of Tycho makes it an excellent place to see an impact crater's central peak. Tycho isn't the largest crater on the Moon, but it is among the most well studied.

What to observe

11. Archimedes
Size: 83 km **Type:** Impact Crater **Appearance:** A large impact crater lacking any central peak in the Mare Imbrium, but a huge rim that at its peak is 2 km high. Crater cones, craterlets and even possible volcanic vents have been spotted on its surface. View it at sunrise for some amazing shadows.

12. Hadley Rille
Size: 120 km **Type:** Rille **Appearance:** Located at the foot of Apennines explored by Apollo 15, this sinuous rille is 1.5 km wide and 400 metres deep. Best seen on a low-angle morning or with evening illumination, can you determine if lava once flowed here?

13. Proclus
Size: 28 km **Type:** Impact Crater **Appearance:** While Proclus is a small impact crater, it's 600 km long, asymetrical ray system created by impact is very interesting. As a very bright lunar object, its best seen after the full moon.

14. Mare Crisium
Size: 740 km **Type:** Volcanic Basin **Appearance:** This large, dark spot is visible with the naked eye and in most conditions. This is the site of Luna 15's crash, the unmanned Soviet spacecraft that was trying to beat Apollo 11 back to Earth with soil samples.

15. Petavius
Size: 177 km **Type:** Impact Crater **Appearance:** Petavius isn't just any impact crater, it also has a domed and fractured floor. The best way to observe this phenomenon is to view the formation when its eastern wall is on the evening terminator.

16. Schroter's Valley
Size: 168 km **Type:** Rille **Appearance:** A great, zig-zagging rille that is 10km at its widest. Originally planned as a site for Apollo 18, it's believed to be volcanic.

17. Posidonius
Size: 95 km **Type:** Impact Crater **Appearance:** An interesting site surrounded by other much smaller craters, and a noticeable central impact inside the main crater. Viewing it at local sunset, you'll see an illuminated ring effect, where the floor is pitch black, but the rim of the crater is lit up.

18. Rima Hyginus
Size: 219 km **Type:** Rille **Appearance:** Rima Hyginus is fairly unique in terms of lunar rilles in that there are a number of small impact craters throughout its length, including the much larger Hyginus crater half-way down. This rille and crater are easily viewable in most conditions.

19. Rupes Altai
Size: 427 km **Type:** Mountain Range **Appearance:** The most prominent lunar escarpment is actually difficult to locate during a full moon. However, it appears as a bright, winding line about five days after the new moon, and casts a long, irregular shadow about four days after the full moon.

20. Rimae Triesnecker
Size: 215 km **Type:** Rille **Appearance:** Next to the crater Triesnecker is a family of rilles that split off from each other to form what looks like a series of streams and rivers on the lunar surface. Wait for lower sun angles to get the best view of it.

Proclus
The rays from the impact spread for hundreds of kilometers in one direction

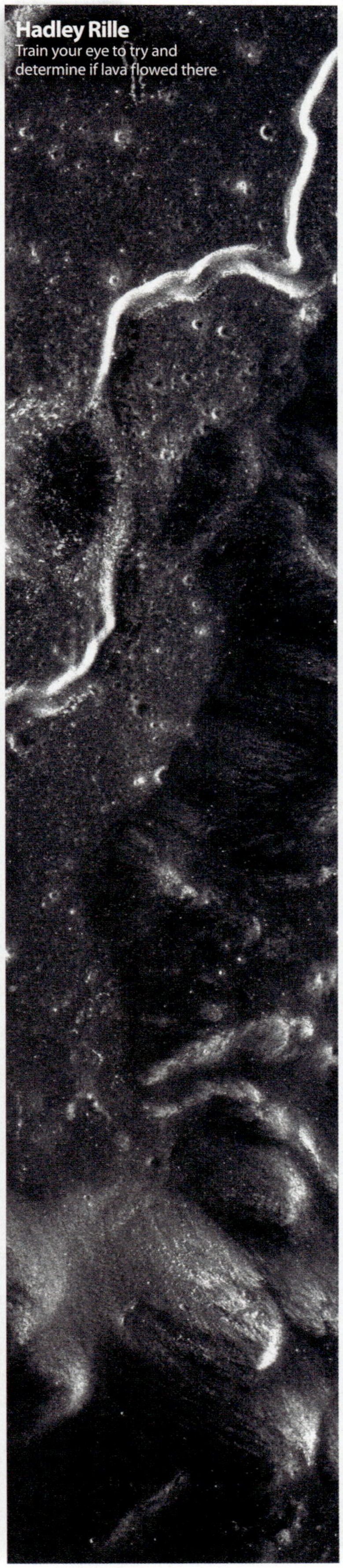

Hadley Rille
Train your eye to try and determine if lava flowed there

Posidonius
Posidonius is full of interesting craters and lunar geography

©ESO

Rima Hyginus
The hyginus crater is believe to have been caused by volcanic activity, possibly causing the rille

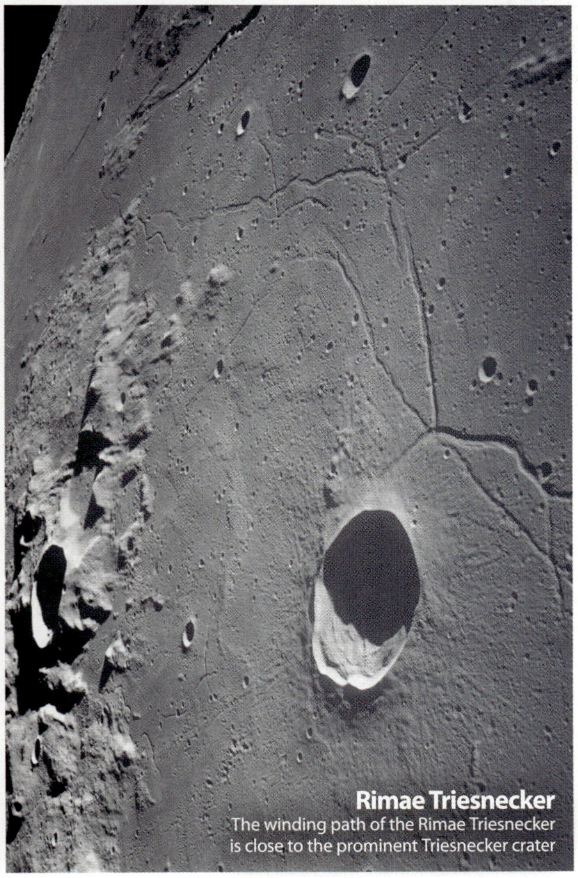

Rimae Triesnecker
The winding path of the Rimae Triesnecker is close to the prominent Triesnecker crater

View 20 famous stars

Discover how to locate and view the 20 most famous stars in the sky, and for a lot you don't even need a telescope

There's a reason we consider our most celebrated performers to be 'stars'. Both brilliant and beautiful, the real stars have been revered since the dawn of humanity, often worshipped as avatars of the gods, or admired as tranquil windows to heaven. But there are celebrities in the sky, too. Some of the stars in the night sky have become so well known that they pervade popular culture, whether by their value for navigation, or their sheer brightness in the sky, and you can admire many of them without a telescope. Join us as we take a look at five of the biggest highlights of the night sky. From the fabulous red supergiant Betelgeuse, which can be found in the Orion constellation, to the brightest star in the sky, Sirius, which is situated in the Canis Major constellation; these are the stars among the stars. Get out there and track them down.

"Some of the stars in the night sky have become so well known that they pervade popular culture"

Polaris (Alpha Ursae Minoris)

Constellation: Ursa Minor (Little Bear)
Right ascension: 02h, 31m, 49s
Declination : +89 deg, 15', 51"
Distance: ~430 ly

Many a nomad has found his way home thanks to the Polaris – the Pole Star. It sits very close to the north celestial pole. Throughout the age of sail and the ensuing globalisation, Polaris was relied upon for navigation, and today aids astronomers in the northern hemisphere to correctly align their equatorial mounts for accurate tracking of the celestial sphere. Polaris is the most useful North Star in human history, so it's no surprise that its common name reflects its position. It marks the tip of the tail of the Little Bear.

Sirius (Alpha Canis Majoris)

Constellation: Canis Major (Big Dog)
Right ascension: 06h, 45m, 09s
Declination: -16 deg, 42', 58"
Distance: 8.6 ly

Scorching, searing, glowing – these are all words that spring to mind when we think of Sirius, the brightest star in the sky. Sirius is actually a binary star with a tiny white-dwarf companion. With the powerful Hubble Space Telescope, astronomers have been able to photograph the pair. From northern temperate latitudes, Sirius often spends much of its apparition in the atmospheric soup, flashing almost every colour of the rainbow. It joins Procyon and Betelgeuse in the Winter Triangle asterism.

Vega (Alpha Lyrae)

Constellation: Lyra (Harp)
Right ascension: 18h, 36m, 56s
Declination: +38 deg, 47', 01"
Distance: 25 ly

The fifth brightest star in the sky is of great importance to astronomers. Not just because it was the first star other than the Sun to be photographed; but because it was chosen as the benchmark by which astronomers would judge the brightness of all other objects in the night sky. This honour was originally granted to Polaris, but eventually Vega replaced it. This was because Vega was discovered to be an incredibly stable star, in terms of variability, whereas Polaris was found to change brightness and could not be relied upon. Astronomers now use a more accurate reference, but Vega remains very significant to modern astronomy.

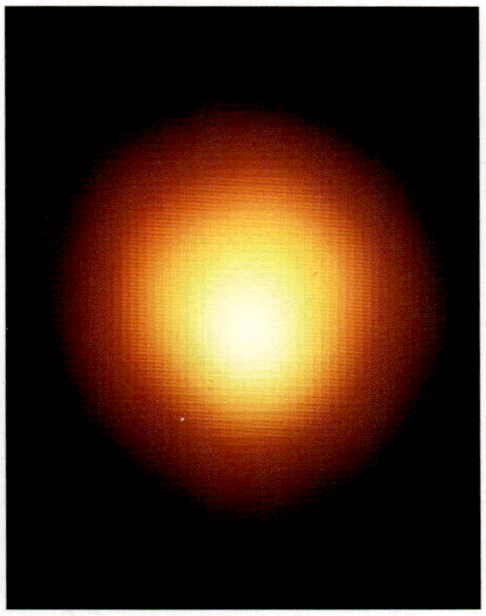

Betelgeuse (Alpha Orionis)

Constellation: Orion (Hunter)
Right ascension: 05h, 55m, 10s
Declination: +07 deg, 24', 25"
Distance: ~700 ly

Betelgeuse is a huge red supergiant star nearing the end of its life. It's expected to die in a spectacular supernova explosion, with recent observations leading astronomers to predict it might happen within the next million years. Unfortunately, this will punch one of the pivotal dots out of one of the most beautiful constellations. Constraining the star's colossal size is tricky, but astronomers believe it might be large enough to swallow everything inside the orbit of Saturn if it replaced our Sun.

Rigel Kentaurus (Alpha Centauri)

Constellation: Centaurus (Centaur)
Right ascension: 14h, 39m, 36s
Declination: -60 deg, 50', 02"
Distance: 4.3 ly

Our nearest neighbouring star system, Alpha Centauri, hosts two very Sun-like stars, of which one is now known to harbour an Earth-sized planet. Could it be that a habitable Earth-like world has co-habited our little corner of the Milky Way? If so, we may be on the verge of discovering it, and this would become the most exciting exoplanet discovery to date. With today's technology it would take over 50,000 years to travel there. With one more revolution in physics, the 4.3 light year gulf to Alpha Centauri might be very manageable indeed. For now, we'll just have to admire the system from afar.

What to observe

Barnard's Star

Constellation: Ophiucus
Right ascension:
17h, 57m, 48s
Declination:
+04° 41′ 36″
Distance: 6 ly

The closest star to Earth after the Alpha Centauri system, and also a low mass red-dwarf. Although it is too dim to see with the naked eye, but fine to see with a telescope. It's also extremely bright in infrared compared to visible light.

Proxima Centauri

Constellation: Centaurus
Right ascension:
14h, 29m, 42s
Declination: -62° 40′ 46″
Distance: 4.2 ly

Sister star to the Alpha Centauri binary star, Proxima Centauri is the closest star to Earth other than the Sun. It's also a red dwarf, making it the closest red dwarf to Earth. It can only be seen through a telescope, although it undergoes random increases in brightness.

Antares

Constellation: Scorpius
Right ascension: 16h, 29m, 24s
Declination: -26° 25′ 55″
Distance: 550 ly

The brightest star in the Scorpius constellation, and a red supergiant star. It's one of the brightest stars in the night sky, and its apparent magnitude is just below +1. Even at such a great distance, it's much more visible than nearer red stars.

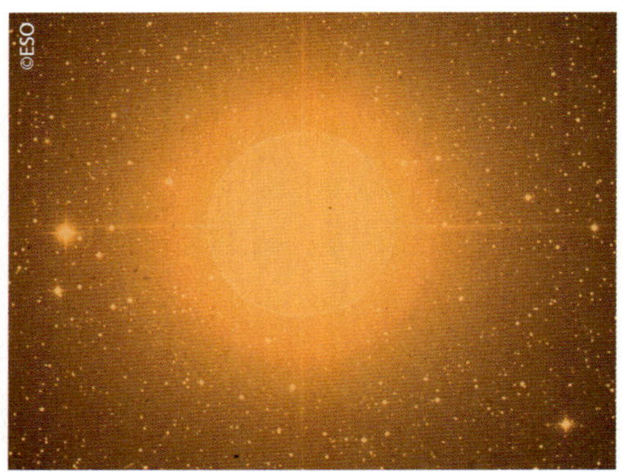

Procyon

Constellation: Canis Minor
Right ascension: 07h, 39m, 18s
Declination: +05° 13′ 30″
Distance: 11.5 ly

The brightest star in Canis Minor, and the eighth brightest star in the night sky. It's actually a binary star, and much like Sirius has a small white dwarf companion. It's part of the winter triangle comprised of Betelgeuse and Sirius.

Canopus

Constellation: Carina
Right ascension: 06h, 23m, 57s
Declination: -52° 41′ 44″
Distance: ~310 ly

The brightest star in the Southern sky, and the second brightest star in the night sky. It's also a supergiant star, and looks very white to the naked eye. It's best seen in the southern hemisphere in the summer.

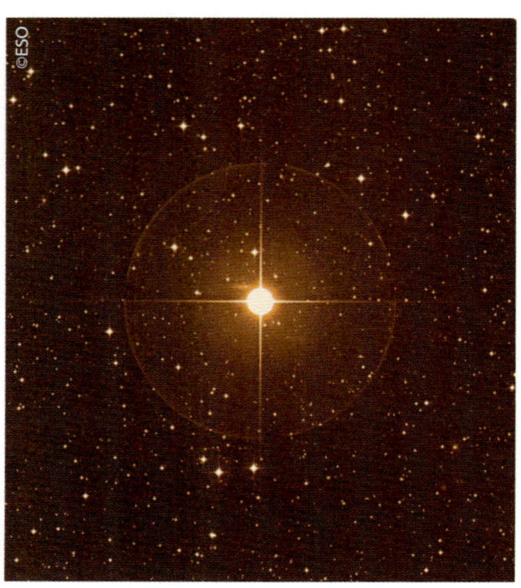

Sigma Octantis

Constellation: Octans
Right ascension:
21h, 08m, 46s
Declination: -88° 57′ 23″
Distance: 270 ly

If Polaris is considered the North Star, then Sigma Octanis is currently the closest thing we have to being the South Star. Its magnitude isn't particularly good though, so unfortunately it doesn't command the same prominence as Polaris does in the north.

Arcturus

Constellation: Bootes
Right ascension:
14h, 15m, 39s
Declination:
+19° 10′ 56″
Distance: ~36.7 ly

The brightest star in the northern celestial hemisphere, and very close to zero magnitude. Arcturus is an orange giant, believed to have exhausted all its hydrogen and now fusing helium. It will likely end its life by becoming a white-dwarf inside of a nebula.

Capella

Constellation: Auriga
Right ascension: 05h, 16m, 41s
Declination: +45° 59′ 52″
Distance: ~42.2 ly

Another bright northern star, although this one is special as it's actually made up of four stars in two binary pairs. The first pair are giant stars with a radius ten times greater than the Sun's. The other two are red dwarfs.

Altair

Constellation: Aquila
Right ascension: 19h, 50m, 46s
Declination: +08° 52′ 06″
Distance: ~16.7 ly

The name Altair comes from an Arabic phrase that means the flying eagle, very apt for a star in an eagle constellation. Altair actually spins incredibly fast, causing its poles to flatten due to this, making it non-spherical.

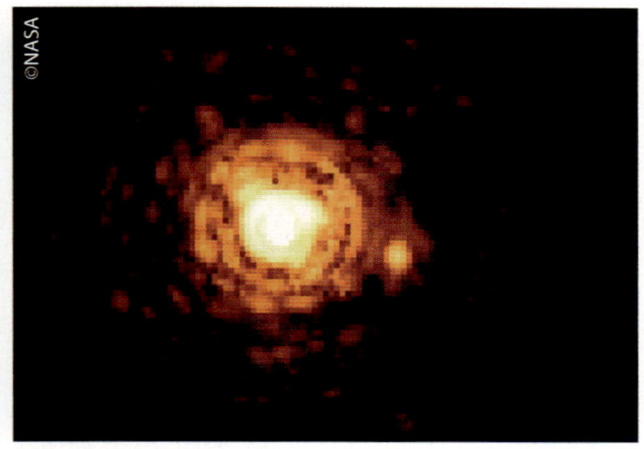

Kapteyn's Star

Constellation:
Right ascension: 05h, 11m, 40s
Declination: -45° 01′ 06″
Distance: ~12.8 ly

Named after noted Dutch astronomer Jacobus Kapteyn, who discovered galactic rotation. It's a red dwarf star that was named after him when he noticed that it had a very high proper motion, moving across the sky noticeably every year.

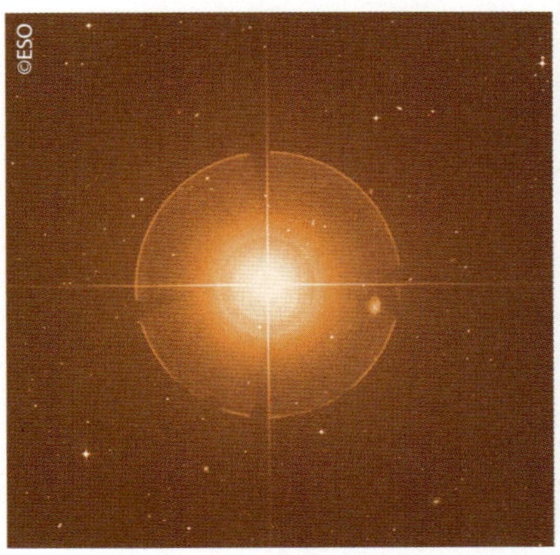

Tau Ceti

Constellation: Cetus
Right ascension: 01h, 44m, 04s
Declination: -15° 56′ 14″
Distance: 11.9 ly

A very interesting star – it's the nearest solitary star like our Sun. While it was originally believed there were no planets orbiting it, evidence now suggests that there are five planets in the system, and one possibly being habitable. Are we catching a glimpse of our first exosolar colony?

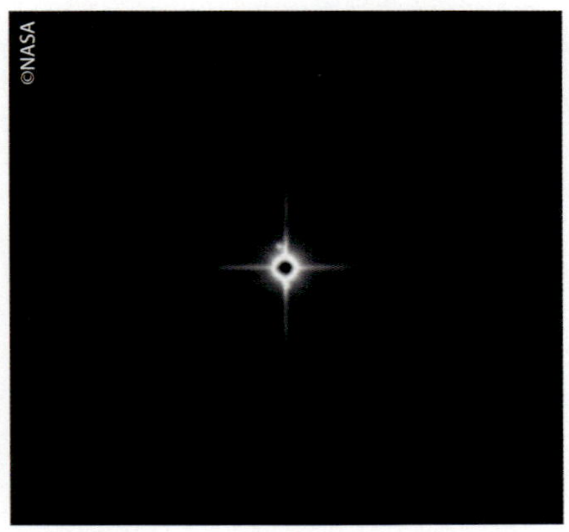

Pollux

Constellation: Gemini
Right ascension: 07h, 45m, 18s
Declination: +28° 01′ 34″
Distance: ~33.8 ly

Pollux is an evolved giant star, with a distinct orange hue, and is the brightest star in the Gemini constellation. This star is important as its spectrum is used as a reference to classify other stars. It also has an exosolar planet orbiting it.

Rigel

Constellation: Orion
Right ascension: 05h, 14m, 32s
Declination: -08° 12′ 06″
Distance: ~860 ly

Made famous by *Star Trek*, Rigel is a blue-white supergiant star and the brightest star in Orion. It's almost 20 times heavier than our Sun, and has 74 times the radius. Even at such a vast distance from Earth, it outshines smaller, much closer stars.

Alnilam

Constellation: Orion
Right ascension: 05h, 36m, 12s
Declination: -01° 12′ 06″
Distance: ~1300 ly

The brightest star in Orion's Belt is a blue supergiant. It's the middle star of the trio, along with Alnitak and Mintaka. It is one of the 57 stars used in celestial navigation, and is another star whose spectrum is used as a reference for others.

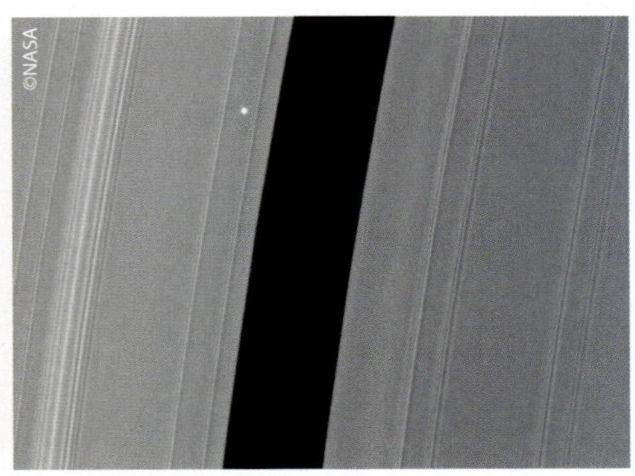

Aldebaran

Constellation: Taurus
Right ascension: 04h, 35m, 55s
Declination: +16° 30′ 33″
Distance: ~65 ly

Another red giant star, and the brightest star in the Taurus constellation. Its name means the follower, as it seems to follow the Pleiades in the night sky. It has about 44 times the radius of our Sun, but isn't even quite twice as heavy.

Seeing double stars

It's a little known fact that around 50 per cent of all the stars in the night sky are double or multiple stars…

Double stars can either be stars which look very close to each other due to a line of sight effect for us here on Earth, or they can actually be bound to each other through gravitation – in other words, they orbit around their common centre of gravity. These are arguably the most interesting as their position relative to each other can change over time.

There are a couple of 'naked eye' double stars we can see from Earth, but for most you will need a telescope. The rule of thumb here is that bigger is better, so the larger your telescope, the more double stars you are likely to be able to resolve as two distinct stars, otherwise known as 'splitting'. Some doubles are so close that, even with the largest telescopes on Earth, you can never discern them as individual stars. Sometimes the stars can look like a single egg-shaped star as they are apparently very close to each other. Others are relatively easy to split and often can be of differing brightness or colours. For close doubles, you'll need to use a fairly high magnification if you can, around 100x or so.

> "The larger the telescope, the more double stars you are likely to be able to resolve"

©Alamy

Mizar and Alcor

The two stars which make up this pair have separate names, which is unusual for double stars. They are also a good test of eyesight as you should be able to make out these two stars without any optical aid. Sometimes also called the 'Horse and Rider' this double star is interesting for several reasons: not only is it a visual binary, it's also a multiple star system which consists of six stars. The system lies 83 light years from Earth, while Mizar and Alcor are 1.1 light years apart from each other.

How to find it: Mizar and Alcor make up the 'star' in the middle of the handle of the famous 'Plough' or Big Dipper asterism. Look closely and you will be able to see that it's actually two stars.

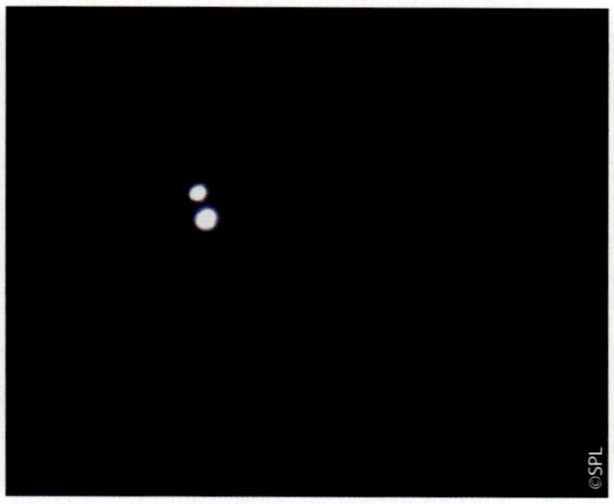

Winnecke 4

Back in 1764, Charles Messier was hunting for a nebula in the constellation of Ursa Major but never found it. Instead, he came across this double star and catalogued it. Also known as Messier 40, this object has caused much confusion, some thinking that Messier made a mistake in listing a double star. Recent observations suggest this is an optical double rather than a true binary star. These stars are too faint to be seen with the naked eye and require a telescope to make them out.

How to find it: Winnecke 4 lies just above the star Megrez which connects the handle of the 'Dipper' to the 'Bowl'. It is approximately 510 light years from Earth.

Epsilon Lyrae

Another popular and famous double star is Epsilon Lyrae, or the 'Double Double'. With this star you get two for the price of one, as each star is itself a double star, so this is a quadruple star system. Binoculars will split the pair easily but you'll need a medium-sized scope to be able to split each star into its further components. The main stars are around 162 light years away from us and orbit each other, although they are so far apart it is thought they take hundreds of thousands of years to circle each other.

How to find it: Epsilon Lyrae can be found close to the bright star Vega in the constellation of Lyra the Lyre. It can be viewed just above the 'square' of the main part of the constellation.

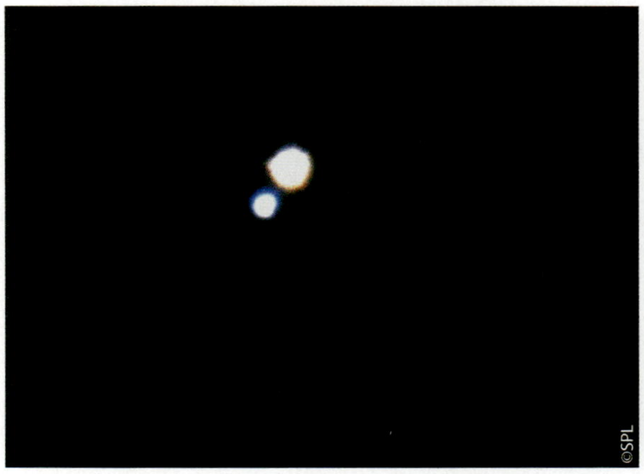

Almach

Another golden/blue contrasting pair of stars is Almach or Gamma Andromedae. It is not as well known as Albireo, maybe because the components are closer together and therefore harder to see as separate stars. However, this is still a beautiful double which, like Epsilon Lyrae, is in fact a quadruple star system, but these others are too close to be seen as individual stars. The main pair can be easily split in a medium-sized telescope at moderate power and the colours are quite stunning and well worth the time to find. Almach lies 350 light years from Earth.

How to find it: Almach is the left-hand star at the end of the 'Y' shape of the Andromeda constellation. It is best seen in the autumn months.

Albireo

This lovely double star is an easy target for even a small telescope or binoculars. The brightest of the pair is a golden yellow colour which contrasts with the fainter bluish coloured secondary and is a striking colour contrast. This is probably one of the most popular double stars to view in the entire night sky as it is so easy to find and such a well-contrasted pair. The stars are 35 arcseconds apart and it is not yet known if they are orbiting around each other. Albireo lies around 430 light years from us.

How to find it: Albireo is the star marking the head of Cygnus in the constellation of the Swan. Best seen in the summer when it rides high in the night sky.

Interacting stars

There are binary stars, two stars that orbit around their common centre of gravity, that can interact with each other physically. These are often in a very close orbit and sometimes consists of a red dwarf star which is having matter pulled away from it by a white dwarf star. This matter forms what is known as an 'accretion disc' around the white dwarf. This will then fall on to the surface of the white dwarf.

Through this interaction the stars will vary in brightness as the matter from the 'ordinary' star crashes on to the white dwarf causing it to flare up often at irregular intervals due to nuclear fusion reactions converting hydrogen to helium at a very fast rate. It is known that these stars have intense and complex magnetic fields surrounding them. Stars such as these often form the basis of 'novas', stars which will suddenly increase in brightness many hundredfold.

If the stars are massive enough then such interactions can trigger a supernova explosion.

Observing variable stars

It is not very well known that more than half the stars in the night sky vary in brightness...

It is strange to think that so many stars vary in brightness, but most only vary by a small amount. Often this is almost undetectable with the human eye. Even our own Sun is a variable star over its 11-year cycle. As the number of sunspots increase and decrease so does the light output. However, there are some stars which have a huge change in brightness, going from a moderately bright star in our skies to only being detectable in medium to large telescopes at other times.

What causes this odd behaviour? There are several reasons for this and there are also several types of variable star. We can therefore classify many variable stars into groups. Some of these stars vary in how quickly they change their brightness. Some can change in a matter of days, while others can take years, decades or even centuries to complete a cycle.

One type of variable star is known as an 'eclipsing binary'. This is where there are two stars orbiting around each other and from our perspective here in our Solar System they line up so that one star seems to pass in front of the other. Often there is a larger, brighter star being orbited by a smaller, dimmer one, and when the smaller passes in front of the larger, the amount of light reaching us appears to dip. Then, as the smaller star seems to disappear behind the larger, the amount of light dips again but not by so much. The most famous of this type of eclipsing binary star is Algol in the constellation of Perseus. These stars are too close together to be seen individually from Earth-based telescopes, but we know there are definitely two stars in the system.

There are several other reasons why the brightness of some stars fluctuates. Some stars actually vary in size, they pulsate like a balloon being filled with air and then let down again. Most well known of this type are the Cepheid variables. They swell and shrink very regularly, so regularly in fact, they can be used as a distance measuring device.

> "As the number of sunspots increase and decrease so does the Sun's light output"

In 1912, an astronomer by the name of Henrietta Leavitt worked out that by measuring how bright the stars appeared compared to their rate of variability meant it would be possible to figure out the distance to them. Edwin Hubble used this to work out the distance to the Andromeda Galaxy. Variable stars can be put into two basic groups, short period and long period, with a third group of irregular and semi-regular variables, which have no pattern to the variation of their light output. One type of star in this category is the 'Mira Variable'. This type is named after the star Mira or Omicron Ceti. It is a cool, red supergiant which has large pulsations that increase and decrease its brightness. It does have a rough period of around 332 days during which time it undergoes a dramatic drop in brightness to well below naked eye visibility. There are also stars similar to R Coronae Borealis, which appear to fade quite markedly at odd intervals and then climb back up to their original brightness. This is due to the buildup of carbon dust in the star's outer atmosphere. As the dust is dispersed, the star regains its brightness. Another type of variable star is the 'Gamma Cassiopeiae' class, which fluctuate their light output due to it throwing off material around its equator because they rotate very quickly.

These are just a selection of the different types of stars whose apparent brightness as seen from Earth can vary. Observing variable stars is a fascinating and very popular area for those interested in stargazing.

Mira

Otherwise known as the 'wonderful' Omicron Ceti, 'Mira' is a pulsating giant star and is the brightest of the 'red' long period variable stars. It has a period of around 332 days, although its exact maximum is never predictable. It has the widest variation of brightness to dimness of any celestial body which can be seen with the naked eye, outside of our Solar System. It lies in the constellation of Cetus and doesn't get very high in the sky as seen from mid-northern latitudes. It lies in a fairly sparse region of the sky, which can make it difficult to find.

How to find it: Follow a line of stars from Aldebaran in Taurus into Cetus. A star chart will help you pin it down. It lies roughly midway between eta Eridanus and alpha Pisces.

Delta Cephei

This is the prototype Cepheid variable star, which has a cycle of 5.37 days. This type of star pulsates in a period in proportion to how bright they are and it is this relationship that allows astronomers to determine how far away they are.

How to find it: You can find delta Cephei at the lower easternmost corner of the constellation of Cepheus.

©SPL

Algol

Possibly the most famous of the eclipsing binary stars, Algol has given its name to this particular type of variable star. It has an interesting double dip in brightness every two days, 20 hours and 49 minutes. The second dip can only be detected with electronic sensors as it is too shallow to be noticed by the human eye. This second dip occurs when the smaller star passes behind or is occulted by the larger. Algol is one of the best stars to start practising on while learning how to observe these fascinating objects.

How to find it: If you draw an imaginary line between the star Aldebaran in Taurus and the star Shedir or alpha Cassiopeia, Algol lies halfway along this line.

©SPL

©ESO

Gamma Cassiopeiae

The central star in the 'W' of Cassiopeia is known as 'gamma'. It's an unstable very hot star and can vary in brightness randomly, although it hasn't changed much in over 40 years, so it might just flare up again sometime soon! We know this star to be a powerful source of X-rays although it is still uncertain why this is. There is no danger to us from this though, because it also lies a very long way from us at 550 light years distance.

How to find it: Cassiopeia looks like a letter 'W' or 'M' in the night sky low down in the north during February. The middle star is 'gamma'.

Betelgeuse

This bright orangy-red coloured star sits at the top left of the constellation of Orion. Many people are unaware that this star is unstable and variable in brightness, although not by a huge amount. It fades and brightens fairly slowly with a period of about six years. It's thought that in the next million years or so, Betelgeuse will explode as a supernova. That will be really worth seeing! In fact, you'll probably be able to see it in daylight at least for a while.

How to find it: Orion is easy to find during the winter in the northern hemisphere. Betelgeuse is the star above and to the left of Orion's 'belt'.

See five amazing star clusters

In the dark night of winter all you need are binoculars or a small telescope to pick out some beautiful clusters of stars which will take your breath away…

All images ©NASA

The winter night skies are ever popular for star gazing. On cool, clear nights you'll have a welter of objects which you can see either with the naked eye, binoculars or a small telescope. Some of the most stunning of these can be detected as tiny jewels of light against the blackness of the sky with just a glance. Binoculars will turn these, only hinted at treasures, into glorious fireworks to feast your eyes upon. Here, we'll show you some of the very best of the bunch and tell you a little bit about them and where to find them.

The Pleiades

Constellation: Taurus
Right ascension: 03h 47m 24s
Declination: +24° 07′

High in the south on clear winter evenings, you can't fail to notice a small group of stars sparkling away. If you are away from towns or cities and have sharp eyes, you should be able to count seven or more stars in the group. If you turn binoculars on to it, you'll see a lot more. This cluster is also known as the 'Seven Sisters'. However, there are in fact up to 150 stars in this cluster. It marks the shoulder of Taurus the Bull, one of the 12 constellations of the Zodiac. In long-exposure photographs, you'll see the thin clouds of gas near these stars which is reflecting their light. These stars are relatively young at less than 100 million years old. Unusually for a cluster, some of the stars are named, with two of the cluster's brightest known as Alcyone and Merope.

The Hyades

Constellation: Taurus **Right ascension:** 04h 27m **Declination:** +15° 52′

Just to the south-east of the Pleiades star cluster lays the Hyades 'open' cluster. Easily seen with the naked eye, the Hyades cluster, a V-shaped pattern of stars lying on its side, represents the head of Taurus the Bull. It is much older than the Pleiades at some 625 million years but is the nearest open cluster to us at a mere 153 light years away! It is thought these stars are slowly moving apart and so in millions of years the cluster will no longer exist. If you look at the Hyades through binoculars or a small telescope you will see hundreds of diamond-like stars suspended in the blackness. The brightest star, the red giant Aldebaran, is not part of the cluster, it just happens to lay on the same line of sight.

The Double Cluster

Constellation: Perseus **Right ascension:** 02h 20m **Declination:** +57° 08′

'Like diamonds on black velvet' is a good description of this beautiful pair of star clusters, which can be seen almost directly overhead from mid-northern latitudes during the winter months. These clusters can be made out as a faint misty patch with the naked eye and look simply stunning in binoculars. They're said to represent the 'jewelled sword' of the Ancient Greek hero Perseus who is remembered in the stars for killing Medusa by cutting off her head. Fortunately, nothing as unpleasant happens when you look at these two groups of stars, one lying 6,800 light years away and the other around 7,600 light years distant. They are thought to be quite young clusters, similar in age to the Pleiades.

Messier 35

Constellation: Gemini **Right ascension:** 06h 09m 01s **Declination:** +24° 21′

Messier 35 is a gorgeous open star cluster due east of the Hyades cluster. It is quite different in character, however, being more tightly compact than the loose collection of stars of its near neighbour. It lays about 2,800 light years away from us and covers an area of sky about the same as the full Moon. It consists of at least 120 stars and can be just about picked up with the naked eye from a dark site and shows up well in binoculars and small telescopes. It lays just off the 'foot' of Castor, marked by three stars in a row, the twin of Pollux in the constellation of Gemini the Twins. In the picture it is shown next to the smaller cluster NGC 2158, which can be seen in the same field of view through binoculars.

The Beehive Cluster

Constellation: Cancer **Right ascension:** 08h 40m 04s **Declination:** +19° 41′

About midway up in the eastern night sky during mid-December you might be able to detect a faint misty patch of light with your naked eye. As winter progresses, it will climb higher and be easier to spot. If you turn binoculars on this object, the view will light up with a host of stars. This is the Beehive Cluster. The stars here are about 600 million years old and it lays 577 light years distant. It contains both red giant and white dwarf stars. Galileo was the first person to study the Beehive Cluster with the aid of a telescope. Charles Messier, the famous French astronomer, added it to his catalogue in 1769. The ancient Chinese gave this cluster a colourful description, calling it the 'exhalation of rotting corpses'!

Tracking meteor showers

Meteors, commonly known as 'shooting stars', often come in regular showers. Here we'll look at how to get the best views of them

Meteors consist of tiny particles, often no larger than a grain of sand or, at most, a pebble. This material is shed from comets as they orbit the Sun and if a comet's orbit happens to cross the orbit of the Earth, every year at around the same time we will pass through this stream of debris in space.

There are several of these debris fields through which the Earth passes. As we travel through the densest part of the field it leads to a peak of intensity in the meteor shower. This means that showers can be predicted with some accuracy although not perfectly. The number of meteors we are likely to see from these encounters is known fairly well, but is never definite. The peak of a meteor shower usually lasts for several hours, which is the best time to observe them. As the Earth moves through this field it causes the meteors to appear as if they are all radiating from one point in the sky. This point in the sky will seem to lay in a particular constellation and so the shower takes the name of its 'parent' constellation, for example, the Geminids appear to emanate from a point in the constellation of Gemini.

Here are some of the most spectacular meteor showers and how to get the best views of them.

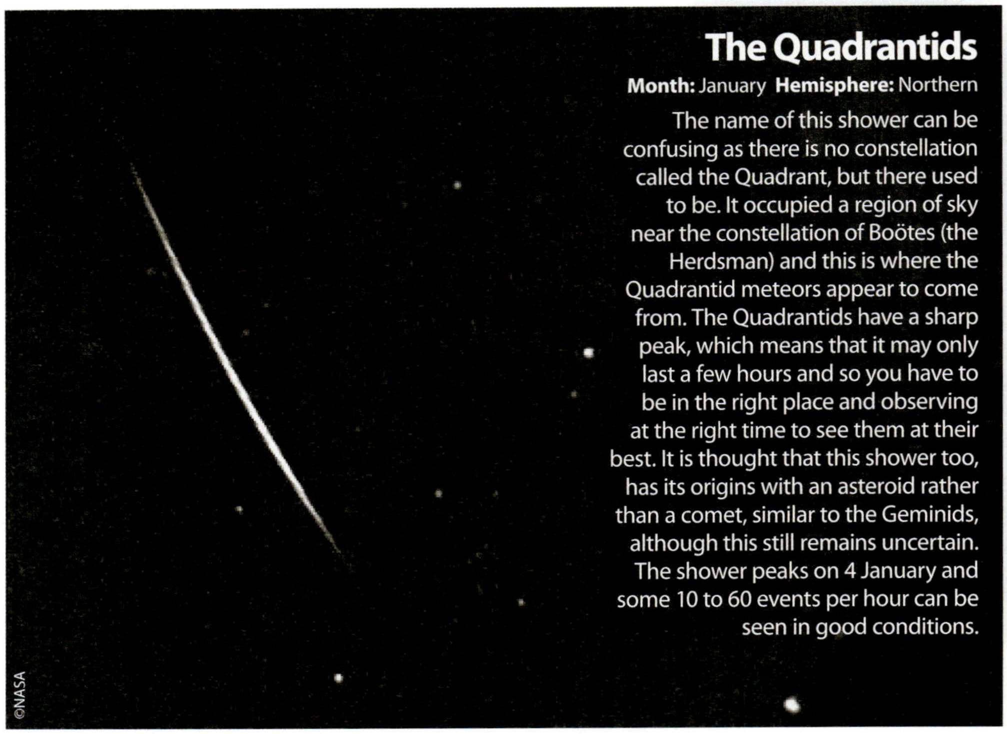
©NASA

The Quadrantids

Month: January **Hemisphere:** Northern

The name of this shower can be confusing as there is no constellation called the Quadrant, but there used to be. It occupied a region of sky near the constellation of Boötes (the Herdsman) and this is where the Quadrantid meteors appear to come from. The Quadrantids have a sharp peak, which means that it may only last a few hours and so you have to be in the right place and observing at the right time to see them at their best. It is thought that this shower too, has its origins with an asteroid rather than a comet, similar to the Geminids, although this still remains uncertain. The shower peaks on 4 January and some 10 to 60 events per hour can be seen in good conditions.

©Alamy

The Orionids

Month: October **Hemisphere:** Northern and southern

As the name suggests, the radiant point for the Orionid meteors is in the constellation of Orion (the Hunter), just above the bright red supergiant star Betelgeuse. The shower peaks on 21 October each year and can produce fireballs, where a meteor explodes in the upper atmosphere due to the intense heat generated by the speed at which these small grains of material enter it, travelling at some 230,000 kilometres per hour (140,000 miles per hour)! There is only one other shower known to produce faster moving meteors. The parent comet for the Orionids is the famous Halley's Comet. These meteors are not particularly numerous; you might see as many as ten events per hour in a dark sky. The setting of the late autumn sky makes this shower very attractive.

©Alamy

The Geminids

Month: December **Hemisphere:** Northern and southern

The object which gives rise to the Geminids is not a comet, but an asteroid. It is known as 3200 Phaethon. It is one of the most consistent of the regular meteor showers with 120 to 160 events per hour being observed, although this is at the peak and in perfect conditions. This is one of the best showers of the year and seldom disappoints. These are slower meteors than some of the other showers, with the particles travelling at a mere 126,000 kilometres per hour (79,000 miles per hour)! Because of the slower speed of these events, observers often find them easier to spot and their trains have been reported to be colourful. They peak on the night of 13/14 December and make a lovely pre-Christmas light show if conditions are good.

©Navicore

The Leonids

Month: November **Hemisphere:** Northern and southern

The Leonids are another meteor shower known to produce very bright 'fireball' events. What's more, the actual shower is known to produce meteor 'storms'! Every 33 years, the Earth passes through a thicker part of the debris field and so the number of shooting star events we can see here from the surface of the planet increases dramatically. The last time this happened was during the years 1998 through to 2002. The highest recorded peak was in November 1833 when thousands of meteors per hour could be seen – it looked as if it was raining meteors! The peak of the shower is usually on the night of 17/18 November and it is well worth spending some time outside to see how many you can spot.

©ESO

The Perseids

Month: August **Hemisphere:** Northern

Probably the most famous meteor shower of the entire year, the Perseids reach their peak in early August and so can often be seen on balmy summer evenings. The parent comet which gives rise to the dust and debris for this shower is called Swift-Tuttle and swings by every 133 years to replenish the stock of material. Depending on which part of the meteor stream we pass through, we see more or fewer shooting stars, the thickest part of the stream obviously producing more events. The Perseids are often fast and bright and can leave persistent trains across the sky – another reason they are popular. As with all meteor showers, they are best observed after midnight, when the rotation of the Earth turns us into the body of the stream.

Observing tips

Meteor showers can be difficult things to observe. Sometimes they peak during the day, sometimes a bright Moon will wash out the fainter events and sometimes the weather will conspire to prevent you looking. Here are some tips that will help you maximise your chances of seeing some.

Check to see when the peak of a particular shower is likely to occur. You'll find lots of information on the internet about this as well as prospects for a good show with regards to the position and phase of the Moon. Check your local weather forecast and always wrap up warm – it can get cold at night, even in the summer. Be prepared to stay out for at least 20 minutes – the longer the better. Don't look directly at the radiant point, you'll do better viewing about 30 degrees away in any direction, or, alternatively, just look straight up.

Viewing The Big Dipper

Let's take a closer look at one of the most easily recognisable patterns of stars in the northern hemisphere

The Big Dipper goes by several different names, including the 'Plough' and the 'Saucepan'. It is, though, very recognisable with its bowl-shaped pattern of four stars connected to a 'handle' of three more. This is a group of stars which has been recognised from time immemorial and by nearly all cultures around the world.

It is not a constellation in its own right, but just an easy-to-spot pattern of stars which form part of the larger constellation of Ursa Major, or the Great Bear. Patterns of stars like this that are only a part of one or more constellations are known as 'asterisms'.

It's a really useful asterism for several reasons, one of the most important is that it can help us find Polaris or the 'pole star', which in turn helps us understand where true north lays, so it is of great benefit to navigators to know how to use the Big Dipper to aid finding this. The two end stars, opposite the handle, are called the 'pointers', because if you draw an imaginary line through these stars heading out of the 'bowl' the next bright star you will arrive at will be Polaris. By sheer chance Polaris sits almost over the north celestial pole. If you drop an imaginary line directly from this point to the horizon, you will know the position of true north.

For anyone whi happens to be living north of the latitude of southern Spain, the Big Dipper is circumpolar. This means that from these latitudes it never appears to set or disappear below the horizon. It rotates around the north celestial pole as do all the other stars and constellations, but because it resides near the pole it can always be found in the night sky.

The star in the handle which lays higher than the others is interesting; as if you look closely you'll see it is two stars. This is a naked eye double star and unusually for double stars they both have names. These are Mizar and Alcor. If you have good eyesight you should be able to make out both stars.

What is particularly interesting about this binary or double star is that each component is also a multiple star system. Mizar itself has four stars in orbit around their common centre of gravity, so all in all, this double star is in fact a sextuplet system, although most of these stars cannot be resolved using even the largest Earth-based telescope. We know of their existence from spectroscopy, whereby the light from the star is split by a prism into its constituent colours.

All the seven stars in the Big Dipper have names. The two stars of the pointers are called Merak (the lower of the two) and the other, at the top of the 'bowl', is called Dubhe. This is the brightest star in the group. Ursa Major plays host to several amazing deep sky objects including several galaxies. You can use the stars of the Big Dipper to find a couple of them. If you draw an imaginary line from the bottom left star in the bowl through the top right one (Dubhe) and keep going for roughly the same distance again, you will come across a beautiful pair of galaxies known as M81 and M82. If you form an equilateral triangle with the two end stars of the handle, Mizar/Alcor and Alkaid as the base, at the other point of the triangle you will find the galaxy M101.

The Big Dipper is also a great signpost to other constellations. If you use the two stars in the bowl nearest the handle, Megrez and Phad, as pointers but head away from the pole star, you can find the bright star Regulus in the Leo constellation. Again if you use the handle as a signpost, the next bright star you'll come to is Arcturus in the constellation of Boötes.

All this means that you should now be able to see what an amazing and useful group of stars the Big Dipper really is.

The stars of the Big Dipper shine through the Northern Lights. The auroral light is translucent which allows the faint starlight to shine through it

The stars that make up the Big Dipper

1. Dubhe
The second brightest star in the Big Dipper and is one of the pointers to the pole star, Polaris. It is a giant star which lays approximately 123 light years distant.

2. Merak
Beta Ursae Majoris is the other star in the 'pointers' to the pole. It's 2.7 times more massive than our Sun and lays 79.7 light years away.

3. Phad
Also known as Phecda, Gamma Ursae Majoris is 83.2 light years from us. It was one of the original stars that was used to classify the spectra or light signature of other stars.

4. Megrez
This is the dimmest of the seven stars in the Big Dipper. For all that, Megrez is still 63% larger than the Sun and 14 times as bright!

5. Alioth
The brightest star in the Big Dipper and the 31st brightest star in the sky, Alioth is 82 light years away from Earth.

6. Mizar/Alcor
Consisting of the four-star system of Mizar and the double-star system of Alcor, this six-star grouping is a good test of vision. Only the two brightest stars are visible with the naked eye.

7. Alkaid
The last star in the handle of the Big Dipper is the third brightest in the asterism and one of the brightest in the entire night sky. It is around 10 million years old.

8. Polaris
Although the pole star isn't a member of the Plough or Big Dipper constellations, the pointers show the way to this important star around which all others seem to revolve.

Searching for constellations

Discover how to locate the constellations in the sky, and when's the best time to see them

From ancient times, mankind has seen patterns in the stars. Getting to know these star patterns can help you feel at home in the night sky and being able to recognise just a couple can help you find many others.

In the past, every culture had its own way of seeing patterns in the stars. These patterns, or constellations, were connected with stories and folk legends. In the west we have settled on a set of constellations largely described by the ancient Greeks with a few more recent additions, and these patterns are used by professional and amateur astronomers alike to describe shapes and positions of stars and objects in the heavens. Each constellation represents a figure in mythology – an animal, bird or object. There are 88 internationally recognised constellations overall. These patterns fall inside a defined box or area and divide up the whole of the night sky. Depending on where you live you may be able to see many but probably not all of them. In the northern hemisphere, for example, you probably won't be able to see constellations such as Octans the Octant or Pavo the Peacock.

Often the brightest stars in a constellation will have names, such as Betelgeuse in Orion or Regulus in Leo. You can use a whole constellation, part of it or even just a couple of known stars to point yourself to another, perhaps less familiar pattern. Some star patterns aren't constellations in the strict definition of the word and are known as asterisms, but are easily recognised and very useful. The Plough, or Big Dipper, in the Ursa Major constellation is an asterism which can be used to navigate to other constellations. For example, you can use the two end stars in the bowl of the Plough or Big Dipper to point you towards the Pole Star, Polaris, in Ursa Minor. You can use the handle of the Plough to find the star Arcturus in Boötes the Herdsman and follow this line down to the star Spica in Virgo the Virgin. You can see that by getting to know just a couple of these constellations, they can act as stepping stones to finding your way around the rest of the night sky.

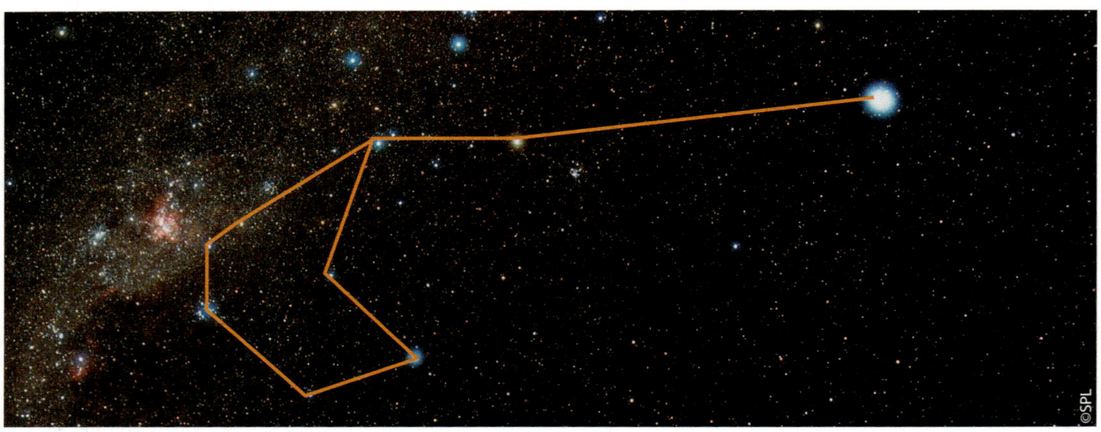

Carina

Southern hemisphere

January is the best time to view the constellation of Carina the Keel with its bright star Canopus high in the south. Carina is the keel of the great ship Argo Navis – once the largest constellation in the sky. Nearby you'll find Puppis the Poop Deck and Vela the Sail, all once part of this huge but now disassembled constellation. Canopus itself is the second brightest star in the night sky yet lies around 320 light years away, which means it must be extremely bright.

Centaurus

Southern hemisphere

May is a great time of year to view the constellation of Centaurus the Centaur. It is quite a large constellation and contains many deep sky wonders such as Omega Centauri, the largest and brightest globular star cluster associated with our Milky Way galaxy. This constellation is also home to the star system of Alpha Centauri, also known as Rigil Kent, the closest star system to our own star the Sun, at just over four light years away. We now know that there are planets in orbit around the stars in this multiple star system.

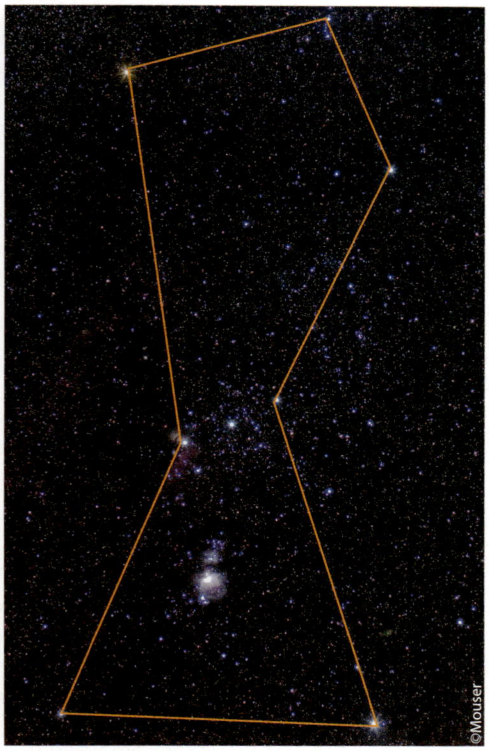

Cygnus

Northern hemisphere

Sometimes known as the Northern Cross, Cygnus the Swan is a very ancient constellation with several stories attached to it. It rides high in the summer skies in the northern hemisphere and sitting as it does in the band of the Milky Way is full of star clusters and nebulas. The star Albireo, marking the head of the Swan, is a double star. You'll need a telescope to see this star as a pair, but it is worthwhile as it's one of the most beautiful doubles in the whole of the night sky, being a lovely contrasting orange and blue.

Orion

Northern hemisphere

Orion the Hunter is an easily recognised constellations thanks to the three stars of the Hunter's belt from which hangs his sword. The bright orange supergiant star Betelguese marks the Hunter's shoulder and the bright white star Rigel, in the opposite corner, his knee. You can use the belt stars as pointers to other stars and constellations. Follow the three stars to the right and you'll come to the star Aldebaran in Taurus the Bull and left you'll find Sirius in Canis Major.

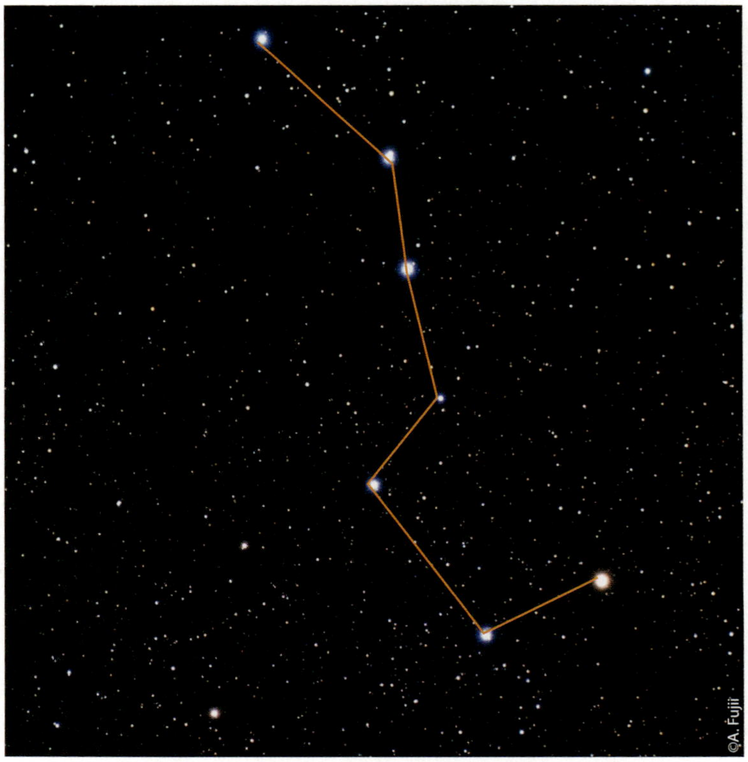

Ursa Major

Northern hemisphere

Ursa Major is the constellation in which you can find the Plough or Big Dipper. The seven stars that make up this asterism are the brightest and most easily recognised out of the whole constellation and possibly out of the entire sky. The second star in the handle of the Dipper is a naked eye double star. If you look closely you should see that it consists of two stars very close together. You can use the two stars in the bowl of the Dipper as pointers to Polaris the Pole Star in the constellation of Ursa Minor the Little Bear.

Crux

Southern hemisphere

You'll find the Southern Cross riding high in the south in June, the four stars describing a diamond or cross shape in the sky. The brightest star, Alpha Crucis or Acrux, marks the bottom of the cross and is 320 light years away from us. Crux lies in the band of the Milky Way and is surrounded by star clusters.

Locate a supernova

At the end of their life, some massive stars explode with such ferocity that they outshine the rest of their galaxy's stars combined…

Stars are exploding all the time, but most of these events happen in distant galaxies where we need large telescopes to detect them. Just occasionally, though, a massive star will end its life in a cataclysmic explosion, known as a supernova, in our own Milky Way Galaxy and when it does it can lead to the sudden appearance of a star so bright it can be seen in broad daylight. This can last for several weeks until the remains of the star fade away.

This is a very rare event, though, and may happen only once in several centuries. Although there are none visible at the moment, we can never tell for sure which stars are going to explode and when but there are candidates, these stars are coming to the end of their lives and could 'blow' at any time. One such star is the red supergiant we know as Betelguese, the bright star which marks the shoulder of Orion the Hunter. There are plenty of other potential supernova candidates, however, and astronomers, both professional and amateur, monitor these regularly. Fortunately, none of the stars near to the Earth are big enough to become supernovas, so we are quite safe.

■ Finding a bright supernova can be an exhilarating experience

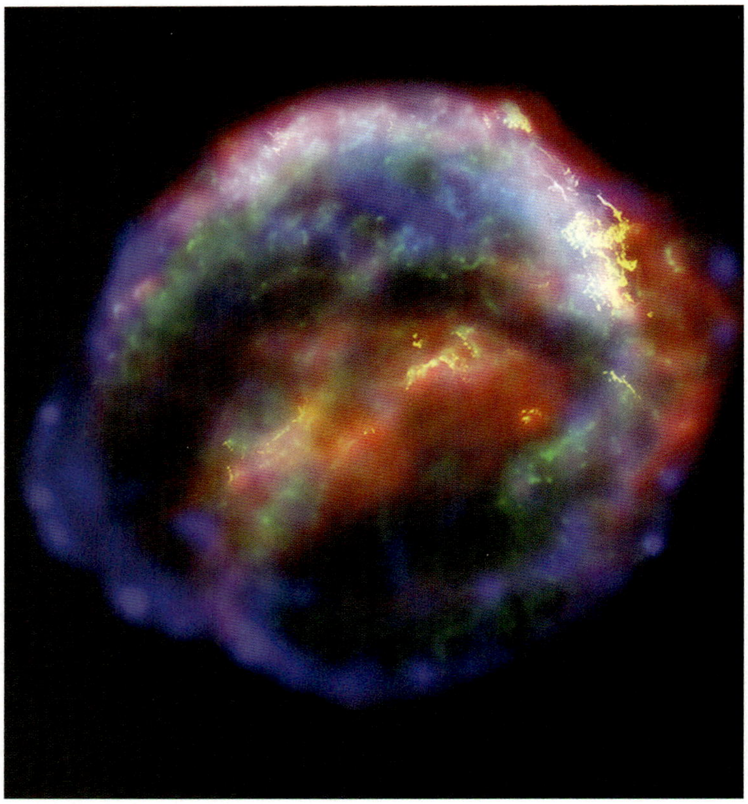

Kepler's supernova

On 17 October 1604, the famous German astronomer Johannes Kepler at his observatory in Prague recorded a supernova in the constellation of Ophiuchus so bright that it was seen in daylight for more than three weeks. It is the most recent known naked-eye supernova so far. The star was around 20,000 light years away in our own galaxy and when it exploded it outshone every other star and planet in the night sky except for Venus. The supernova remnant is still a focus of a lot of study by astronomers and astrophysicists.

How to find it: Kepler's supernova remnant lays near the easternmost foot of Ophiuchus the Serpent Bearer, about halfway between Sagittarius and Scorpius. It is best seen in the summer months for mid-northern latitude observers.

The Veil Nebula

The Veil Nebula is a cloud of ionised gas which is just a part of the larger Cygnus loop, the remains of a supernova which exploded some 5,000 to 8,000 years ago. The cloud of gas has been expanding ever since and now covers an area of sky approximately six degrees in diameter. The progenitor star itself has never been identified. Some sections of the 'loop' are quite bright and have been recorded as separate nebulas; the loop itself is divided into the eastern and western halves. The most famous of these sections is the Witch's Broom Nebula, NGC 6960.

How to find it: The Veil Nebula lays to the southwest of the star Gienah, the bright star in the southern wing of the Swan. It is faint, though, and in order to locate it you may find that you will need to be using a telescope with an Ultra High Contrast filter.

Tycho's supernova

The supernova of 1572 recorded by Tycho Brahe was one of the most important celestial events in history as it helped to usher in a new way of thinking about the cosmos. Despite being discovered by many individuals, it was named after Brahe because he wrote an important book about it. It was seen in the constellation of Cassiopeia and like Kepler's supernova, which followed a couple of decades later, it was visible in daylight. It is now so faint it can only be seen with professional telescopes and cameras. It lays some 8,000 to 9,000 light years away from Earth.

How to find it: Although this remnant is beyond the reach of amateur telescopes, it lies to the north of the right-hand 'v' of the 'w' shape of the Cassiopeia constellation.

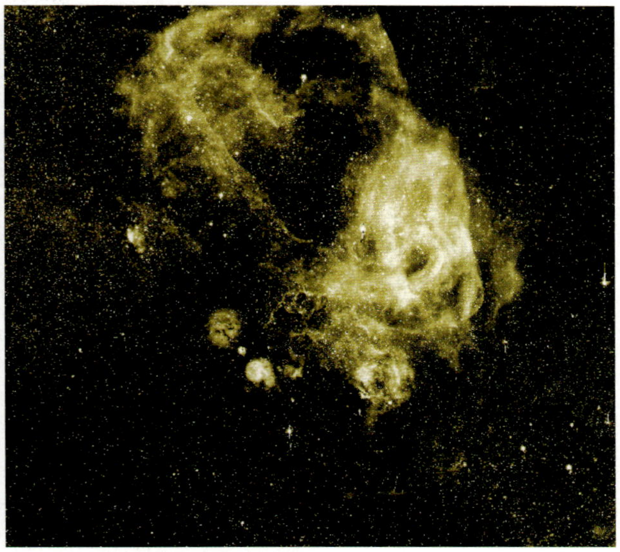

Vela supernova

The Vela supernova remnant is the remains of a star which blew itself to pieces somewhere between 11,000 and 12,300 years ago. This supernova was one of the closest known to us at a distance of approximately 825 light years. The star which exploded formed the Vela Pulsar, which was proof for astronomers that such supernovas form neutron stars.

How to find it: The Vela supernova remnant lays to the southeast of the bright star Suhail in the Vela constellation. It is very faint and requires photography to show it up well.

The Crab Nebula

In 1054, a star in the constellation of Taurus blew itself apart and was seen and recorded by Chinese astronomers. It was bright enough to show in daylight for many days. As the star faded the remnants of it expanded into space and this growing cloud of gas was noted by Charles Messier in his catalogue in 1758. Because of its shape it became known as the Crab Nebula. The star itself collapsed and became a very dense spinning neutron star. This was subsequently discovered to be pulsating at 30 times a second; one of the first pulsars to be found.

How to find it: You will need a telescope to see it now as a faint misty smudge of light just north of the star Zeta Taurii, the tip of the left hand horn of the Bull.

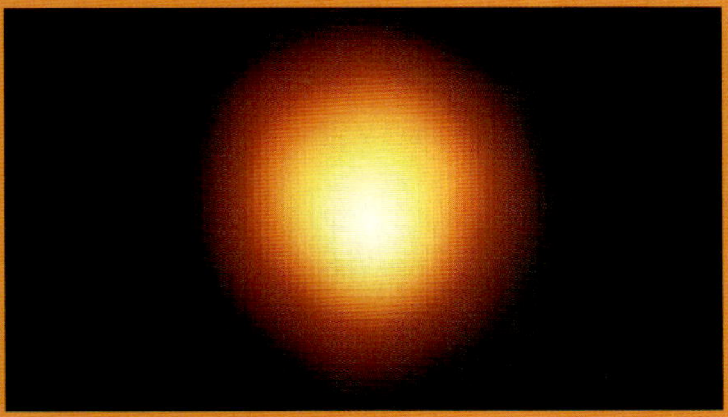

The next supernova

It really is difficult to predict when and where the next supernova will explode in our galaxy. We just have to keep a careful watch. There are some candidates, however, which we know are large stars that are reaching the end of their lives. One of the most well known of these candidates is Betelgeuse in the Orion constellation. This is the bright orange star which marks the Hunter's right shoulder on the left of the constellation as we see it.

How do we know it is coming to the end of its life? Well, its size for one thing tells us this. It is a red supergiant star and lays about 630 light years from us, so when it does finally blow it will be one of the most spectacular sights to ever be seen in the heavens. When is this likely to happen? Again, we just don't know. It might not happen for another million years, or it could happen next week. When it does eventually blow it will be easily seen in daylight, probably for several weeks. It will then fade away and will radically alter the look of the constellation. All we can do is watch and wait.

Five amazing night sky sights

You don't need an expensive telescope to enjoy astronomy, here's five fantastic night sky objects you can view with inexpensive binoculars

Portable, with ample light-gathering powers and big fields of view, binoculars are ideal instruments with which to explore the night skies and glimpse a wide selection of bright deep-sky objects. From virtually any observing site away from artificial lights, tens of thousands of stars, along with hundreds of nebulae, star clusters and distant galaxies are within the reach of binoculars as small as 7x30s. With the broad swathe of the Milky Way arching high overhead, the Northern Hemisphere's spectacular summer skies (the Southern Hemisphere's winter skies) host a wealth of celestial treasures. The following is just a sampling of the brighter deep-sky objects on display.

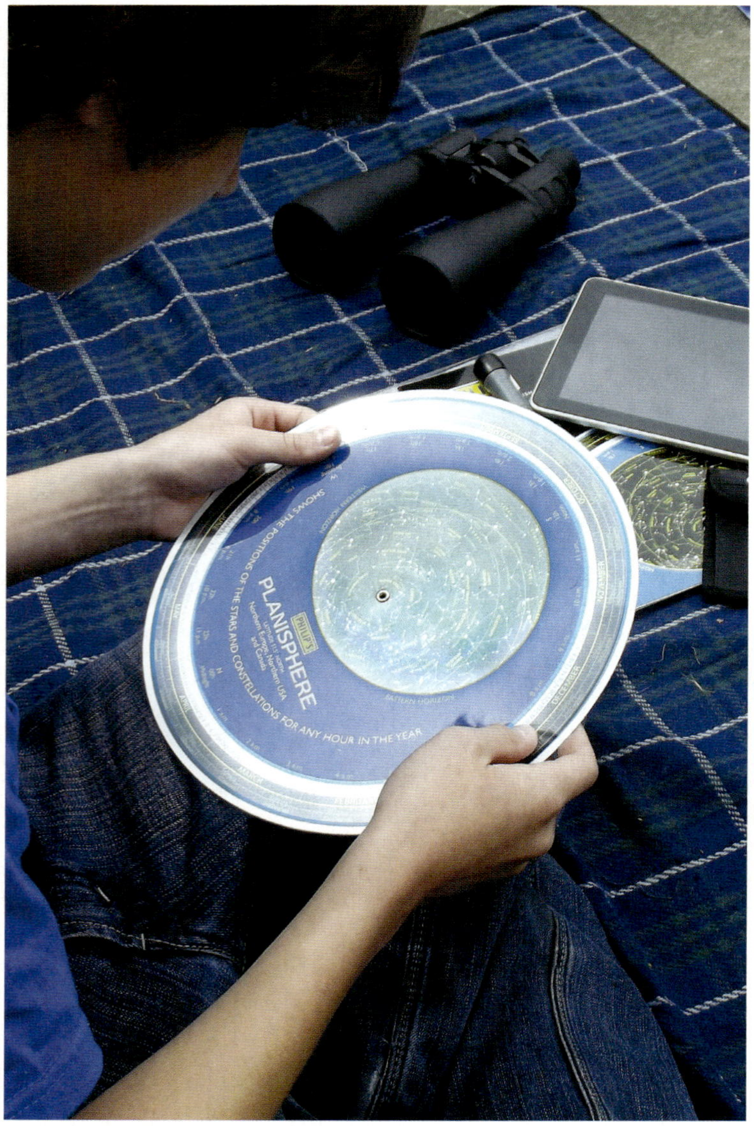

Using a star chart will help you get the most from the night sky's delights

The Double Cluster (NGC 869 & 884)

Northern Hemisphere

Constellation: Perseus

Distance: 6,800 ly (2,085 pc)

One of the grandest sights in the northern night skies, the Double Cluster (NGC 869 and NGC 884) is a glorious side-by-side pair of open star clusters.

How to find it: It is located in the northwestern corner of Perseus, midway between the constellation's brightest star Mirphak and the central star in the prominent 'W' asterism of neighbouring Cassiopeia. NGC 869 and NGC 884 can be glimpsed as a hazy patch with the unaided eye. Both clusters fit in a single binocular field. More than 300 blazing blue-white supergiants in each cluster contrast nicely with a number of nearby red stars. Both clusters formed in the same nook of the Milky Way less than 6 million years ago and are very young by cosmic standards.

The Coalsack / Jewel Box (NGC 4755)

Southern Hemisphere

Constellation: Crux

Distance: 6,440 ly (1,970 pc)

The Coalsack is a patch of inky darkness some four degrees wide that covers the southeastern portion of the far southern constellation of Crux, overlapping the adjoining constellations of Musca and Centaurus, making it rather easy to locate.

How to find it: First find beta Crucis, the most eastern star in the Crux constellation, slowly move your aim southeast one and a half degrees to find The Coalsack. Although it looks pitch black, it is actually faintly illuminated by starlight and is a little brighter than the background of deep space. Just to its north, a small misty spot can be discerned with the unaided eye. This is the Jewel Box (NGC 4755) a marvellous open star cluster.

The Dumbbell Nebula (M27)

Northern Hemisphere

Constellation: Vulpecula

Distance: 1,360 ly (417 pc)

Straddling the Milky Way, the inconspicuous constellation of Vulpecula is home to the Dumbbell Nebula (M27), the finest planetary nebula north of the celestial equator.

How to find it: M27 can be found by first locating the small but clearly discernable constellation of Sagitta and sweeping just three degrees north of its brightest star Gamma Sagitta (magnitude +3.5). Visible in the same binocular field as Gamma, M27 is easily visible as a well-defined glowing patch, surprisingly large at some eight arcminutes across (a quarter the full Moon's diameter) with a magnitude of +7.5. Closer telescopic scrutiny reveals the nebula to be shaped like a misty apple core with a greenish hue.

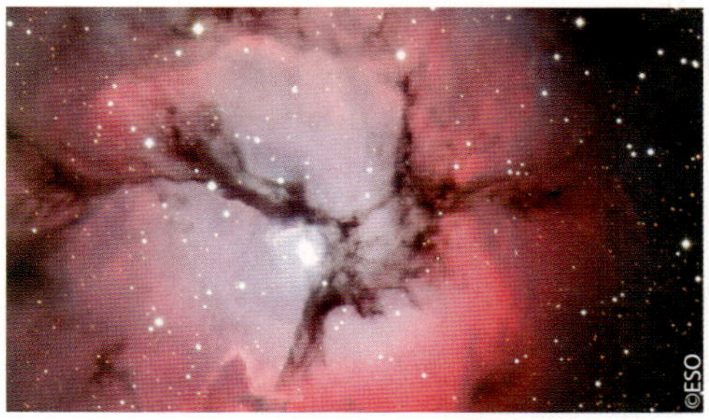

The Trifid Nebula (M20)

Northern & Southern

Constellation: Sagittarius

Distance: 5,200 ly (1,595 pc)

Sagittarius doesn't rise very high above northern temperate horizons but it is easy to locate and several of its brighter stars can be seen from dark locations. Most of the constellation's deep-sky treasures lie in its western half.

How to find it: First, you'll need to locate the Lagoon Nebula (M8) a few degrees north of the 'spout' on the Sagittarius tea pot. North of M8 lies the Trifid Nebula (M20). At magnitude +6.3, binoculars show M20 as a pinkish patch measuring approximately half a degree across. Through a large telescope it assumes a good degree of structure, including three dark dust lanes (Trifid means 'divided into three').

The Sombrero Galaxy (M104)

Northern & Southern

Constellation: Virgo

Distance: 35 million ly (10 million pc)

Southwestern Virgo hosts numerous bright galaxies, of which the Sombrero Galaxy (M104) is prominent. At magnitude +9.0 it is well within the grasp of binoculars.

How to find it: Find the bright star Spica (magnitude +1.0) and sweep 11 degrees to its west. Binoculars reveal M104, an edge-on galaxy, as an elongated smudge eight arcminutes long. Larger telescopes show its nucleus bulging from spiral arms, while a dark dust lane runs through its centre. Our view towards Virgo is angled to the plane of the Milky Way into intergalactic space. Virgo contains a cluster of up to 2,000 galaxies.

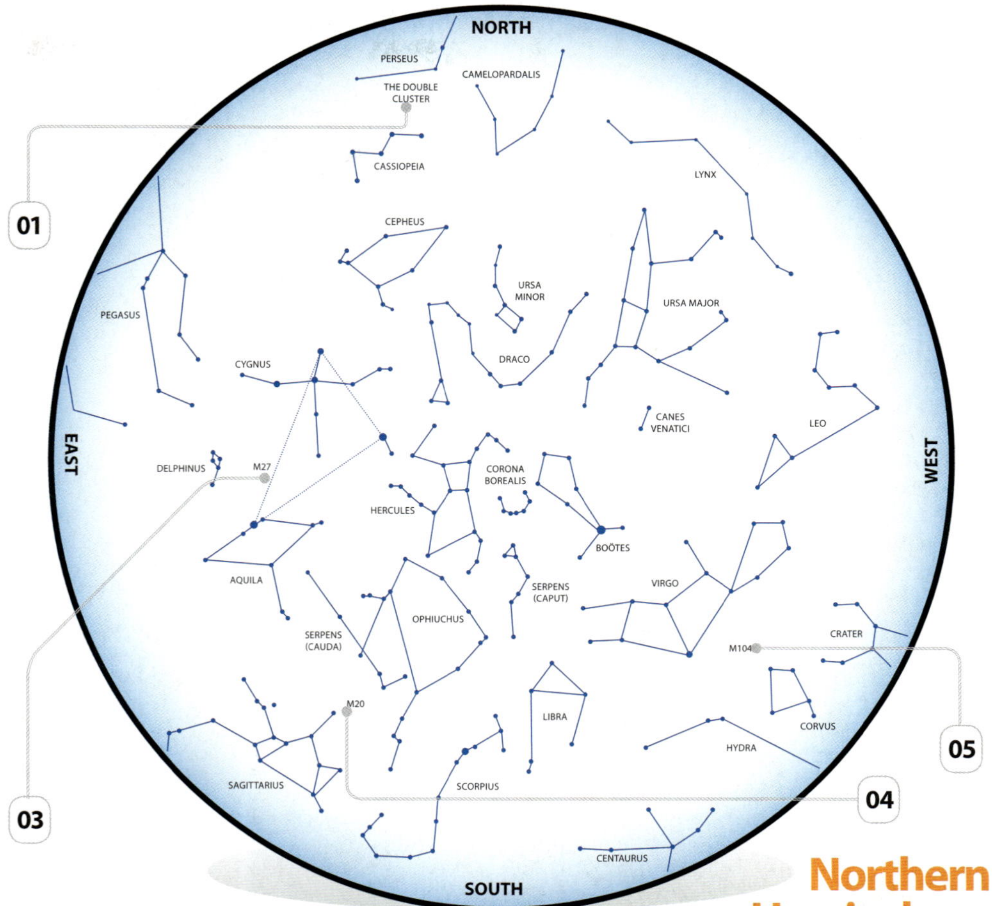

Northern Hemisphere

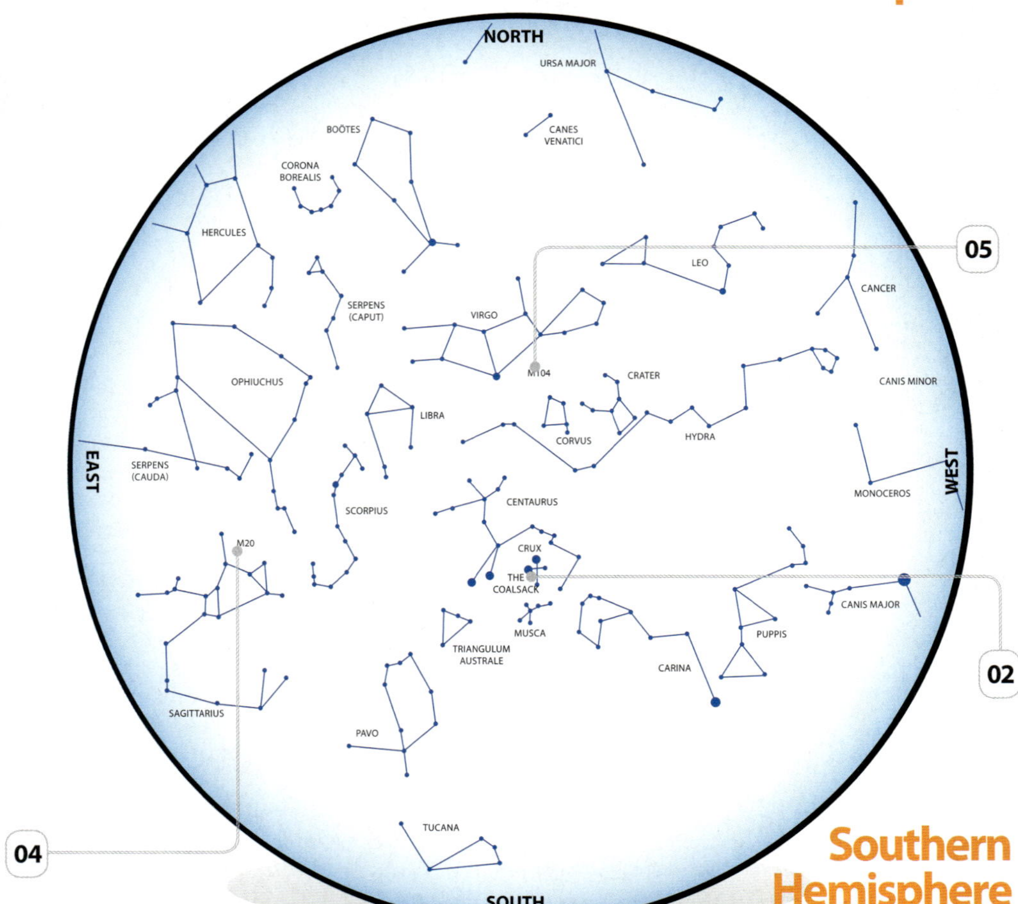

Southern Hemisphere

Operate a telescope remotely

Controlling a large telescope – as far out as Australia or Hawaii – from the comfort of your very own home has never been easier

We all know that amateur astronomers use telescopes of all different types and sizes to scan the heavens. However, what some don't know is that the telescopes found in observatories atop mountains where the air is thin and the climate is exotic, isn't always the sole preserve of professional scientists. It is also possible for amateurs to get involved simply through the touch of a computer keypad. The incredible thing is that you don't even need to be in the same country, let alone next to the telescope that you're operating. In other words, you are using these powerful instruments remotely, similar to the scientists that control interplanetary robotic spacecraft that image the Moon and travel long distances to planets, from here on Earth.

In the current times of high-speed internet access and advanced browser-based programming languages, anyone with an internet connection can now escape cloudy skies to some of the clearest in the world. Not only can you skip through the skies of New Mexico and Spain to Australia and elsewhere, you will also be using equipment that would otherwise be out of financial reach to many.

While you don't actually get the chance to look through the eyepiece as you would at home or at a society meeting, controlling an observatory in another country or even another hemisphere is mind-boggling in its own right. With a few clicks of a mouse, and affordable rates per hour of observing time (usually quoted in points), you could be using a telescope under a pitch-black foreign sky, observing and imaging deep-sky objects that you might never have seen before, in addition to distant comets and asteroids. Now the universe really does lie at your fingertips like never before!

"You are using powerful instruments remotely, similar to the scientists that control interplanetary robotic spacecraft"

The ultimate remote telescope – Hubble is operated by several space agencies

Global Rent-A-Scope
www.global-rent-a-scope.com

Hailed as the best facility for the advanced amateur astronomer, the Global Rent-A-Scope (GRAS) operates a network of some ten telescopes in three locations across both the Northern and Southern Hemispheres – six of which are situated in New Mexico, three in Australia and one can be found in Israel.

Being in two different hemispheres gives GRAS a huge advantage. If you find that the skies are not as clear as you'd have hoped in one hemisphere, or one site is down because of adverse weather, you can simply switch to the other. So many telescopes also means observers are given a huge choice in camera and focal length configurations including a CCD that is aimed at near-infrared observations.

Time using the telescopes can be bought in packages ranging from a starter trial at $19 up to a larger sum of $289 per month supplying you with 11 hours observing time as well as the added bonus of being able to schedule your telescope time. Free time is also offered to new users, allowing you to try out the system.

Faulkes Telescope Project

www.faulkes-telescope.com

A partner of the Las Cumbres Observatory Global Telescope Network (LCOGTN), the Faulkes Telescope Project provides free access to its two-metre robotic telescopes – just slightly smaller than the Hubble Space Telescope – situated in Hawaii and Australia to encourage teachers and students to get involved in research-based education. Similar to other organisations that host overseas telescopes, the Faulkes Telescope Project provides comprehensive training for any individual or group wanting to get the most out of amateur astronomy, either online or by running workshops across the UK as well as selected events in Europe.

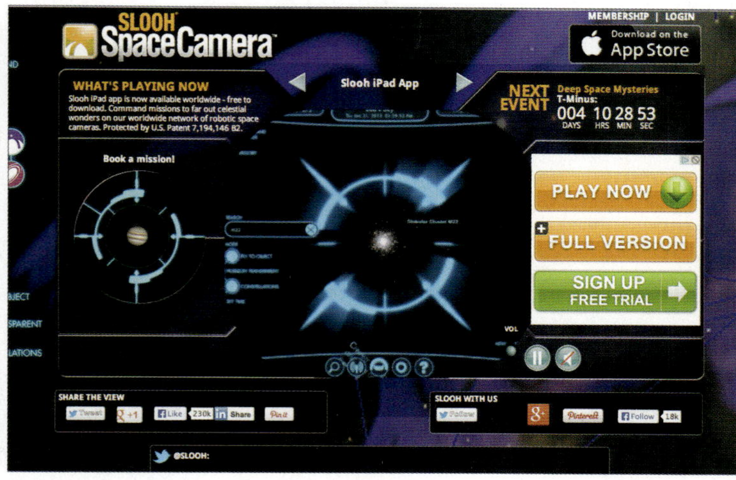

Slooh

http://events.slooh.com

With only two telescopes per site, Slooh does not offer a network that is as extensive as GRAS but does offer membership to use its telescopes at a free level. Using Slooh, you'll also find that you have the option to be guided through live imaging sessions by an astronomer.

Slooh is also very simple to use, with comprehensive guidance on controls that allow you to plan and make observations. This robotic telescope is so simple to use in fact, that children can get involved and there are observing programs for the young astronomer – without parents having to worry about large telescope bills!

LightBuckets

www.lightbuckets.com

Amateurs can join LightBuckets for free, however you need to purchase telescope time to use the five telescopes situated in France. These robotic telescopes are geared towards beginners to astrophotographers as well as the serious amateur or professional astronomer.

LightBuckets' interface presents a simple setup that leads the user through choosing an observatory, a target as well as setting up an imaging run and retrieving data. LightBuckets will also automatically produce final full-colour images, so there's absolutely no need to know anything about image processing. If you see yourself as an advanced observer, then you have the option of having complete observatory control as well as command of your imaging run.

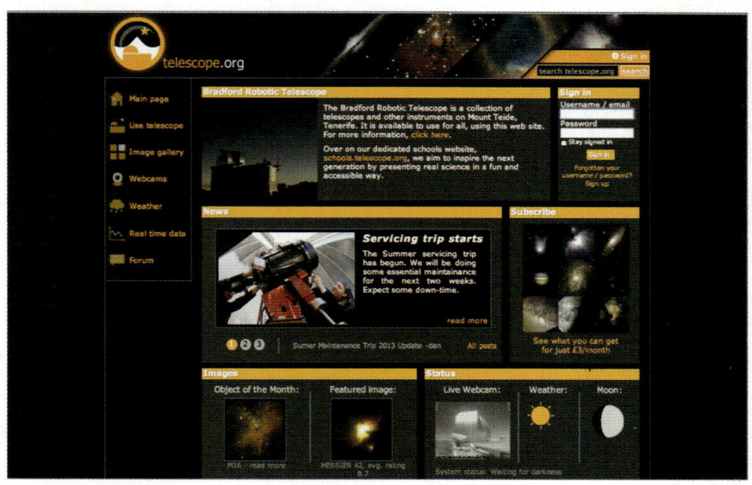

Bradford Robotic Telescope

www.telescope.org

Consisting of four telescopes mounted at the summit of Mount Teide in the Canary Islands, the Bradford Robotic Telescope (BRT) is often used by schools and colleges, making it one of the favourites for astronomy outreach. It boasts over 75,000 registered users, many of which are at educational establishments. The BRT is also free to use, unfortunately meaning that telescope-time is heavily over-subscribed. However, requests to use the BRT are usually processed fairly quickly.

Completely automated, the system features multiple power backup and can cater for any teething troubles that it may encounter. At a height of over 2,377 metres altitude, the telescope is high above cloud level and allows users to monitor local conditions with the guidance of an online display.

Astrophotography

"You should find everything you need to get up and running with astrophotography here"

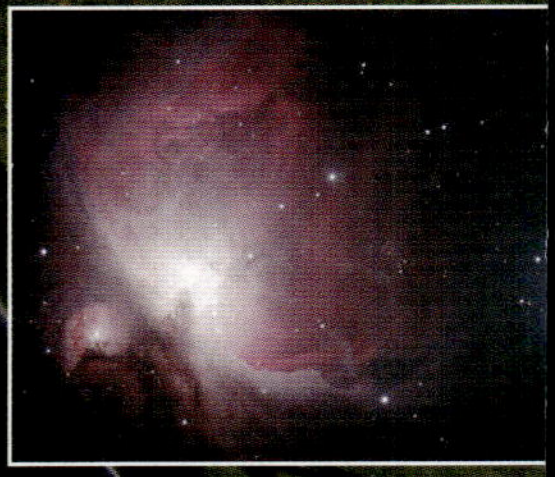

Discover astrophotography

From the Milky Way to distant nebulae, we take you on a photographic journey to space with our guide to astrophotography

The sky at night. The sense of wonder and awe we all experience whenever we gaze up at a canopy illuminated by millions of tiny points of light is something everyone can relate to. It's one of the most awe-inspiring things that a human being can look upon.

Whenever something amazes us, one of the first urges we get is to capture an image of it. Our earliest ancestors carved images of the constellations into the walls of caves and now in the 21st Century we have a wealth of high-tech equipment available to us. However, taking great photos of the night sky is harder than it looks. In fact, a convincing case could probably be made for astrophotography being more challenging than almost any other kind of photography.

As an astrophotographer striving to capture compelling images of the night sky, you need to build up your reserves of patience, be willing to drive for miles when you'd rather be tucked up in bed and be prepared to stay awake all night, even if you work the next day. Successful shoots will also need a large amount of planning and a good understanding of the equipment you're using. And then there's the science. Decent astronomical and meteorological knowledge is definitely an advantage, rapidly becoming a necessity if you want to take close-up portraits of the Moon and stunning images of distant galaxies and nebulae.

You can't take great shots of the heavens on any given night of the year, and this is why, as previously mentioned, one of the first virtues astrophotographers need is patience. For example, if there is any kind of cloud coverage, the stars will be obscured and great images will be difficult to obtain, even with extensive equipment. This is one reason why the stars often seem brighter on cold, winter nights as the low temperature is in part due to an absence of cloud allowing heat to escape from Earth and disperse into the atmosphere.

Another reason for the vivid sparkles of winter skies is that the Sun drops below the horizon by a much greater degree than in summer. Though it's almost imperceptible to the naked eye, during the height of summer there is some degree of sunlight interfering with the clarity of the night sky for all but a few hours. Astrophotographer Phil Young believes the weather should never be overlooked or taken for granted when it comes to astrophotography: "You are at the mercy of the weather, which cannot be predicted that far in advance."

However, not all of the challenges faced by astrophotographers come down to the raw science of astronomy and meteorology. Human activity also greatly affects the chances of obtaining a clear view of the canopy of stars. For example, the summer

■ Astrophotography can be an expensive hobby, but it doesn't have to be

"You're at the mercy of the weather, which can't be predicted far in advance"

The North America nebula in Cygnus constellation, captured by Ian Sharp using 15 hours exposure with narrowband filters

Phil used a DSLR attached to an 80mm telescope and an exposure of one second at f6 and ISO 100 tracking on a motorised mount to capture this full moon image

Plan your shoot

1. Check the weather

Keep a close eye on the weather if you are planning an overnight expedition to photograph the night sky – if there's likely to be a lot of cloud around your trip may be in vain.

2. Take a mobile phone

As well as being useful for weather updates, take a mobile phone with you so that you can contact someone if anything at all goes wrong – some of the best astrophotography sites are lonely places.

3. Use a map

Study a map and familiarise yourself with your destination – don't just trust your sat nav to be able to guide you to some of the locations recommended for astrophotography.

4. Familiarise yourself

A simple star chart, such as those designed for children, can be an excellent way of familiarising yourself with what the sky has to offer at each time of year.

months can present a problem if smog and general air pollution from dust particles and exhaust fumes gather in the atmosphere during a period of prolonged high temperatures and poor airflow. And this isn't the only kind of pollution astrophotographers have to contend with.

Perhaps an even bigger problem is light pollution and it's the combined effects of air and light pollution that force those searching for the clearest views of the sky out into the most isolated and dark areas they can find, which is also the reason why large-scale scientific observatories are often constructed hundreds of miles from the nearest city.

The glow of several thousand lights burning all night long in the big cities affects both the visual clarity of the starlight and also plays havoc with long camera exposures, presenting itself as an orange glow that competes for attention with the main attraction in the skies above. As Phil Young says emphatically: "Light pollution is the biggest problem that astrophotographers will encounter. You need to be away from street lights in towns and cities, and even then you might still have problems caused by light pollution."

A final factor that can come into play in certain locations is aircraft activity, and in areas close to major airports it's unlikely that any amount of careful planning or preparation will allow you to avoid man-made lights in the sky.

Astrophotography is, without doubt, a huge subject and one we're covering in greater depth within this section of the book. From taking great images to offering up inspiration to help you understand the types of images that you'll be capable of taking, you should find everything you need to get up and running with astrophotography here.

■ Phil made sure we spent some time reviewing the images that we'd taken, before packing up for the night at about 2am

■ Even a basic DSLR will be able to provide impressive shots of the night sky

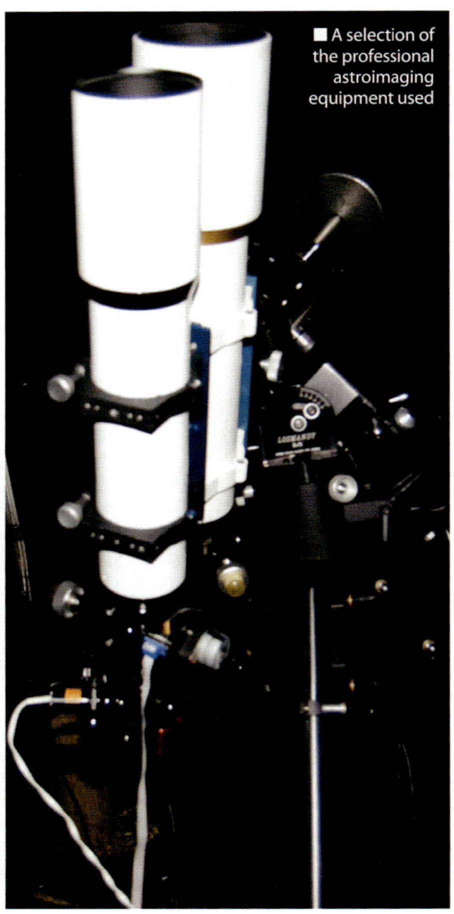
■ A selection of the professional astroimaging equipment used

Astrophotography for as little as £15

While results will differ depending on the kit used, it's not necessary to spend a lot of money to create an astrophotography setup. All you need is a decent quality telescope, a good DSLR camera and a method of connecting the two. This can be done with a simple and inexpensive T-Ring which simply replaces the lens of the camera allowing you to connect a T-Adapter and image directly through your telescope. Our picture here shows a Nikon D80 attached to Sky-Watcher's Quattro f4 Imaging Newtonian using a generic Nikon T-Ring. The ring is £15 from **www.astronomia.co.uk** and is the only part needed to make the connection.

Orion Nebula (Ian Sharp)
Originally imaged by Henry Draper in 1880, the Orion Nebula was the subject of the first instance of astrophotography.

Horsehead Nebula in Orion (Ian Sharp)
This is definitely one of the most popular nebulae to photograph and appears on most astrophotographers' checklists.

The Milky Way (Ian Sharp)
As Ian Sharp says: "The beauty of the Milky Way stretching across a dark sky is difficult to beat." The exposure was 20 seconds at f2.8 and ISO 400.

A professional setup

Ian Sharp talks us through the most essential equipment for deep-space imaging

"Here is a photograph of a typical setup for deep-sky imaging. The telescope is a small 75mm Pentax APO Refractor that I often use for wide field nebulae imaging. The camera is at the end in red and just in front is a black filter wheel so that I can choose Luminance, Red, Green or Blue filters, or maybe H-Alpha or OIII for narrow-band imaging.

Then the key to accurate guiding – the Off-Axis Guider (OAG) unit, which is at 90 degrees to the optical path. It has a small 'pick-off' prism inside that directs a small part of the light to a second small camera which has the white cable connected to the top. This feeds back to the mount controller and makes very tiny drive corrections every two or three seconds. I choose a guide star in the OAG and the software ensures that this star stays spot-centre. It uses a centroid algorithm so it can actually guide to sub-pixel accuracy. In this way I take images up to one hour, or, more typically 30 minutes, to reduce the chance of spoiling an image due to a cloud etc. I would typically process 12 hours or more together to produce a final image. More images stack to reduce noise. The camera operates at about 30 degrees below ambient.

"You can use a separate, dedicated guide scope in parallel with the main scope, but you find that small flexures between the scopes can take the edge off the guiding, especially when using larger scopes than the little Pentax."

1. Finder scope
2. Guiding CCD camera
3. Cable to mount computer
4. Imaging CCD camera
5. USB to laptop
6. Mount controller
7. Filter wheel
8. OAG unit
9. Telescope

Amateur astrophotographer's gallery

Get inspired by this collection of fantastic images of the night sky

Since the dawn of time people have been looking to the stars, wondering what secrets they hold. We're still wondering but now we can see them a whole lot closer with an amazing range of telescopes, zoom lenses and DSLRs. We're always amazed by the quality of photos taken by amateur astronomers, so we thought we'd find some of our favourites for you to enjoy, get jealous of and attempt to better.

You've given us stars, moons, galaxies – basically everything that makes the universe wondrous. We've tried to pick out a range because, incredible as it is, no one wants to sift through lots of snaps of the Andromeda Galaxy! Hopefully the images here will show what you'll be capable of with your telescope, and demonstrate that anyone – with the right equipment – can take some incredible images.

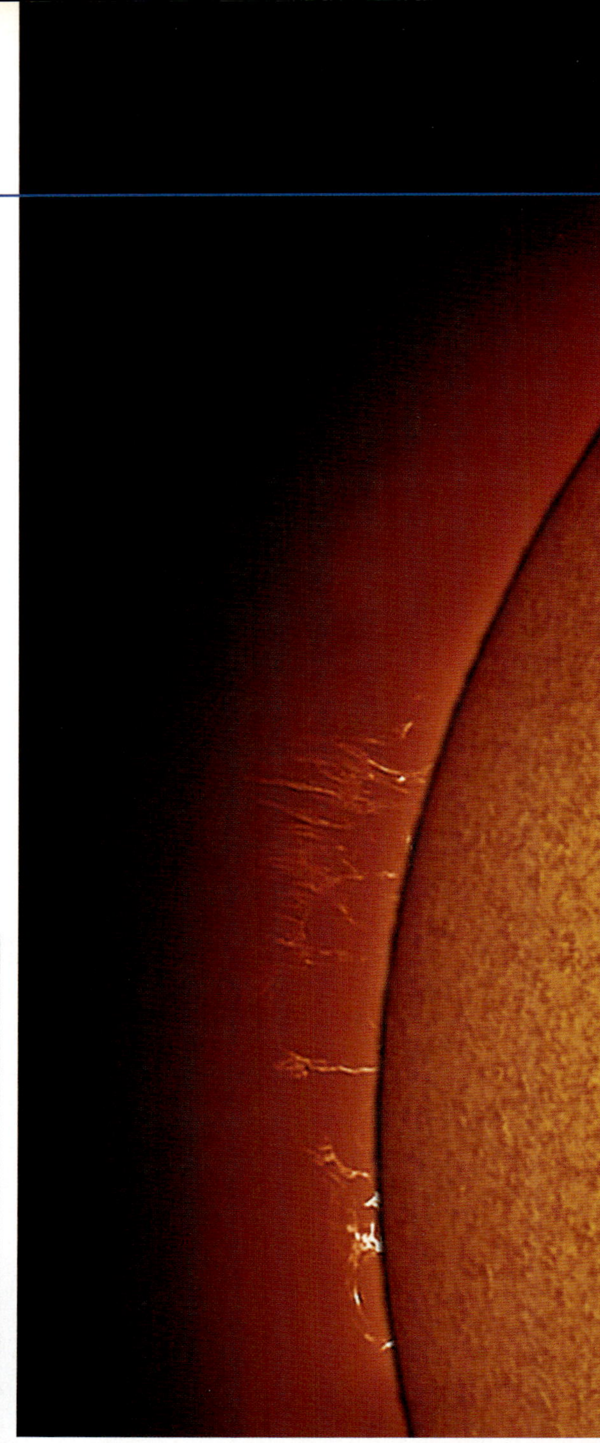

Bill Schlosser

■ n/a

I currently use a QSI 583 WSG with a TEC 140 and an AT65EDQ for scopes. I also use Astrodon filters and had a Celastron CGEM DX mount, but I sold it and bought the new CGE PRO mount which I haven't been able to use yet.

Brian Johnson

■ Meade LX200GPS/Televue NP-127

I live on the outskirts of Brighton with its terrible light pollution. As such, I try to photograph the night sky when travelling in my motor caravan to Kelling Heath star parties and going to Scotland for the dark skies.

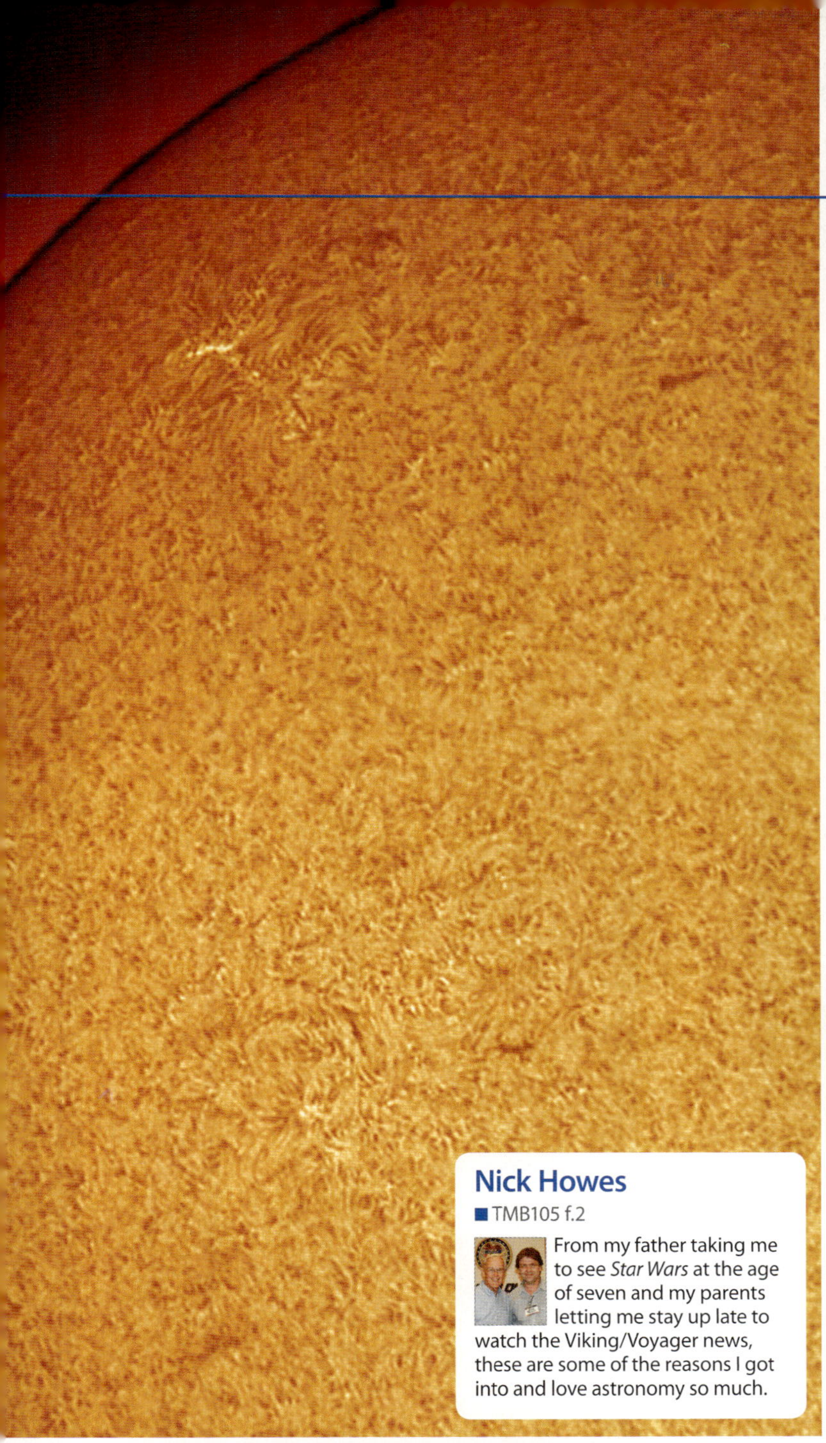

Nick Howes

TMB105 f.2

From my father taking me to see *Star Wars* at the age of seven and my parents letting me stay up late to watch the Viking/Voyager news, these are some of the reasons I got into and love astronomy so much.

Daniel Sundstrom

Meade 102mm APO and 37-minute exposure with a Nikon D80 mounted on an unguided NEQ6 Pro

Just wanted to share my latest harvest from the grey and very wet autumn here in Arvika, Sweden. M31, the Andromeda Galaxy, is seen here heavily light polluted by the Moon unfortunately, but nevertheless it is my best amateur picture.

Sarah Lewis

n/a

I had always been into astronomy but didn't explore it much until I heard about the ISS passing over. I started taking long exposure images of it that displayed its path as it floated over.

Paul Wharton

Sky-Watcher 200P

This was taken at Craigavon Lakes in County Armagh, Northern Ireland in my unsuccessful viewing attempt of the Venus transit. I've also adapted an Xbox Live camera and a Trsut WB-5400.

Sonia Gee

Sky-Watcher 10" Dobsonian

I got into astronomy when I was seven after my parents bought me a Tasco telescope. When it comes to astrophotography, I focus mainly on constellations and the Moon, as well as the International Space Station!

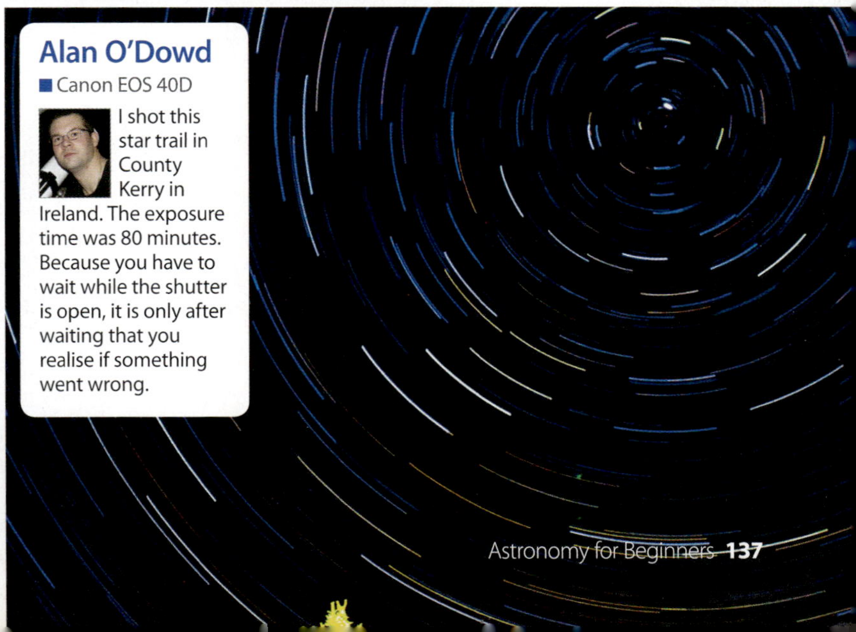

Alan O'Dowd

Canon EOS 40D

I shot this star trail in County Kerry in Ireland. The exposure time was 80 minutes. Because you have to wait while the shutter is open, it is only after waiting that you realise if something went wrong.

Astrophotography

Steven McConnach

■ Canon 500D and Celastron Advanced GT8 telescope

I am lucky enough to live on the north coast of Scotland, where we have beautiful dark skies. These photos were all taken in my back yard. Living so far north also means we get the best chance to see the Northern Lights from mainland Britain.

Daryl Jewell

■ Sky-Watcher Explorer 130PM

I'm a very keen and very amateur astronomer. The planets, the Moon and the Sun are my favourite views. The Sky-Watcher Explorer 130PM is an affordable and simple telescope that's great to use.

Robert Chadwick

■ Meade 4504

I want to be an a scientist or an astrophysicist. I was introduced to astronomy by my dad. I enjoy looking at most visible planets. This is an image of the star Sirius.

Steve Mansfield

■ ED80 D5-Pro

This is the first image I've taken with this scope and mount. I took it from the skies in Preston, Lancashire with a total exposure time of four hours. I've been interested in astronomy all my life since my father bought me a 70mm reflector when I was 12.

Philip Pugh

■ Skywatcher 127mm Maksutov telescope

My best images are of Jupiter, taken on 18 November. No piece of equipment cost more than £500 so all affordable stuff and many were taken with a compact digital camera.

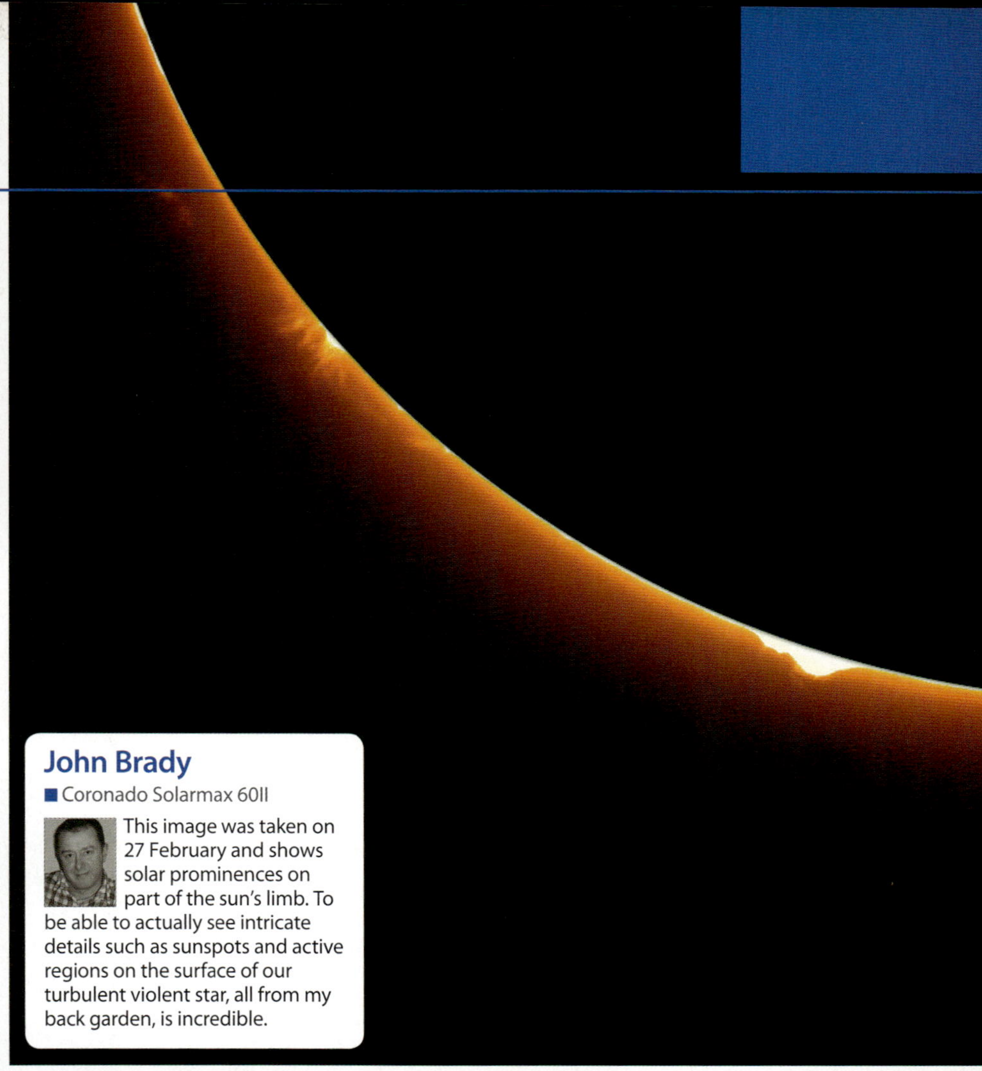

John Brady

■ Coronado Solarmax 60II

This image was taken on 27 February and shows solar prominences on part of the sun's limb. To be able to actually see intricate details such as sunspots and active regions on the surface of our turbulent violent star, all from my back garden, is incredible.

Andrew Beech

■ Sky Watcher Skyliner 150P

This image of the Moon is my first astro image taken afocally using a 10 megapixel compact camera held to a 15mm eyepiece. I'm pretty pleased with it for a first attempt.

Tanja Carruthers

■ Celastron 11" CGEM DX

My dad introduced me to the stars at a young age, but astrophotography is a recent hobby. I love the challenge of shooting something the eye can't see, my favourite imaging objects being nebulae and galaxies, or anything spectacular!

Jathin Premjith

■ 7D DSLR camera mounted on a Celaston CPC-800 eight inch reflective telescope

This photo of the transit of Venus was taken at sunrise through the telescope without a solar filter. The telescope was in solar tracking mode and I managed to capture the gradation from dark red to yellow.

Astrophotography

Dean Watson

■ Canon EOS 450D DSLR

Here is my image of the galaxy NGC 6946 and the open cluster 6939 on the Cepheus/Cygnus border. I live in Lincolnshire, am a keen astrophotographer and thought you might enjoy this attractive but slightly unusual target on the outskirts of our galaxy.

Gordon Haynes

■ Paramount ME, Takahashi FSQ106ED

I've been interested in astronomy for most of my life but about five years ago I started taking it more seriously. I specialise in narrow band imaging using the HST palette. This image is of SH2-155, the Cave Nebula, using the HST palette with an exposure time of 24 hours.

Matthew Estabrook

■ Astroscan 2001

This is a photo of my five-year-old son using my 30-year-old Astroscan 2001, perfect for a budding astronomer! He's taking a good look at the moon high above!

Paul Wharton

■ itelescope.net

You don't even need to own a telescope to do astrophotography. There are a few websites that let you control and take images from their telescope. It's a simple way to get into astro imaging and it doesn't cost you a penny.

John Slinn

■ William Optics Zenithstar 66 refractor

I have visited La Palma twice with my Astrotrac 320XX system and taken some excellent images, even getting nominated into the top 100 astrophotographers comp run by the Royal Observatory Greenwich in 2010.

Marco Frissen

■ Nikon VI camera

Here is a high-resolution of the Moon and Jupiter in conjunction. It was actually the first time I had tried this setup. Note that it is not a single image, but rather a combination of two images.

Ralph Wilkins

■ 115mm Altair Astro triplet refractor

I'm usually found in a dark field with a medium-sized refractor and my DSLR camera to image the Moon, planets, galaxies, star clusters and nebulae.

Stuart Gotsall

■ Canon 5D MkII

This shot with the house in the foreground is the ISS just before it went into the Earth's shadow. I set the focus on the Moon in auto then switched back to manual focus to keep it there throughout the shot.

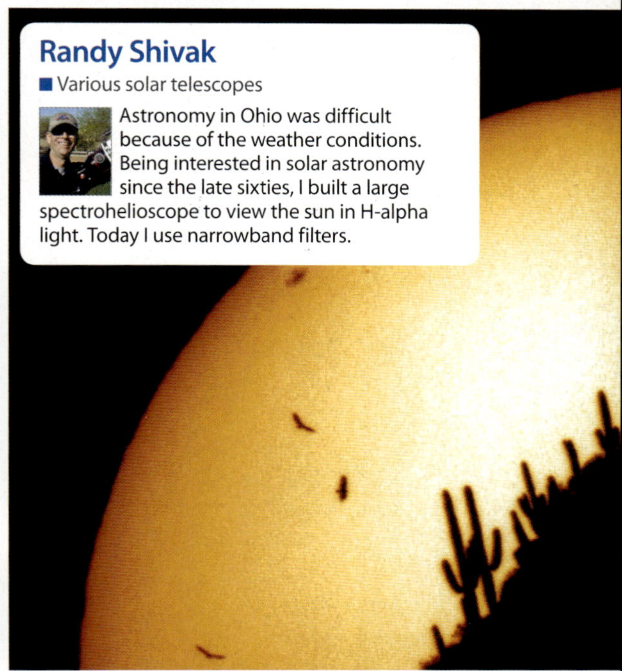

Randy Shivak

■ Various solar telescopes

Astronomy in Ohio was difficult because of the weather conditions. Being interested in solar astronomy since the late sixties, I built a large spectroheliosope to view the sun in H-alpha light. Today I use narrowband filters.

Paul Hill

■ Sky-Watcher 127mm Mak

I am that rare beast, an observer recording what I see in graphite. While many objects fill my sketch books, lunar craters are my passion and my scope allows me to sit 1,600km above the surface and draw these dramatic and ancient objects.

Matthew Robinson

■ Skywatcher Heritage 130P

Since I've had my telescope, I really have enjoyed looking at the many phases of the Moon as well as Jupiter and its moons. I am particularly looking forward to the Geminad meteor shower and Saturn rising at dawn.

The next step

150
20 amateur discoveries

154
The best apps

"Join a club and you'll be able to get advice and share your experiences"

144 Join a club

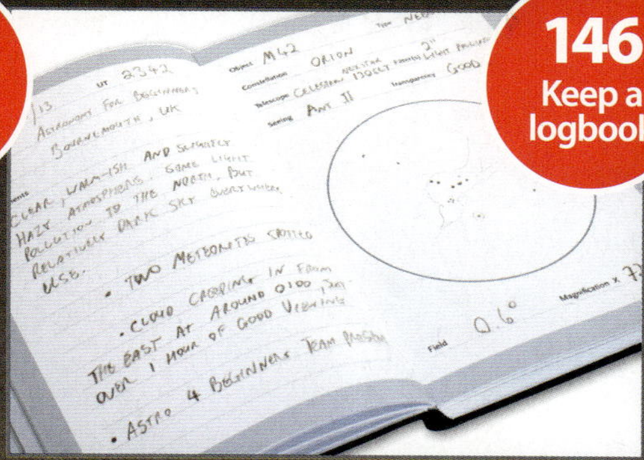

146 Keep a logbook

148 Report a discovery

Joining a club

Enrolling in an astronomy club need not be daunting. Here we provide a lowdown on what to expect when joining your nearest astronomical society

Why join?

If you are new to astronomy, perhaps one of the first pieces of advice you have been given is to join an astronomy society or club. Whoever gave you that advice was talking a lot of sense; from mixing with like-minded people and learning a few new things with the chance to have a play with observing equipment thrown into the bargain, joining an astronomical society near you is very likely to give an extra dimension to your hobby. In short, you won't regret it.

At an astronomy club, you're likely to come across experienced members in the field of amateur astronomy. This in itself is a godsend as asking advice from them will very likely save you a lot of time, money and aggravation when it comes to choosing new observing equipment. Astronomy

Don't worry!

The important thing to remember before you join a new club is not to worry – you are extremely likely to receive a warm and friendly welcome and, whether you're a beginner, intermediate or fully fledged expert on astronomy, clubs are organised in such a way that everyone is catered for, whatever your age or needs.

You may feel that you're so inexperienced that you won't be able to be of any use to the other members when it comes to sharing advice. That's untrue given that there will usually be someone with even less experience than you. Some of the best teachers are individuals who are still learning the ropes and so can empathise with a complete beginner, so make sure you pitch in whenever you can.

clubs are strongly focused on helping their new members with everything from purchasing new equipment to finding your way around the night sky and locating objects such as star clusters and planets. You may even be able to share your experiences to help others learn and enjoy the hobby.

Astronomy clubs can also serve as a "try before you buy" outlet where members are sure to bring along their own instruments such as their newly bought binoculars or trusty telescope that has been nothing short of reliable on those cold nights throughout their hobby. At a club, chances are that a member has a telescope or eyepiece that you've had your eye on for the past few weeks. If your club allows it, you may be able to borrow equipment to tide you over before you settle. Because astronomy speciality stores are quite rare in most cities, you are likely to have to buy expensive equipment over the internet. Unsure of buying expensive items without seeing them first? Then you should get yourself to an astronomy club.

How to join

The first step is to find an astronomical society near you. If you are not aware of any in your area, then calling the nearest observatory, planetarium, science centre or by contacting the physics and astronomy department at your local university or college should provide you with information on not just your local astronomy club and ways to contact them, but possibly a review of the club and what you can expect. If you are an avid reader of astronomy magazines, then you are also likely to find a resources page dedicated to astronomical clubs and what's happening at that particular club on certain dates. You can also use our directory to find an astronomical society nearest to you.

The next thing to consider is that some astronomical societies may ask for a fee to become a member and usually offer a newsletter on top of the events, meetings and observational evenings they have on offer. Some however, are free of charge. For clubs that require a membership fee, prices vary, with some charging for a yearly or seasonal membership while others may charge per meeting. Costs are usually reasonable and will usually differ for adults, concessions and under 16s.

Most, if not all, astronomy clubs have a website with details on how to join. The most common method is to download a membership application form from a particular astronomical society's website and fill it out enclosing either your bank details or a cheque that is made payable to a membership secretary. If you find that the society in your area does not have a form, then don't panic – there will usually be a contact email address or telephone number.

Club meetings

Attending an astronomy club meeting can be one of the most exciting and rewarding experiences when it comes to getting involved in amateur astronomy. Not only do you have the opportunity to interact with other members, but you will also be able to take part in a variety of different activities.

Whatever astronomical society you decide to become a member of, there's likely to be some kind of structure where your society meets on particular days of the week or fortnight. These evenings usually take the form of observation sessions or presentations.

As you may have found out, observing by yourself can be quite lonely. Most clubs often schedule regular observing sessions, where you can loan the society's observing equipment or bring your own, at least on weekends near the new Moon – when the Moon is not visible, making observing easier without glare – as well as other times during the month too. A huge selection of societies also periodically organise field trips to extremely dark observing sites, arranging for discounts on food and accommodation if required. Additionally you will also be able to attend regularly scheduled presentations, ranging from astronomy-related videos to planetarium programs to lectures presented by some of the very best and knowledgeable people in astronomy – these are often university lecturers, observatory and museum workers as well as members of your club. Many also hold workshops that can give you advice on building your own observatory or telescope as well as astrophotography. If your society has a club library, you may also get to use their night sky guides, back issues of astronomy magazines and other reference materials.

During the warmer months, your club will likely offer day trips to local space centres, observatories and museums, weekend star parties as well as science festivals. Some societies usually throw in a summer or Christmas meal too.

Keeping a logbook

Recording the observations you make not only helps you to learn about the night sky, it will also hold your fondest memories. This guide will show you how to keep your very own logbook

If you've looked through the eyepiece of a telescope or those of a pair of binoculars, you most likely have a favourite night sky object that leaves you in awe time and time again. You remember what the object is, what type of instrument you used to observe it, you have an obvious recollection of how you felt when you first saw it hanging in the sky and probably how cold you felt in the night air, rubbing your hands together to keep them warm as you changed your telescope's eyepieces. However, you only vaguely remember what time and evening you first clamped eyes on your favourite object. This is where the logbook can become an astronomer's best friend as it stores the fiddly little details that you're most likely to be struggling to remember right now.

Your sessions under the stars have the scope to become a book of memories which, over time, will allow you to gain familiarity with the treasure trove of objects held by the night sky. Keeping a logbook not only allows you to relive your experiences, but it also allows you to relocate objects, document any unusual sightings and even predict patterns in what our universe has to offer. As well as being of sentimental value, your logbook might be useful if there's a gap in the data of a professional astronomer or researcher.

So what information do you need to keep in a logbook? Choose a notebook, diary or even computer software and read on to start making the most out of your evenings.

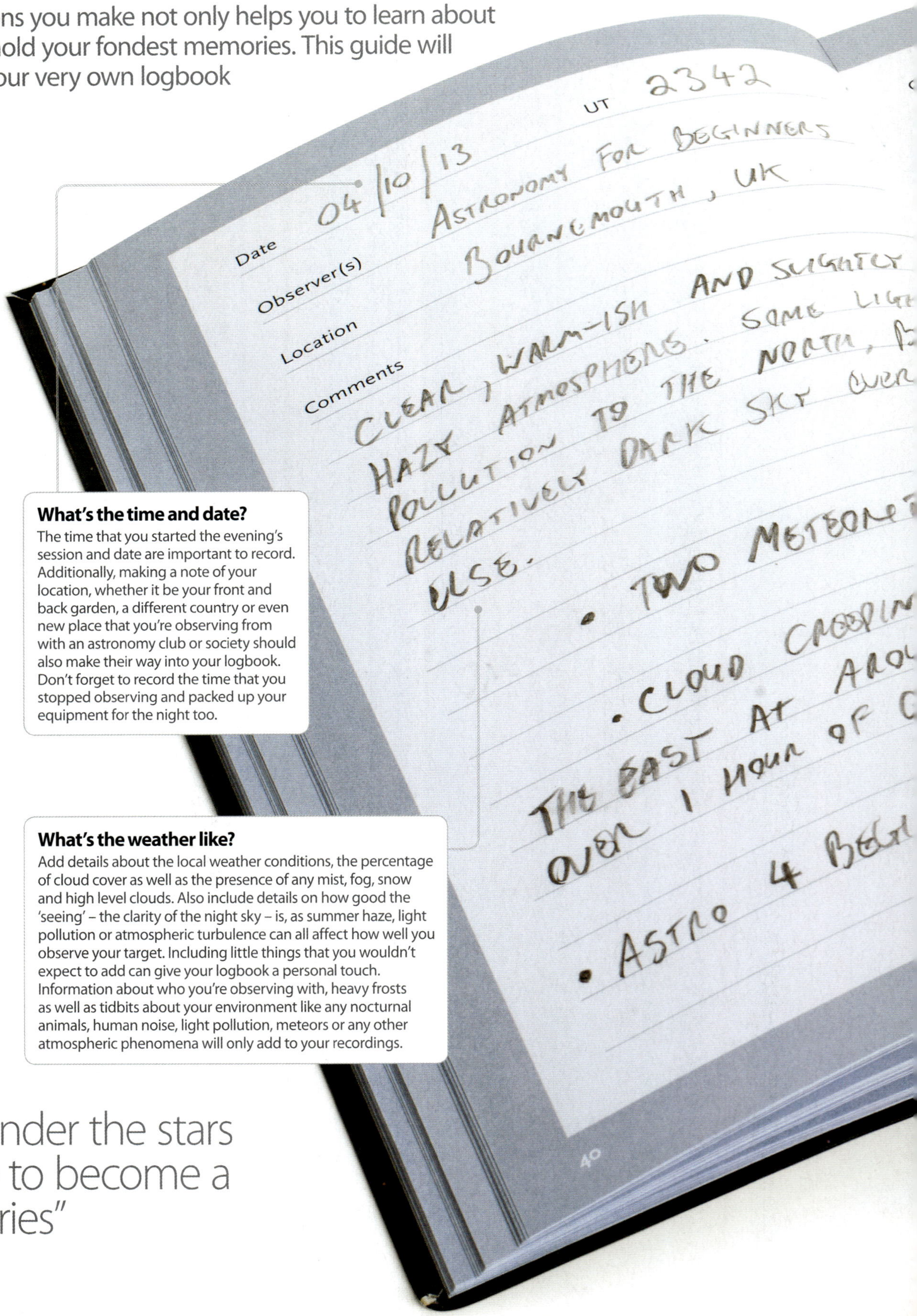

What's the time and date?

The time that you started the evening's session and date are important to record. Additionally, making a note of your location, whether it be your front and back garden, a different country or even new place that you're observing from with an astronomy club or society should also make their way into your logbook. Don't forget to record the time that you stopped observing and packed up your equipment for the night too.

What's the weather like?

Add details about the local weather conditions, the percentage of cloud cover as well as the presence of any mist, fog, snow and high level clouds. Also include details on how good the 'seeing' – the clarity of the night sky – is, as summer haze, light pollution or atmospheric turbulence can all affect how well you observe your target. Including little things that you wouldn't expect to add can give your logbook a personal touch. Information about who you're observing with, heavy frosts as well as tidbits about your environment like any nocturnal animals, human noise, light pollution, meteors or any other atmospheric phenomena will only add to your recordings.

"Your sessions under the stars have the scope to become a book of memories"

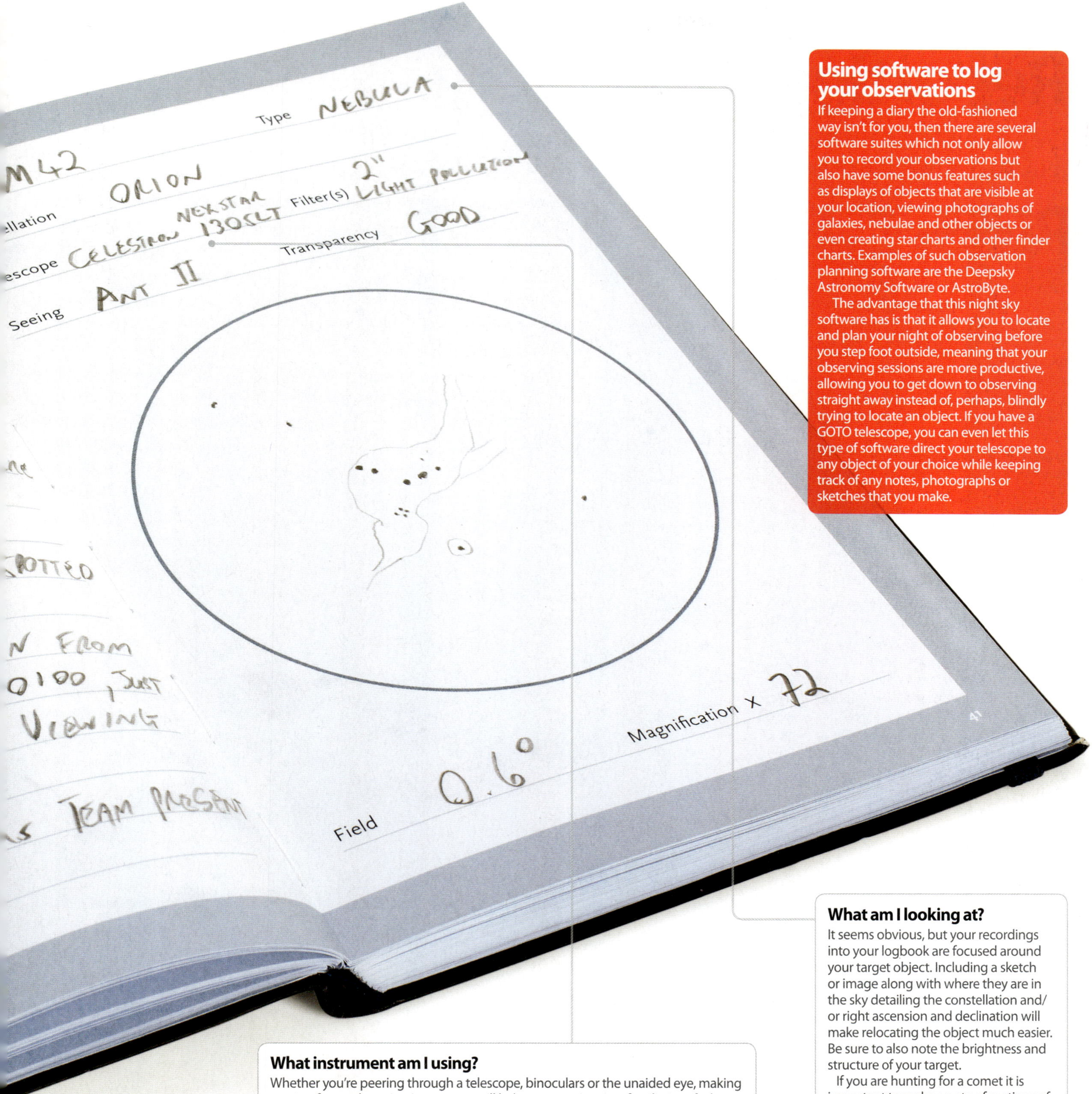

Using software to log your observations

If keeping a diary the old-fashioned way isn't for you, then there are several software suites which not only allow you to record your observations but also have some bonus features such as displays of objects that are visible at your location, viewing photographs of galaxies, nebulae and other objects or even creating star charts and other finder charts. Examples of such observation planning software are the Deepsky Astronomy Software or AstroByte.

The advantage that this night sky software has is that it allows you to locate and plan your night of observing before you step foot outside, meaning that your observing sessions are more productive, allowing you to get down to observing straight away instead of, perhaps, blindly trying to locate an object. If you have a GOTO telescope, you can even let this type of software direct your telescope to any object of your choice while keeping track of any notes, photographs or sketches that you make.

What instrument am I using?

Whether you're peering through a telescope, binoculars or the unaided eye, making a note of your observing instrument will help you to gain some familiarity of what object requires which tool, making sure that you're well equipped when it comes to observing the object again.

Keeping note of your telescope's type, focal ratio or length, eyepieces used, magnification, apparent Field of View (FOV), plus comments on the accuracy of your motor drive or GOTO encoders or drives, can only help when it comes to considering your instrument's performance and whether you need an upgrade. If you're an astrophotographer, be sure to keep notes on camera settings and exposures.

What am I looking at?

It seems obvious, but your recordings into your logbook are focused around your target object. Including a sketch or image along with where they are in the sky detailing the constellation and/or right ascension and declination will make relocating the object much easier. Be sure to also note the brightness and structure of your target.

If you are hunting for a comet it is important to make a note of sections of sky you sweep through noting any star clusters, Messier objects or other objects that you have never encountered before. In general, anyone hunting for objects such as supernovae, novae, comets or variable stars must document precise details of everything they see and do.

Reporting a discovery

Our universe is vast, holding a treasure trove of new objects to be found. But what do you do if you think you've made a discovery? We take you through the steps to successfully report it

Peering through your telescope on one of many evenings under the night sky, you've come across an object that you've never seen before. You look once, and you look again before bringing your faithful instrument into the light, making sure that there's no damage or fingerprints on your telescope's lens. Nothing. But you clean it just to make sure before heading back out to relocate the object. Could this be the moment you've been waiting for? Have you really made a new astronomical discovery?

Reporting discoveries isn't just for professional astronomers; amateurs can also play a part in flagging up previously unidentified objects that they've spotted in the night sky, making astronomy one of the few sciences that allows everyone and anyone to stake claim on a discovery. The sky is large enough for everybody, holding a bounty of objects waiting to be discovered as well as being the result of many amateur astronomer success stories. New asteroids, comets, novae and supernovae are all well within reach of amateur astronomers to discover.

In 1993, Carolyn and Gene Shoemaker and David Levy scanned the starry skies to find a comet orbiting Jupiter. That same speeding chunk of ice, named Shoemaker-Levy 9, smashed into the heavyweight gas giant around a year later, adding fuel to discussions about the possibility of objects colliding with our own planet. And this isn't the only comet that has been spotted by amateur astronomers – Hale-Bopp and comet ISON are another pair that were picked up by the telescopes of enthusiastic stargazers. Asteroids are also being found in great numbers by amateurs.

However, amateurs are not limited to just planets, asteroids and comets. British amateur astronomer Tom Boles holds the record for discovering many supernovae, with 153 discoveries to his name from his personal observatory in Suffolk.

Finding completely different objects, these amateurs had to go through varying channels. The Shoemakers and Levy who found comets, had to approach the Central Bureau for Astronomical Telegrams (CBAT) with their discovery as did Boles with his reports on the supernovae he found, so that others could confirm their discoveries. The CBAT is also the organisation to report observations of novae and outbursts from unusual variable stars.

Keep monitoring the night sky and you might just find a new discovery

However, those who have located asteroids or planets will find that they must report to the Minor Planet Centre, while any new variable stars should be made known to the American Association of Variable Star Observers or the variable star section of the British Astronomical Association.

Last but not least, fireballs and meteorites can be flagged up to the Fireball Data Center of the International Meteor Organisation.

"Astronomy is one of the few sciences that allows everyone and anyone to stake claim on a discovery"

Think you've found a new planet?

Planets around other stars are too faint to be seen with back garden telescopes – specialised professional telescopes and cameras in exotic locations such as Hawaii, the Canary Islands, or even space, are required. However, these telescopes produce so much data that scientists need the public's help to search through it all.

Many enthusiastic amateurs use the citizen science project – Planet - Hunters – which forms part of the Zooniverse project and some have successfully found an exoplanet around another star by studying data yielded from this project on their computer. Could you be the next?

■ Join a friend in your star-searching quest

01 What type of object have you found?

After you have checked that your finding is real and not a trick brought about by your binoculars, telescope or CCD camera, and you have confirmed your observation on a second night and have multiple photographic exposures (an independent confirmation is very important), you're now ready to look into what type of object you've found. How does it move? If there's definite or small movement, of if it's placed in a galaxy it could be a comet or minor planet. If there doesn't seem to be any movement, then you might well have found a supernova or nova.

02 How bright is it?

Your next task is to look at how bright your object is as this, combined with the object's movement, can give you some clues as to what your target could be. If the brightness changes, but you're sure it's not a nova or supernova, you might have detected a variable star. You may have spotted the outburst of an unusual variable star, a cataclysmic variable or even one of the more familiar types of variable star.

03 Consult a list of known objects

Before you can think about reporting your discovery, you need to check where your potentially new found object is located. As soon as you have noted the Right Ascension (RA) and Declination (Dec), you can then make use of a sky atlas such as WIKISKY or the Digitized Sky Survey to check and make sure your object hasn't already been catalogued.

04 What do I need to include in my report?

If you can't find your object on any of the catalogues, then you are now ready to make an exciting step – reporting your discovery. Make sure that you have noted an accurate position and time, written a description of you object including its magnitude, your full name and contact details, information on your observing location and the instrument you used to detect it as well as information on the sources you used to check that the object is new.

05 Where do I report my discovery to?

Depending on what you think you've found, there are several organisations to report to. For comets, supernovae, and outbursts of unusual variable stars, contact the Central Bureau for Astronomical Telegrams (CBAT), for minor planets and asteroids you should report to the Minor Planet Centre and either the American Association of Variable Star Observers should be contacted for the more routine or new variable stars.

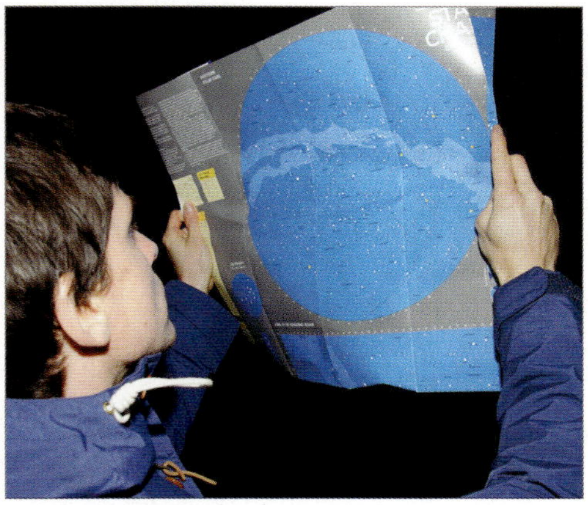

■ Keep track of constellations so you can spot changes

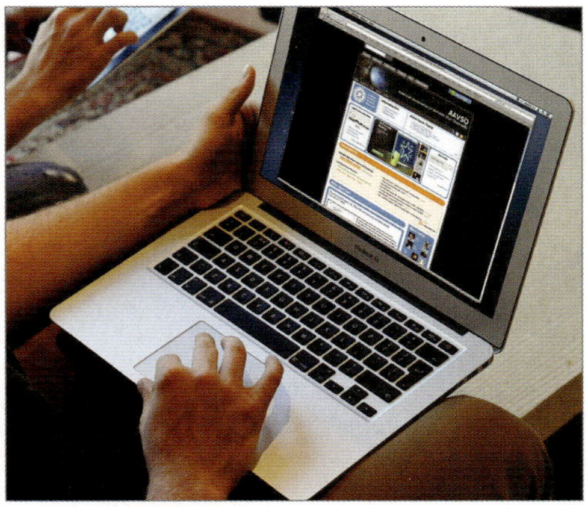

■ Swap a telescope for a computer and use an online service

20 amazing amateur discoveries

Be inspired by some of the fantastic discoveries made by amateurs through the ages

You'd think that with the proliferation of Earth-based observatories, space telescopes and probes there would no room for amateur astronomers. Yet, agencies like NASA are enthusiastic about pro-am collaborations. As an amateur, you can be involved in hunting for meteors, comets and even exoplanets.

This is because amateurs can fill in the gaps left by automated observatories and professionals who concentrate on limited areas of study. Often, the amateur can just get lucky and spot something straightaway, or they might spend years of diligent observing. As an example, it took British amateur George Alcock six years looking for a comet, and then five days later he found another one. In contrast, Thomas Bopp, co-discoverer of the Hale-Bopp comet, almost spotted it by chance.

With modest equipment or even just a computer screen, you have a greater chance of becoming an amateur space pioneer than ever before. And if you need proof, check out these examples.

© NASA

Jovian moons Io, Europa, Ganymede and Callisto

Discoverer: Galileo Galilei **Discovered:** January 1610

Using a telescope with a 20x magnification, Galileo noticed what looked like four stars near Jupiter. For two months, he continued observing these objects and determined that they were satellites orbiting Jupiter. This discovery undermined the Ptolemaic belief that the Earth is at the centre of the universe and showed the effectiveness of telescopic observations.

© NASA

The planet Uranus

Discoverer: William Hershel **Discovered:** March 1781

Herschel was a musician based in Bath, UK, whose interest in mathematics and lenses led him to build his own telescopes. Using his own equipment, he took on the task of looking for double stars. During these observations, he spotted what he first thought was a comet, but analysis of its position determined it was a planet orbiting beyond Saturn.

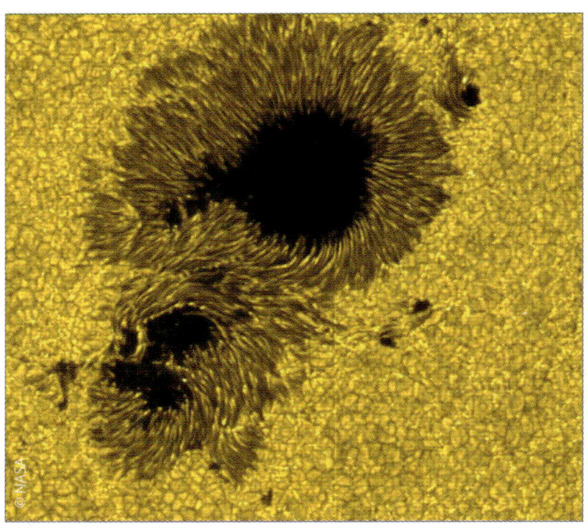

Sun spot cycle

Discoverer: Heinrich Schwabe **Discovered:** 1843

German amateur, Heinrich Schwabe, spent virtually every day for 17 years recording the position of sun spots. His aim was to discover the hypothetical planet Vulcan, orbiting between Mercury and the Sun. When he reviewed his data, he noticed a ten year cycle of sun spot activity, which was revised to 11 years when further data was analysed.

© ESO

Nova Cygni 1920

Discoverer: Will Denning **Discovered:** 20 August 1920

Denning was originally trained as an accountant, but was absolutely devoted to amateur astronomy. He discovered four comets and two Novas. It was when looking for meteors that he quickly spotted a bright new star in the Cygnus constellation. This was named Nova Cygni 1920 (V476 Cygni), and was a particular highlight in his viewing career.

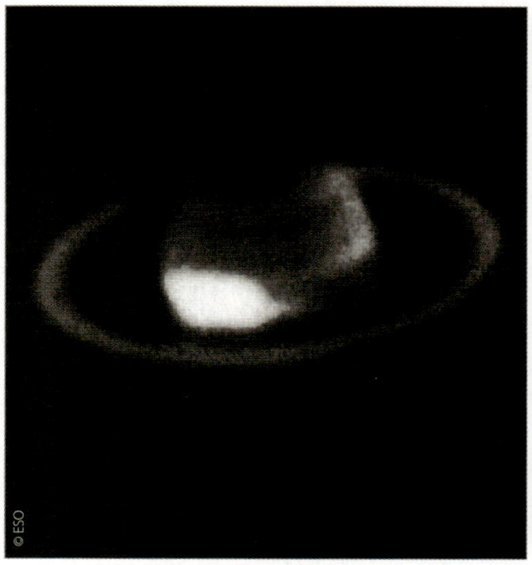

Saturn's white spot

Discoverer: Will Hay
Discovered: 3 August 1933 at 22:35 GMT

The British comedian, Will Hay was a Fellow of the Royal Astronomical Society and had his own observatory. Using his 6-inch (152mm) Cooke refractor, he was the first to spot a large bright area in the Equatorial region of Saturn. The huge storm was visible for several months before it faded away.

Lunar surface details

Discoverer: Patrick Moore
Discovered: 1945 onwards

Patrick Moore inspired generations of amateur (and professional) astronomers, with his enthusiasm and knowledge of the subject. The Moon was his specialist interest, and his detailed maps were used by the Russians to check the images captured by Lunar 3 in 1959, and by NASA when preparing for the Moon landing.

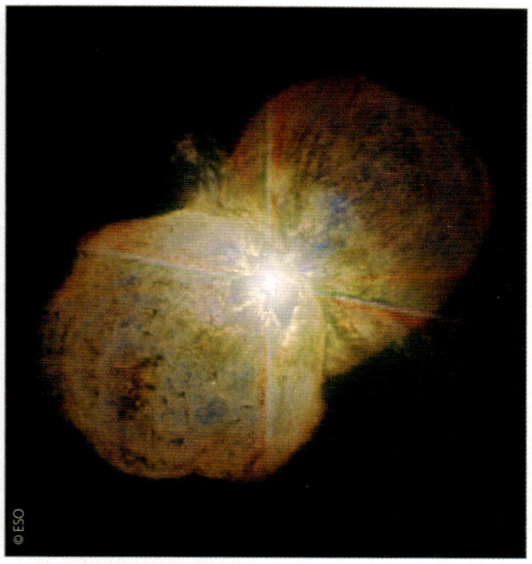

Multiple variable stars

Discoverer: Michiel Daniel Overbeek
Discovered: 1951 onwards

South African, Daniel Overbeek, is credited with viewing a record 250,000 variable stars, over a period of 40 years. At the age of 15 years old, he used a reading glass and a pocket microscope to make his own telescope. The data he collected about variable stars was used to schedule observing time for the Hubble Space Telescope.

Multiple supernovas

Discoverer: Owen Robert Evans **Discovered:** 1955 onwards

In a period spanning over 40 years, Robert Evans, a minister for the Uniting Church in Australia, is the proud discoverer of one comet and 40 supernovas. He also succeeded in memorising the position of a staggering 1,500 galaxies, making it easy for him to quickly scrutinise them for these elusive and powerful stellar explosions.

Comet C/1959 Q1 (Alcock)

Discoverer: George Eric Deacon Alcock **Discovered:** 27 August 1959

After taking an interest in meteor showers, Alcock concentrated on searching for comets and novas. Like Robert Evans, he memorised the position of thousands of stars to enable him to spot any new arrivals. Over a span of 24 years, he discovered five comets. In addition, he spotted four novas, the last being nova V838 Her, in 1991.

The next step

Comet C/1995 O1 (Hale-Bopp)

Discoverer: Thomas Hale, Alan J. Bopp **Discovered:** 23 July 1995

Two amateur astronomers in the USA independently spotted one of the brightest comets to appear in the 20th Century. Alan Hale saw the comet through his telescope on the driveway of his home. On the same evening factory manager, Thomas Bopp, saw it through a friend's telescope.

OGLE-2005-BLG-071

Discoverer: Grant Christie, Jennie McCormick
Discovered: April 2005

With data supplied by these two New Zealand amateur astronomers, who were members of the Microlensing Follow Up Network, a new exoplanet was confirmed. It was determined to be 3x the size of Jupiter, at a distance of 15,000 ly.

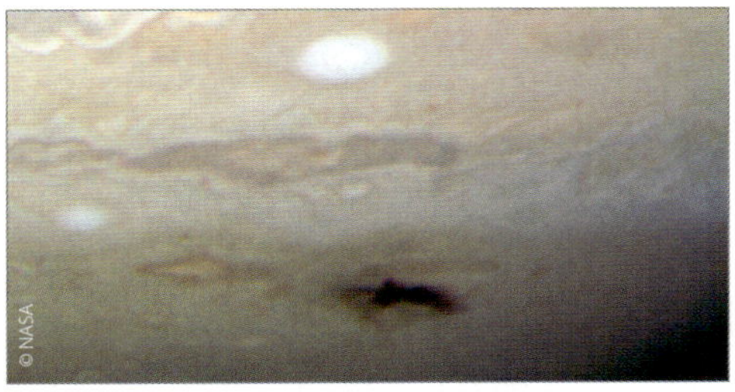

Jupiter asteroid collision

Discoverer: Anthony Wesley
Discovered: 19 July 2009

Using his 14.5 inch Newtonian telescope at his home observatory in NSW Australia, Wesley captured images of a spot moving over Jupiter. This turned out to be an asteroid colliding with the planet, now nicknamed the Wesley Impact.

Saturn storm

Discoverer: Erick Bondoux, Jean-Luc Dauvergne, Jim Phillips, Don Parker
Discovered: 25 January 2006

The two French men working together, and the two US amateurs working independently, are members of the Association of Lunar and Planetary Observers, and spotted a white patch on the surface of Saturn. NASA used this to confirm the presence of a storm detected by its Cassini space probe.

NGC 4449 galaxy star streams

Discoverer: Robert Jay Gabany **Discovered:** April 2010

Robert is a pioneer in using digital cameras and small telescopes to capture long exposure images of stars and galaxies. He has worked with the Max Planck Institute for Astronomy in Germany to obtain images of previously undetected star streams. His skills contributed to the mapping and analysis of a stellar stream in the halo of the nearby dwarf NGC 4449 starburst galaxy.

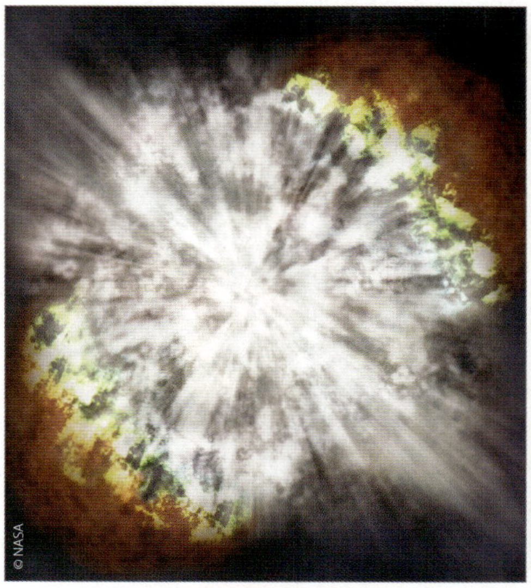

Supernova 2010lK

Discoverer: Dave Grennan
Discovered: 17 September 2010

Dave Grennan is a software developer who spotted this supernova in Raheny, north Dublin, making it the first to be discovered in Ireland. Using his self-built garden shed observatory, he obtained images of the same area of sky over a two month period and compared them to find this 300 million-year-old supernova.

Kn 61 planetary nebula

Discoverer: Matthias Kronberger
Discovered: January 2011

Austrian Matthias Kronberger spotted this intriguing soccer ball/raspberry shaped nebula in the Cygnus constellation. It consists of an ionised shell of gas surrounding a blue coloured central star. He is a member of the Deep Sky Hunters group that exchanges data between amateurs and professionals.

Comet Lovejoy (C/2011 W3)

Discoverer: Terry Lovejoy
Discovered: 27 November 2011

Information technologist, Terry Lovejoy, has specialised in spotting comets using modified digital camera technology. Using this equipment at his home in Queensland, Australia, he has discovered three comets. His rarest discovery so far was of C/2011 W3, which is a Kreutz Sungrazing comet.

Comet C/2012 S1 (ISON)

Discoverer: Vitali Nevski, Artyom Novichonok
Discovered: 21 September 2012

This is another sungrazing comet, which was spotted by Vitali Nevski and Artyom Novichonok, both of whom are members of the International Scientific Optical Network (ISON) survey program. ISON was certainly a comet for everyone to keep their eye on when first discovered, as scientists thought it could be much brighter than Comet Lovejoy on its pass through the Sun's atmosphere in November 2013. In fact, there were strong rumblings at the time that it could potentially be the 'comet of the century'.

Exoplanets

Discoverer: Roy Jackson
Discovered: 2012 ongoing

As part of the Planet Hunters project, these volunteers sifted through data supplied by the NASA Kepler Space Telescope, to discover the existence of 42 potential exoplanets. Fifteen were identified as being in the habitable zone of its parent star, indicating they could support life forms. For this research, web browsers are used instead of telescopes to find exoplanets missed or overlooked by the professionals. One volunteer was 71-year-old Roy Jackson, a retired police officer in Gateshead.

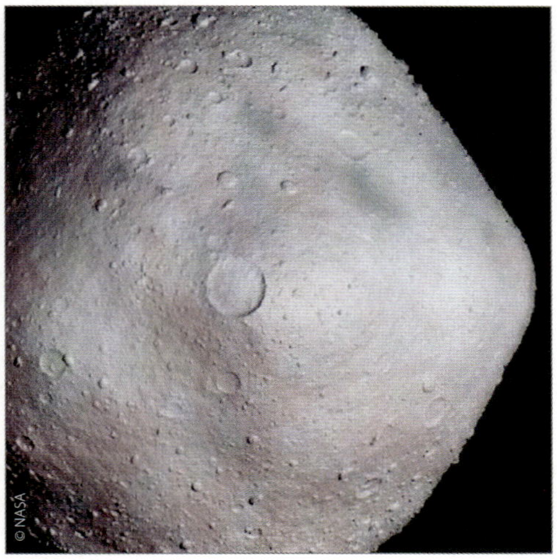

Asteroids

Discoverer: NASA volunteers
Discovered: April 2012

In 2016 NASA is planning to launch the OSIRIS-REx spacecraft to collect a small sample from the near-Earth carbonaceous asteroid (101955) Bennu. To support this mission, NASA's Target Asteroids! project is encouraging volunteers to measure the position, brightness and spectrum of these near Earth objects. You can use your own equipment or online robotic telescopes to carry out this work. This data will be compared with that collected by the spacecraft to identify asteroids for future missions.

The best astronomy apps

Essential space-based mobile apps

"As far as space apps go this is one of the best out there, and we'd definitely recommend giving it a try"

01 SkySafari Pro

For: iOS/Android **Price:** £27.99 ($39.99)/£22.99 ($36.99)

It might carry a high price tag, but there's little doubt that SkySafari Pro is one of the most professional astronomy apps out there with a whole host of amazing space information and features. It boasts a large database, with half a gigabyte's worth of data, so make sure you've got enough space to hold this app. It gets the majority of its data from the Hubble Guide Star catalog, over 15 million stars to be exact, as well as comets and asteroids. You can even use the app as a 'GOTO' device to control a full-sized telescope, while the app can be used as an augmented reality tool to point up at the stars and identify objects in the sky. It's the pure size of data on offer, though, that really sets SkySafari Pro apart from the rest.

02 NASA App

For: iOS/Android **Price:** Free

For all things NASA related this app is the way to go. Boasting a multitude of detailed information on all current missions plus a whole host of other features. For starters you get daily featured images, while you can also watch NASA TV live when there's a show or press conference on air. The app also does a good job of connecting with social networks by allowing you to browse all the latest tweets from the various NASA subsidiaries. The app can be bland in places, but there's detailed information here on pretty much anything you want to know, from launch sites to past missions. There's plenty of other nifty features – such as the International Space Station locator – that will keep you coming back for even more.

03 Brian Cox's Wonders Of The Universe

For: iOS **Price:** £3.99 ($5.99)

If you're looking for an informative and fun guide to the Solar System, Milky Way and the universe, then who better to turn to than loveable BBC presenter Dr Brian Cox. In this amazing app the professor's work across a whole host of TV shows including *Wonders Of The Solar System* and *Wonders Of The Universe* are seamlessly brought together to provide users with an interactive guide to all things space. You can pinch and zoom your way through a 3D space environment and glean information in the form of test, images, videos and illustrations along the way. As far as space apps go this is one of the best out there, and we'd recommend giving Brian Cox's app a try.

04 Star Walk

For: iOS **Price:** £1.99 ($2.99)

For stargazing on the go you'll be hard-pressed to find a better app than Star Walk. This app presents you with real-time positions for pretty much every celestial object in the night sky, including artificial satellites, allowing you to pinch and swipe with your phone to locate a multitude of constellations on your phone and then find them in real life in the night sky. Amazingly, Star Walk uses augmented reality to make this even easier. Simply point your phone at the sky and you'll be able to locate objects with the app. There's a ton of information on offer here as well, including the motions of planets across the night sky and the positions of various constellations. This is a great companion for amateur astronomers on the go.

05 Redshift

For: iOS **Price:** £7.99 ($11.99)

For a definitive guide to the stars, constellations and galaxies, Redshift is the perfect app. It doesn't come cheap but Redshift is packed full of data and glorious graphics. The search functionality is also impressive, allowing users to find objects by their name or browse through different categories quickly and easily.

Redshift is a brilliant educational tool but it lacks a 'fun' factor. Aside from using it as a reference tool you might tire of zooming up to distant stars only to be presented with a few mundane statistics. That being said you can still while away the hours browsing through the universe, and if you need an app to help with amateur astronomy then you'll definitely want to pick this up.

06 Mobile Observatory - Astronomy

For: Android **Price:** £3.99 ($5.99)

If you need an astronomy app for your Android device then this is a great solution. Mobile Observatory lets you see the night sky and a top-down view of the Solar System to explore to your heart's content. It's packed full of features and information, which can be a little disconcerting at first but you'll soon be learning new things with ease. The app also points out key events that are coming up, such as solar eclipses or meteor showers. Like Star Walk for iOS this app also boasts augmented reality features, allowing you to point your device at the sky and locate constellations, stars, planets and more. If you need an astronomy app for your Android then we'd definitely recommend this one.

Dark sky sites around the world

How to beat light pollution and get some great views of the night sky

When it comes to astronomy, light pollution is a problem for most populated areas of the world. Things like streetlights, houses and more can hamper your attempts to view the stars.

Thankfully, there are places across the globe known as 'dark sky sites' that are kept free of artificial light pollution and are intended to give you the best possible view of the universe. Organisations such as the International Dark-Sky Association preserve these sites for people to come and enjoy astronomy.

Almost all of these sites, often found near parks or reserves, are free to the general public. Some are rated on the 'Bortle Scale', which denotes how dark they are, but generally whichever site you choose to visit will likely afford you a better view of the night sky than you have ever had before.

"There are places across the globe intended to give you the best view of the universe"

Galloway Forest Park

Found in Dumfries and Galloway in Scotland, this huge woodland park covering 780 square kilometres (300 square miles) welcomes nearly a million visitors every year to marvel at its pitch-black skies.

Sark

Sark, located in the Channel Islands, was the first populated island in the world to be designated a dark sky site. A ban on cars and an absence of public lighting ensure that Sark's skies stay free from light pollution.

Brecon Beacons

This mountain range in South Wales boasts the large Brecon Beacons National Park, which was designated as a dark sky site in February 2013 thanks to its wide-open and light pollution-free landscape.

Beaver Hills

The Beaver Hills Dark-Sky Preserve was founded back in 2006. It is located in Central Alberta, Canada, with an area spanning 300 square kilometres (115 square miles) preserved for night sky observations.

Mont Mégantic

The Mont Mégantic Observatory in Québec is the second largest telescope in Eastern Canada, and an area of 5,500 square kilometres (2,120 square miles) surrounding it was designated one of the world's first dark sky sites.

Hortobágy National Park

The Hortobágy National Park in Eastern Hungary is a designed dark sky site that is preserved by local people to ensure it retains the natural beauty of its black night sky.

Ring of Brodgar

While not an official dark sky location, the fantastic setting around the Neolithic henge known as the Ring of Brodgar in Orkney, Scotland provides both fantastic scenery and amazingly dark skies.

Lake Hudson

The Lake Hudson State Recreation Area is found near Clayon, Michigan. Its huge and spread-out campsites enable multiple groups of people to simultaneously get a great view of the night sky.

Natural Bridges National Monument

In San Juan County, Utah, United States can be found the Natural Bridges National Monument, an area of stunning scenery that has been designated a dark sky site thanks to continued efforts to preserve its skies.

Cherry Springs State Park

Some of the most fantastic views of the Milky Way can be found at the Cherry Springs State Park in Pennsylvania, USA, which was named an official dark sky site in June 2007.

Astronomy Q&A

We have gathered together the most frequently asked astronomy questions to help you on your way

I want to buy my first telescope. Do you have any advice?

On choosing your telescope, one of the things that first time buyers make the mistake of looking out for is the best magnification. In reality you should be looking for the optimum aperture diameter of the instrument, avoiding small telescopes that claim to have some impressive magnification power of 400x, or even 500x, at all costs.

Aperture diameter is extremely important and here's why; in order to pick up faint objects, your telescope needs to be able to collect as much light as it possibly can. The wider the diameter of the telescope tube, the larger the aperture and the fainter the object you can see.

If you decide to go for a refracting telescope, the minimum aperture that you'll require is around 100mm while a reflector, like a Dobsonian, should have an aperture of at least around 100-150mm. A good beginners' telescope should cost in the region of between £200 and £500.

Can amateur astronomers contribute to real science?

Astronomy is one of the few sciences where amateurs can make real contributions to the professional research conducted by professional astronomers. Researchers in astronomy and astrophysics can often be found working closely with teams of amateurs where discoveries can be made. Amateurs still discover comets, asteroids, novae and supernovae, for example, while their observations of more familiar objects are also vital for our continued studies of them. For example, many astronomers have observing campaigns for Jupiter, observing the planet on every clear night that it is visible. They are the first to see changes in its zones or belts, or even the flashes of meteors through its atmospheres. Because professional astronomers have to compete for telescope time and there is no space probe at Jupiter, amateurs are often the first to observe any changes. Variable stars are another area in which amateurs dominate – there are just too many variable stars for professionals to keep track of.

Is a hobby in astronomy expensive?

It can be expensive, but it doesn't have to be! It really depends on what kind of astronomy you want to do and how serious you are about it. As we've seen, astronomy can be conducted cheaply, with the unaided eye or with binoculars. Small telescopes, of four to six inch apertures, can be purchased for £150–£300 minimum. Larger telescopes, which allow you to see more, obviously cost a lot more, as do added features such as computerised mounts and GOTO drives.

If you want to do astrophotography you are going to need a camera, either a DSLR or a CCD which are both expensive, although some limited astrophotography can be done with point-and-shoot cameras or even mobile phone cameras, while planetary imagers have been using cheap computer webcams to excellent effect for many years. The trick is to learn that you don't have to spend a fortune, but if you do want to do more serious astronomy, you don't have to buy everything at once.

Which star is the Pole Star?

Many people mistakenly think that the Pole Star (also called Polaris) is the brightest star in the sky. It's not. In fact, at magnitude +2, it is not even close to being the brightest but it is still readily visible to the unaided eye if you know where to look.

The Pole Star is in the constellation of Ursa Minor, the Little Bear, but it is to the Great Bear, Ursa Major that we go to first to find our way to Polaris. Ursa Major is made up of a famous pattern, or asterism, of stars called the Plough or, if you are in the United States, the Big Dipper. Find the two front stars of the Plough's 'bowl', called Merak and Dubhe and draw an imaginary line through them and up by a distance roughly five times the gap between Merak and Dubhe, and you will come across the Pole Star.

> "Many people think that Polaris is the brightest star. It's not. At a magnitude of +2, it is not even close"

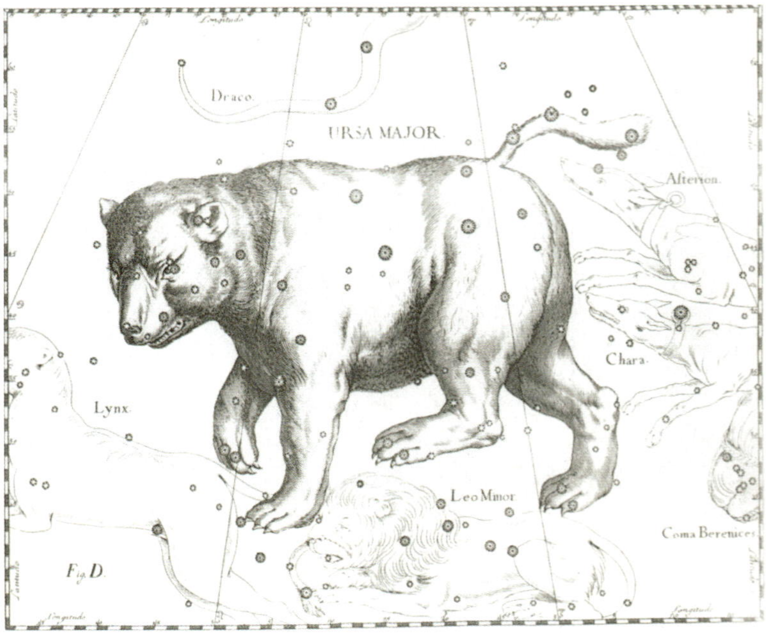

Can you use a telescope to see the flag left behind on the Moon by the Apollo astronauts?

Unfortunately, it is impossible to see the flag, footprints or lunar lander left behind on the surface of the Moon by the Apollo missions. The average distance to the Moon is 384,000 kilometres, while the flag is a few feet across, the lunar lander less than ten metres. At this distance of the Moon the lunar lander has an angular diameter of 0.002 arcseconds. Most amateur telescopes have a limiting resolution of about one arcsecond. The Hubble Space Telescope is limited to 0.1 arcseconds, so even it cannot see the Apollo landers or flag (Hubble is designed to see big things faraway, like galaxies, not to see small things close by). Currently the only thing that can see the Apollo landing sites is NASA's Lunar Reconnaissance Orbiter, which has taken pictures of them showing the landers, footprints and flags.

How should I look after my telescope?

Most modern telescopes are robustly built, but you still have to treat them with care. The most important and delicate part of your telescope is its optics. These can become dusty which can affect the quality of what you see through them. When cleaning them be extra careful. Do not scrub them with a towel or flannel as you will scratch the optics – use cotton wool buds to dab water or cleaning fluid off them. Sometimes you will get spiders and cobwebs in the telescope tubes too, especially if you keep your telescope in the garage!

There are other concerns. A refracting telescope, for example, will need to be collimated on a regular basis to fine tune the sweet spot where the focal point is on the lenses. If you fail to do this, the quality of what you see will degrade. If you have a motorised mount you'll also want to keep the gears well oiled.

Can I name and buy a star?

Some people claim to be able to sell the naming rights to stars, to give as gifts to loved ones, while others even claim to be selling plots of land on the Moon. However, none of these are official and have no legal basis. Furthermore, the stars for which people sell names are faint stars because the bright stars already have names. If you want to buy a star name be aware that no astronomer will ever use the name and it will not be found in any star catalogues. Only the International Astronomical Union have the authority to give names to astronomical orbits, although recently it has begun to accept suggestions from the public when it comes to cooking up the names.

What is meant by Right Ascension and Declination?

Imagine the sky above us being on the inside of a 'celestial sphere'. Declination is the equivalent of latitude on that sphere, whereas Right Ascension would be the longitude.

What type of telescope should I use if I want to get into astrophotography?

You need a telescope with a Right Ascension drive, preferably a motorised one that has the ability to track the sky. You also have to make sure that you possess an adapter to attach to your telescope.

What's the difference between an armchair and amateur astronomer?

An armchair astronomer is someone that often reads about astronomy in books and magazines but doesn't head outside to observe the night sky often (if at all) in comparison to an amateur.

I saw a steady light moving quickly across the sky last night. What could it have been?

These – often fast – moving points of light are communications satellites orbiting our planet. They are quite numerous but often fainter than the International Space Station that can also be seen following a similar path through the night sky.

What type of telescope do I need to look at the planets?

A refractor telescope, which uses an objective lens to concentrate light into the eyepiece at the viewing end, gives better views of the planets as well as the Moon.

I'm new to astronomy and I don't know any amateurs. What do I do?

Joining an astronomy society or club is possibly one of the best things that a beginner can do. Check out our directory to find a club near you and make sure you read our advice on joining a society to find out what you can benefit from. By doing this you'll meet like-minded people who are experiencing the same things as you, and you can share tips.

> "If you want to buy a star name, be aware that no astronomer will use that name"

The next step

Why is the Moon larger when it is close to the horizon?

The Moon isn't really larger when it is closer to the horizon, but it is an optical illusion that makes it appear so. The illusion is really noticeable when a full moon is rising. There has never been a full explanation for this illusion, but one possible explanation is that there are familiar objects such as trees and buildings on the horizon, which we can reasonably estimate the size of, and by placing the Moon behind these it can make the Moon seem bigger than it really is because we know the objects on the horizon are closer, so we mistakenly think the Moon must be too.

What is a blue moon?

Most of us have heard of the phrase "once in a blue moon" to describe something that is rare but what does it mean in astronomical terms? By popular definition, it is the second of two full moons occurring in the same month. The lunar cycle takes 29 days and since most months of the year have 30-31 days we eventually find that a full moon occurs at the beginning and ending of the same month. A blue moon, which has nothing to do with the actual colour of the Moon, happens every two to three years.

A blue moon can also be referred to as the third full moon of four in a single season – i other words the period between a solstice and equinox – or vice versa!

Do you have to have a telescope to do astronomy?

Not at all. Many seasoned stargazers only own binoculars, while many casual observers do astronomy just with their unaided eye. There is so much to see without resorting to a telescope, from the patterns of the constellations and the brightest stars to five of the planets (Mercury, Venus, Mars, Jupiter and Saturn), the phases of the Moon and a host of meteor showers. If you're lucky to be observing from a dark site you may even see the shimmer of the Milky Way. Then there are star clusters such as the Seven Sisters of the Pleiades or the Hyades, both in the constellation Taurus. And the most distant object one can see without binoculars or a telescope is the Andromeda Galaxy, which is 2.5 million light years away, although some experienced observers also claim that they can just about see the Triangulum Galaxy with their naked eyes, which is 2.9 million light years away.

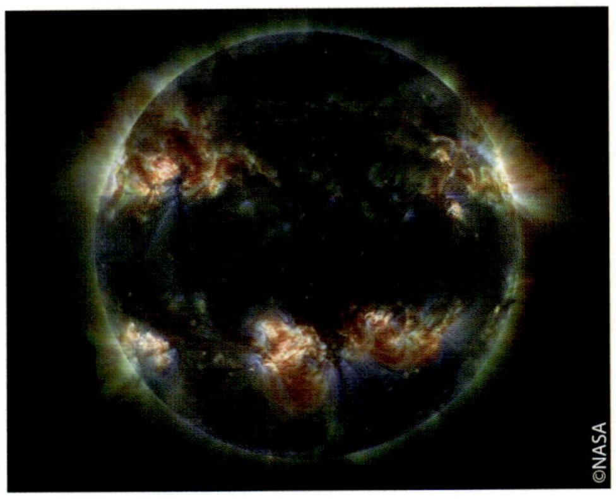

What is a GOTO and are they worth the money?

GOTO mounts are motorised mounts that literally 'go to' any object that you want to see in the night sky. Simply by aligning the telescope with the pole star or some bright stars so the telescope's computer knows which direction everything is, you can then use a hand controller to select an object in the computer's database and command the mount to turn the telescope towards it.

Most GOTO systems work very well and although you may have to pay a few hundred pounds more for them, they have a number of advantages. If you are unfamiliar with the constellations and finding your way around the sky they can do the job for you. Also, if clear skies are rare and you are observing through gaps in the clouds, GOTO telescopes can take you to your target quickly before the cloud draws in again. The disadvantage is that you don't get to learn the constellations as the computer does the job for you.

What can I teach children about the night sky without using a telescope?

Learning the patterns of the constellations and the names of the brightest stars is not only a good way for children to become familiar with the night sky, but it is a great way to involve story-telling too. Many of the constellations represent figures from Greek myth, such as the story of the heroic Perseus, who rode his winged steed Pegasus to save the Princess Andromeda from a sea monster (represented in the night sky by the constellation Cetus) wrought upon her by the Gods after her parents Cassiopeia and Cepheus angered them. All of these appear in the sky as constellations whose patterns children can learn, from the W of Cassiopeia and the Square of Pegasus. As well as the constellations there are the phases of the Moon that children can keep track of over the course of a month, and the movement of the bright planets through the sky.

The view through my telescope is nothing like NASA pictures. Am I doing something wrong?

Not at all – you have to remember that not only are pictures like those photographed by Hubble taken with a much larger telescope in space, but they have also been heavily processed. The wonderful colours in many NASA images are not true colours, but representative colours dictated by the types of filter used. In real life nebulae are often not nearly as colourful. Indeed, in many cases there is not enough light coming into small amateur telescopes for an observer to even discern a colour. Astrophotographers also use filters and heavy image processing to make their pictures colourful, often using the same colour palette as Hubble. But don't let this put you off. That nebula you are looking at may seem faint and pale, but don't forget that it represents the expansive death of a sun-like star the light from which has been travelling for hundreds of thousands of years. Just knowing that is what you are looking at is amazing!

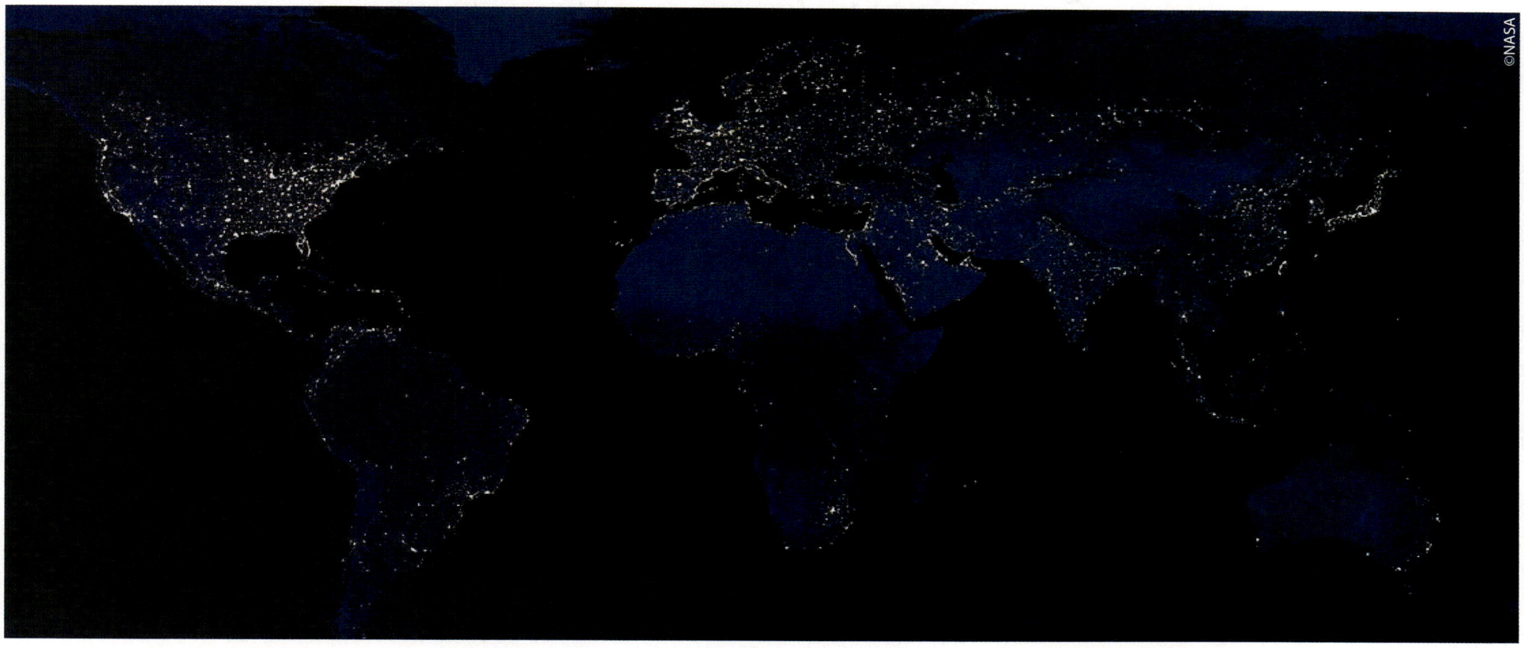

Does light pollution make astronomy impossible?

It doesn't make it easy, which is why astronomers are trying to protect our night skies by campaigning for street lights to be kept to a sensible level. However, astronomy is still possible, even from cities. Bright objects such as the Moon, planets and the main stars are still evident, and binoculars and telescopes will still show many deep sky objects. But fainter stars are drowned out. For example, with the unaided eye you may be able to see only down to magnitude 3 or 4, rather than 5 or 6. A good test of light pollution is whether you can see the Milky Way. Many people have never seen a really starry sky before because of where they live.

You can buy a light pollution filter for your telescope which blocks the sodium light of street lamps, but this only alleviates instead of solving the problem.

What can I see with the naked eye?

Part of astronomy's charm is that you don't need a telescope or a pair of binoculars to get involved. Stepping outside into the night and gazing up at the stars, you are looking at some objects which are similar to our very own Sun as well as others of differing shapes, ages and colours. And that's not all – planets such as Venus, Mars, Saturn and Jupiter can be spotted using just our eyes – not to mention groups of stars gathered in star clusters including the pleiades as well as some galaxies such as the closest spiral galaxy to us, Andromeda, and the dusty track of the Milky Way.

The many patterns of stars – known as constellations – are also great fun to spot and often hold naked eye objects themselves such as the giant red star Betelgeuse and Orion's nebula in the constellation of Orion.

I think I've discovered a new object. How do I report it?

While it is very unlikely that you will find anything new on your first few nights of observing, you should report any discoveries, depending on what you think you've found, to your national astronomy society such as the British Astronomical Association (BAA). You can read about how you should report an object in this bookazine.

When is the best time to see a meteor shower?

The main meteor showers you can enjoy are the Lyrids (April,) Perseids (August), Taurids in (October and November), Aquarids (May), Leonids (November) as well as the Geminids (December).

What's daytime astronomy?

Astronomy isn't just for the night. You can also observe the Moon, the brightest planets as well as the Sun. However, care must be taken when solar observing – you should not stare at the Sun too long or look through a telescope or binoculars at it.

Are binoculars better than a telescope?

Depending on what you wish to observe, both have their own merits. Binoculars are quick and very easy to use and will allow you to sweep the Milky Way, gaze at star clusters and the Moon. A telescope, which is not as free, will allow you to pick up detail on the Moon, planets and galaxies.

Your astronomy glossary

There will be a lot of new terms to learn as you delve into astronomy. Here are some of the most common ones…

A

Accretion disk
A circular disk of stellar matter that has been captured by a large celestial body, such as a sun or black hole.

Accretion disk

Achromatic
A lens that receives light without splitting it into its constituent colours. The opposite is apochromatic, which splits light into red, blue and green.

Albedo
A measure of the brightness of the lunar surface on a scale of zero (no reflectivity) to one (perfectly reflective.) The Moon has an overall albedo of 0.125.

Altazimuth
A telescope mount that moves both vertically (azimuth) and horizontally (altitude).

Ammonia ice
The same chemical you might use for cleaning surfaces, but in Saturn's atmosphere it's frozen and in vast quantities.

Annular eclipse
This is a form of solar eclipse where the Moon does not completely cover the Sun due to being at its furthest from Earth.

Anthelion
An optical phenomenon where a faint halo of light appears opposite the Sun.

Aperture
The diameter of a telescope's front lens or main mirror, usually stated in inches or mm.

Apparition
For any given object in the night sky, the annual window in which it's visible is known as the apparition. For latitude sufficiently far from the equator, there are objects that have no apparition, but are always visible. For everything else, there is a date at which it begins to appear and a date after which it can no longer be seen in the evening.

Apoapsis
The apoapsis is the point at which a body is in the point of its orbit where it's farthest away from the body it oribts.

Apogee
Apogee is the term for apoapsis in regards to the Earth, ie the Moon and any other orbiting satellites.

Arcsecond
Arcseconds and arcminutes measure the angular distance of a body north or south of the equator.

Asterism
An easily recognisable group of stars which may be a part of one or more constellations. Although these groups of stars are unofficial they are often well known in popular culture.

Asteroid
Asteroids are minor planets that are not defined as comets. They're mainly located in the inner Solar System, and orbit the Sun.

Asteroid belt
A region of space between Mars and Jupiter containing millions of asteroids that orbits the Sun with low-eccentricity.

Astronomical horizon
As oppose to the true horizon, the astronomical horizon is the imaginary horizon that lies perpendicular to the direction of gravity.

Astronomical Unit
The average distance between the Earth and the Sun, defined as just under 150 billion km.

Aurora
When charged particles from the Sun meet a planet's magnetic field they get funnelled along the magnetic field lines at the planet's poles. Once they hit the upper atmosphere they cause it to fluoresce.

Aurora

Aurora Borealis
The aurora in the northern hemisphere, colloquially known as the Northern Lights.

Aurora Australis
Where there are Northern Lights, there are also Southern Lights, and the Aurora Australis is the name for the southern hemisphere's aurora.

Azimuth
The angular measurement of an object along the horizon of the observer, relative to the direction of true north.

B

Big Bang
The model describing the start and early stages of the universe, going from a dense hot state and continuing to expand until this day.

Binary stars
These are stars which orbit around their common centre of gravity.

Blue filter (#80A)
Coloured filters are a great tool for observers who wish to tamper with the relative contrast of particular surface features. Each colour is assigned a number, and number 80A represents a medium blue, which has become very popular for Jupiter observing. Sometimes it's known as a 'Jupiter filter'! It darkens the appearance of the planet's belts and festoons, as well as the intricate detail surrounding the larger storms.

Blue moon
The second full moon in a single calendar month. Can also be used to describe the blue tint on the moon caused by volcanic activity.

Blueshift
As an object moves towards you, the wavelengths of light it gives off will shift towards blue in the visible spectrum.

Brown dwarf
An object with all the necessary material to become a star, but not enough mass to accomplish it.

C

Catadioptric
A telescope that uses both refraction and reflection techniques to form an image.

CCD
A charge-coupled device (CCD) is a computer chip which is used to produce digital images by detecting photons.

Celestial body/object
A term used to describe any natural body or object that occupies the night sky, and is located outside of our atmosphere.

Celestial equator
This is an imaginary line splitting the north and southern hemispheres that runs along the Earth's actual equator.

Celestial pole
Like the celestial equator, the celestial pole is an imaginary line from the poles that signifies the axis on which the Earth rotates.

Cepheid variables
These stars pulsate and so the amount of light they put out changes along with this pulsation. It was found that the rate of change of this type of star was proportional to how brightly they seemed to shine. Because of this, it is possible to work out how far away they are by measuring how bright they appear to be and then by timing their pulsations.

Chromatic aberration
If a telescope has only one lens or has a poorly constructed doublet lens, then it might cause bright objects to have a red or blueish halo around them. Even the very best doublet lens can, however, show a little of this, but it is usually barely noticeable if they are of good quality.

Circumpolar
Stars which never seem to rise above or set below the horizon. If you lived at one of the Earth's poles, all the stars you could see would be circumpolar. However, if you lived at the equator, none of them would be circumpolar.

Cloud belts
Saturn does not have a solid surface. It is made of gases, some of them frozen and these gases rotate around the planet as it spins on its axis. This rotation causes the gases to form into 'belts', which we can see as having slightly different colours.

Collimation
Inadvertent knocks to the telescope can affect the alignment of a Dobsonian's primary and secondary mirrors. Both mirrors can be adjusted, altering the direction that they face. The alignment process is called collimation, and reflector users must expect to collimate their telescopes from time to time. Collimation is best done in the light. By looking into the focuser you can identify the primary at the base of the tube and the secondary in its holder. Although elliptical, the secondary appears circular because it's tilted 45 degrees. The aim of collimation is to get everything appearing centred. Collimation instructions are usually supplied with very new Dobsonian telescopes. Astronomical suppliers also sell a number of collimation accessories, such as the Cheshire eyepiece and laser collimator – these are more accurate than just roughly estimating collimation, and they come with full instructions.

Colour index
A term to represent a value to measure the brightness of a star on different frequency bands of the electromagnetic spectrum.

Constellation
A constellation is a grouping of stars marking an area of sky with a defined border. The International Astronomical Union recognises 88 constellations. Some are ancient, with iconic patterns representing fabled heroes or animals, while many others, particularly in the Southern Hemisphere, are less grand, and were imagined and named after inanimate objects during the Age of Sail.

Comet
Small, icy bodies that experiences material melting from it as it approaches the Sun, sometimes causing a tail.

Comet

Commensurability
A ratio comparing the orbit of two objects as they go around the same body, such as Saturn having 5/2 Jupiter's orbital period.

Conjunction
A rare phenomenon when two bodies align in the same right ascension or ecliptical longitude.

Corona
From the Latin for crown, it's the plasma discharged by the Sun that can be easily observed during a total solar eclipse.

Corona

Counter balance
There's a wide variety of astronomical eyepieces and accessories that can be used with a Dobsonian, including heavy ultrawide field eyepieces, Barlow lenses, filters and filter wheels and digital camera mounts. These can add quite a weight and unbalance the instrument. One of the best ways of counterbalancing is to wrap a small bungee cord around the tube near its base and insert a suitably weighted object, such as a small astronomy book, which could also be handy while in the field!

Glossary

Craterlet
The term craterlet applies to any small crater. Colloquially, it is commonly used to refer to a small crater within a larger crater on the lunar surface.

Craters
Once thought to be volcanic in origin, the Moon's craters are now known to have been caused by impacts from asteroids and meteors. There is no atmosphere on the Moon and so no wind or rain to destroy the remains of the impacts which occurred in the early history of the Moon.

Cyclone & Anticyclone
Jupiter is covered with rotating vortices; storms often thousands of miles wide. Whether or not they are cyclonic or anticyclonic depends on latitude and direction of rotation. A storm rotating anticlockwise in the Northern Hemisphere, and clockwise in the Southern Hemisphere is a cyclone. An anticyclone fits the opposite description.

D

Doppler effect
The change in a frequency of a wave for an observer moving relative to its source. This results in a redshift or blueshift.

Double star
A pair of stars that approach near each other in the night sky as we see it from Earth. They may also form a binary star.

Doublet
A lens consisting of two pieces of glass is known as a 'doublet'. Each lens in the system is made to a different shape, one being convex (curving outward) and the other concave (curving inward). This helps to bring the light from the red and blue ends of the spectrum to the same focal point.

Dwarf planet
The official definition is a body in direct orbit of the Sun, large enough for its shape to be controlled by gravity, but has not cleared its orbital region.

Dwarf star
These are small main sequence stars much like our Sun, contrasting giant stars such as Betelgeuse.

E

Eccentricity
The amount an orbit deviates from a perfect circle is known as eccentricity, such as an elliptical orbit.

Eclipsing binary
Two stars in orbit around their common centre of gravity can pass in front or behind one another. When this happens they are in 'eclipse' and the usual combined light of the stars will be dimmed.

Ecliptic
An imaginary line that traces a great circle around the sky. It passes through each of the 12 constellations of the zodiac, and a 13th constellation, Ophiuchus. The ecliptic represents the path of the Sun as it appears on the sky throughout the year.

Electromagnetic spectrum
Light radiation occurs in a range of frequencies that makes up the EM spectrum, from Gamma Rays to Visible Light and Radio Waves.

Ephermis
A table containing the position of objects in the night sky at any given time.

Epoch
A moment in time used as a reference point for co-ordinates or orbital elements of a celestial body.

Equatorial
A mount aligned to the celestial pole, allowing celestial objects to be tracked in just one axis.

Equinox
A position of a celestial body defined by where it lies from the celestial equator.

Evolutionary track
A prediction of how a solitary star will behave through its life span given its mass and composition.

Exoplanet
A planet that is exosolar – outside of the solar system, and orbiting other stars.

Extinction
How dust and gas can absorb and scatter electromagnetic radiation between the object and the observer

F

Field galaxy
A galaxy that does not belong to a larger cluster of galaxies, but is gravitationally alone.

Field of view
The circular area of sky seen through your binoculars or telescope. Binoculars normally have a fixed field of view.

Field star
A star that is in the line of sight of associated stars under study, and is not only unrelated, but may tamper with a study's results.

Flocculus
A prominent region of the solar surface that can be seen by observing through particular wavelengths of the EM spectrum.

Focuser
In order to see the image from the mirrors properly and to be able to magnify it, you need to view it through an eyepiece. This is placed in a moveable tube called the focuser which can be adjusted using the focusing knobs to give the observer a sharp, clear view.

G

Galilean moons
The four largest of Jupiter's moons as discovered by Galileo Galilei in 1610. These are Io, Europa, Ganymede and Callisto.

Gas giant
Refers to a large planet that is primarily composed of rock. An example would be the four outer planets in our solar system.

GEM
A term that is short for German Equatorial Mount, this type of mounting was first invented by Joseph von Fraunhofer. Using a simple T-joint this mount is ridiculously easy to make, as well as being incredibly versatile and accurate. It is also portable enough to pack down for easier astroimaging at a remote site. However, it does have a downside and that is the need for a counterweight.

Geocentric
When an orbit is centered around the Earth, like the Moon or any number of our artificial satellites.

Gibbous
The opposite of a crescent, when a planet or moon is between full and first quarter, looking like a hump.

Globular cluster
The collection of stars that orbits a galaxy's centre as satellites, tightly bound by gravity.

Goto
Some modern telescopes have computers that will 'goto' any object in its database when instructed via the keypad.

Gravitational lens
The effect where light is bent due to the gravitational forces exerted on it between the source and the observer.

H

Halo
An optical phenomenon caused by ice crystals in the atmosphere that results in a ring of light around the Sun or Moon.

Heliocentric
Where as geocentric is revolving around the Earth, heliocentric objects orbit around a central star, such as our Sun.

Heliopause
The boundary of the heliosphere, where the solar winds stop and the interstellar medium begins.

Heliosphere
The bubble of charged particles created by our Sun or another star, protecting the planets from the harsher radiation in space.

I

Interstellar clouds
A denser-than-average region of space comprising of plasma and dust, very similar to a nebula.

Interstellar medium
The region of space between stars, outside of a star's heliopause.

Inverted image
Finder scopes and many telescopes will make the image appear upside down and back to front.

Irregular variables
As the title suggests, these stars will vary in brightness at random intervals unlike many variable stars which still happen to follow a regular pattern to their variations.

■ Charles Messier discovered what is now known as Messier Objects in the 1700s

J

K

Kuiper belt
A trans-Neptunian region comprised of asteroids and other small bodies that is 20 times larger than the asteroid belt.

L

Libration
The Moon wobbles slightly as it orbits the Earth, known as 'libration', which means that sometimes we can see around the 'corners'. Craters, mountains and other features not normally visible will then be seen at very acute angles, but nevertheless are available to view at certain times.

Light year (ly)
Astronomers gauge cosmic distances in terms of the time it takes for their light – travelling at 300,000km per second (186,000 miles per second) – to reach us. One light year measures about ten trillion (ten million million) kilometres – just a quarter of the distance to the nearest star. Our home galaxy, the Milky Way, is 100,000 light years across. The nearest big galaxy is the Andromeda Galaxy, 2.6 million light years away. Binoculars can reveal the ghostly smudges of galaxies many tens of millions of light years distant.

Local group
Our local group of galaxies, including the Milky Way. A total of 54 galaxies make up the local group.

Local standard of rest
The mean motion of material in the Milky Way in the neighbourhood of the Sun, which is not a precise circular motion.

Local/Virgo Supercluster
This is the supercluster than contains both the Virgo Cluster and Local Group, which in themselves contain the Milky Way and Andromeda galaxies.

Luminosity
A measurement of brightness, specifically the total amount of energy emitted by a celestial body.

Lunar
Simply refers to objects and elements relating to the Moon, from the Latin luna, meaning moon.

M

Magnification
Refers to the number of times an object is made to appear larger using the optics found in a telescope or binoculars.

Glossary

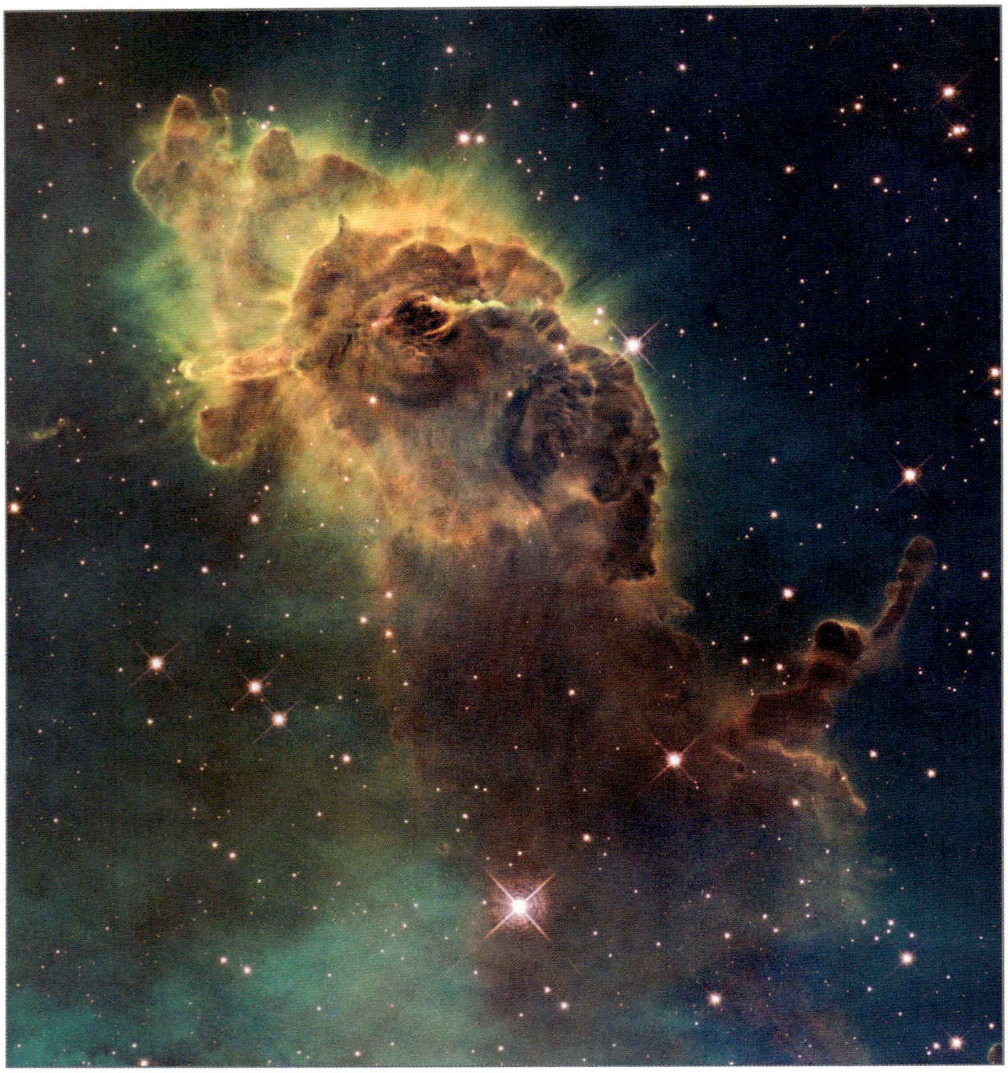

■ Stars and planets can form within a nebula

Magnitude
The perceived brightness of a celestial object is called its apparent magnitude. The brightest star, Sirius, is magnitude -1.4, while the faintest stars visible with the unaided eye under a dark sky are around magnitude +6.0. A pair of 10x50 binoculars will show objects down to magnitude +11.0.

Main sequence
A category of stable stars undergoing nuclear fusion with standard temperature and brightness.

Mare (seas)
We know the Moon has no water, but it was thought a long time ago that it had seas in the darker areas that we can see with the naked eye. We now know these areas are in fact lava plains formed when the Moon was still young and hot.

Mascon
A shortening for mass concentration, it refers to a region of a planet or moon's crust that contains gravitational anomalies.

Meridian
As viewed from Earth, the meridian is a vertical line running through the apparent centre of Jupiter's disk. It's useful to predict the times when features of interest, such as the Great Red Spot, are on the meridian, as this is when they will be best visible. When a feature is on the meridian, as well as being visible from your location, that's the time to grab your equipment and take a look!

Messier object
A list of astronomical objects described by Charles Messier in the 1700s, bodies are designated M1, M2, M3 and so on.

Meteor
The visible streak made by a meteoroid as it enters the Earth's atmosphere.

Meteoroid
Refers to a small rocky or metallic object travelling through space. Meteoroids are much smaller than an asteroid.

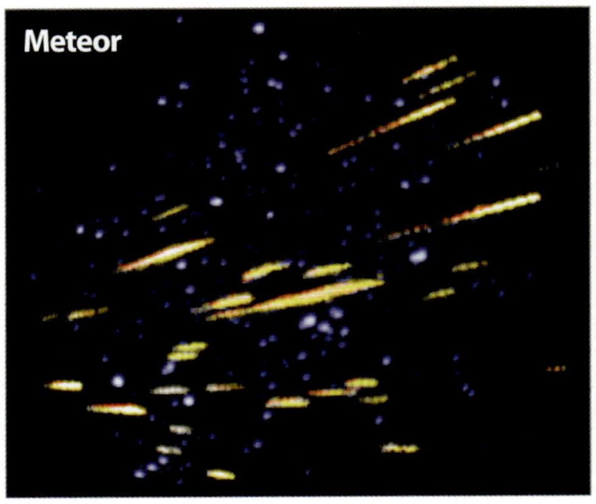

Meteorite
If a meteoroid survives atmospheric entry and impacts with the surface, what remains is known as a meteorite.

Minor planet
An object directly orbiting around the Sun that is neither a planet or a comet.

Molecular clouds
A type of interstellar cloud that possesses the correct conditions in order for molecules to form, including hydrogen.

Mons
Latin for mountain, and used traditionally in the naming of extraterrestrial mountains, such as Mons Olympus on Mars.

Morning width
Also know as the rise width, this is the horizontal angular distance between the rise azimuth of a celestial body and the East direction.

Moving group
A loose collection of stars that move together through space, usually created in the same cloud.

Multicoated optics
Glass is naturally quite reflective and in good quality lenses, each surface should be coated with a special chemical which helps it transmit all the light falling

on to it through the glass. This is then described as 'fully multicoated'. In a doublet lens only the front of the first lens and the back of the second are coated.

N

Nadir
The vertical direction towards the centre of gravity experienced by an object, opposite of zenith.

Natural satellite
Our Moon is a natural satellite; a naturally occurring body that orbits a planet.

Nebula
An interstellar cloud consisting of dust, hydrogen, helium and other ionized gases. Stars and planets can form within them.

Neutron star
Remnants of a dead star that are composed almost entirely of neutrons. They are extremely hot.

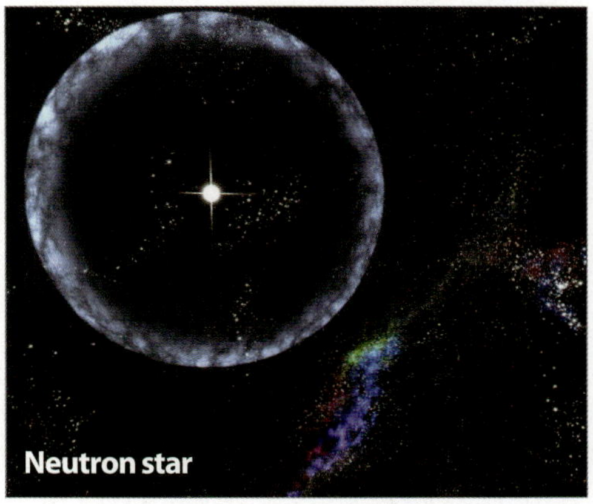
Neutron star

Node
The point at which an orbit crosses a plane of reference, such as when the Earth's orbit crosses the Sun's celestial equator.

Nova
A cataclysmic nuclear explosion in a white dwarf due to it pulling in material from a neighbouring star, characterised by a sudden brightening.

Nutation
The gravitational attraction of other bodies in the Solar System causes changes to a planet's rotation or orbit.

O

OB Association
A group of massive stars that loosely move through space together without being gravitationally bound.

Observable universe
The amount of the universe that can be seen because its light has had enough time since the Big Bang to travel to us.

Occultation
The term for when a celestial object completely obscures another object that is much further from the observer.

Oort cloud
A spherical cloud made up of small, icy bodies that lies at the edge of the Sun's sphere of influence.

Open cluster
A group of up to a few thousand stars that were formed in the same cloud at the same time.

Opposition
When two objects are on opposite sides of the night sky, usually occurring when a planet is closest to Earth.

Outer planets
The four planets beyond the asteroid belt, comprised of the gas giants Jupiter, Saturn, Uranus and Neptune.

P

Parsec (pc)
A parsec is a measurement of cosmic distance based on parallax. Parallax is the change in an object's apparent position with respect to more distant objects caused when the viewing angle changes. Although the stars are at incredible distances, the Earth's orbit around the Sun is almost 300 million kilometres (186 million miles) in diameter, so nearby stars exhibit a small but measurable parallax against the celestial sphere during the course of half a year (from one side of the orbit to the other). Since we know the size of our baseline, the distance of stars displaying a measurable parallax can be ascertained. One parsec is the distance from the Sun to an object with a parallax angle of one arcsecond, and is equal to 3.262 light years. Proxima Centauri, the nearest star, is 1.29 parsecs (4.2 light years) away.

Periapsis
The point at which an object is at its closest to the body it's orbiting around.

Perigee
Perigee is the term for periapsis in regards to the Earth, ie, the Moon and any other orbiting satellites.

Perturbation
The other forces that may affect a body's orbit, such as another gravitational body, resistance, or misshapen bodies.

Phase
The Moon and planets go through specific phases as they travel through space as seen from Earth, full, half, new, etc.

Phase angle
The angle between an orbiting body and the Sun as seen by the observer, determining how much of the body is visible or in shadow.

Plate
The corrector plate shapes the light passing through it to offset the distortion created by the spherical primary mirror. This distortion is known as 'spherical aberration' and would render the images useless without the correcting effects of this specially shaped window.

Polarscope
Larger GEMs often feature a polarscope, which connects to the mount and looks up through the polar axis. The polarscope has a reticule, usually displaying Cassiopeia and the Big Dipper for the northern hemisphere, and a trapezium of brighter stars in Octans for the southern hemisphere. In both cases, the polarscope should be rotated to approximately match the sky as it appears, so that the pole can be set by moving only the latitude and bearing (altitude and azimuth) of the mount.

Pole star
This is the star Polaris which currently resides almost exactly over the rotational axis of Earth at the North Pole. If you extend the North Pole point out into space you get the north celestial pole. From the northern hemisphere all of the stars in the sky seem to rotate around this point.

Power
In astronomy, the term power is often used interchangeably with magnification. Lower powers, like those given by binoculars, afford a relatively wide field of view, while telescope power can be adjusted by changing the eyepiece. Traditionally, the term applied only to the magnifying ability of some element in an optical system (such as a lens or mirror) but now it is usually understood to mean the system as a whole, including the objective and ocular.

Precession
Precession causes different stars to assume the roles of the pole stars. As the Earth spins, it wobbles slowly like a spinning top. The axis running from pole to pole also rotates, a complete cycle taking about 26,000 years. During this time the Sun's position at the equinoxes drifts westward through the zodiacal constellations.

Primary mirror
The main mirror in a Newtonian reflecting telescope is called the 'primary'. The light from the objects which the telescope is pointing at strikes this mirror first and its diameter and quality govern the detail and how bright the objects appear to the observer. It sits on an adjustable support called the 'cell'.

Glossary

Proper motion
The rate of angular motion or change in position of an object over time as seen from the Solar System.

Protostar
The beginnings of a star, as mass forms from the contraction of an interstellar cloud.

Pulsar
A type of Neutron star that is highly magnetised and rotating. It emits a beam of EM radiation that, due to the rotation, seems to pulse.

Q

Quasar
Extremely luminous celestial objects that are distant and with a highly energetic galactic core, surrounding a supermassive blackhole.

R

Radial velocity
An object's velocity along the line of sight of the observer, with a positive value for receding objects.

Radiant
The shooting stars in a meteor shower appear to originate from a common point unique to that shower, known as the radiant. Since the meteors spread out from the radiant none are observed to pass through it, unless they're sporadic.

Radio astronomy
Astronomy using radio waves instead of the visible spectrum, the kind performed by arrays of satellite dishes around the world.

Radio astronomy

Ray system
The radial streaks caused by an impact crater, caused by the fine material thrown off the object that impacted the surface.

Red giant
A star which has used up most of its fuel and has expanded and cooled down giving it a distinctive orange/red tint. These are some of the largest stars in the universe.

Red shift
As an object moves away from the observer, the wavelength of the light and other EM radiation it gives off lengthens.

Refraction
As light passes through a different medium, such as glass, it is bent or – to use an alternative term – refracted. It was discovered that by controlling the shape of the glass (lens) it was therefore possible to vary the point where the image is formed behind the lens. This is known as the focal length of the lens and has a direct bearing on how much the lens can magnify.

■ The intense luminous qualities of a quasar make them a sight to behold

Right ascension and declination

In astronomy, the sky is projected on to a sphere much like that of the Earth's surface. Instead of longitude and latitude, co-ordinates are given in right ascension and declination. The poles have declination of 90 degrees and -90 degrees, and the greatest arc of right ascension is the celestial equator. The Earth's rotation causes everything to appear to drift and a correctly aligned right ascension axis (polar axis) allows us to mitigate the movement by simply tracking against this rotation. The positions of the stars and deep-sky objects are essentially fixed, so a star chart with co-ordinates can be used in conjunction with the setting circles on a good equatorial mount to navigate the sky.

Rille

A rille is a narrow groove in the lunar surface with the appearance of a channel or river. They may be the result of ancient lava tube collapses.

Roche limit

The distance from an object where the tidal forces match the orbiting bodies self-attraction, resulting in it dispersing and forming a ring.

S

Secondary mirror

The secondary mirror in a Schmidt-Cassegrain telescope is suspended in a 'cell' held in place by the corrector plate. This mirror, apart from reflecting the light back through the hole in the primary mirror and through to the focuser, helps to flatten the field of view of the image which would otherwise be curved. The secondary mirror can also be lined up correctly with the optical axis.

Semi-major axis

Circles have a fixed radius, where as an ellipse does not. The semi-major axis is the maximum length the radius can be.

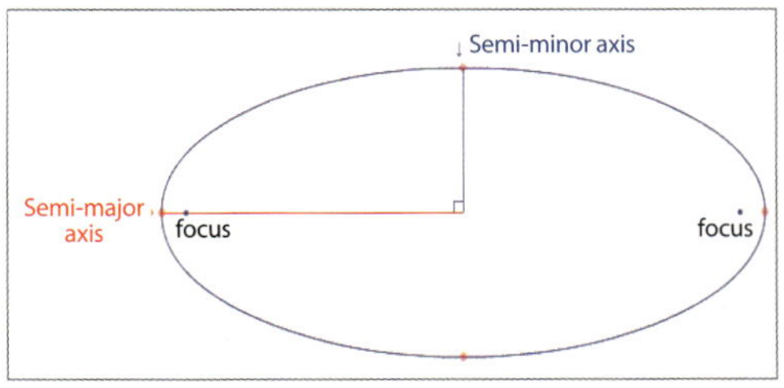

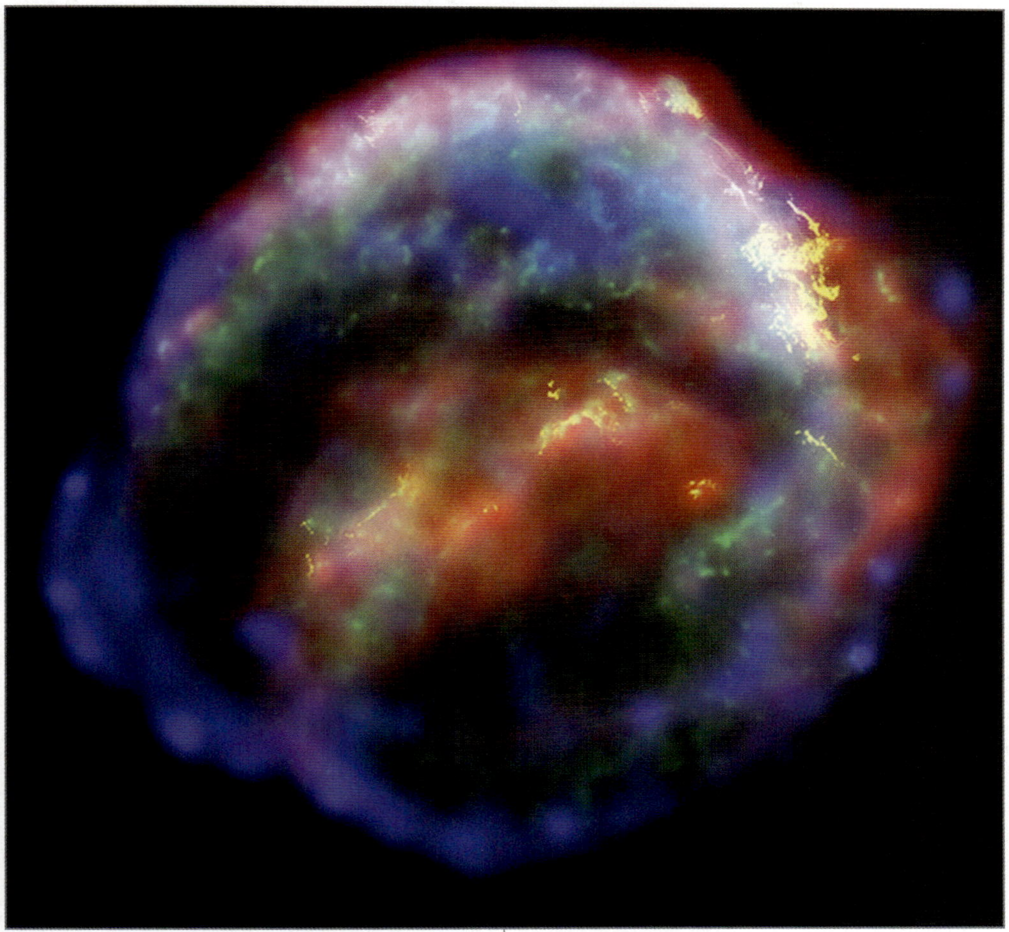

■ As a star expels its material, a supernova is formed

Semi-minor axis

The shortest distance to the edge of an elliptical orbit from the centre, the opposite of the semi-major axis.

Semi-regular variables

These are giant or super giant stars that normally follow a set pattern of change in their brightness but which can sometimes be interrupted.

Shadow transit

When a moon of a planet casts a shadow on the surface of the planet, it slowly moves across the disc as it orbits. This is known as a 'shadow transit'.

Shepherd moon

Small moons that orbit near the edges of a planetary ring, or in the gaps between them. This helps define the ring's shape.

Sidereal time

A time-keeping system based on Earth's rate of rotation to keep track of the location of stars.

Solar apex

The direction the Sun travels in the local standard of rest – its fictional and unreachable destination as it orbits the galaxy.

Solar filters

There are several types of solar filter you can buy for use with telescopes, binoculars and camera lenses. Telescope manufacturers will often make metal-coated glass filters to fit over the front of their instruments. These start from around £50 to several hundred! A cheaper way of obtaining a good solar filter is to use a material called 'astrosolar safety film'. This comes in A4 sheets and looks a little like kitchen foil and is made from a metallised polymer. An A4 sheet costs around £20.

For a more professional finish, you can buy filters using this material in metal rings made to fit the aperture of your telescope. These start at around £40. Dedicated solar telescopes using Hydrogen-Alpha filters start at around £500.

Solar mass

This is a unit of mass based around the mass of our Sun, used to weigh astronomical objects. It's 2×10^{30} kg.

Solar wind

Charged particles blown out by the Sun, consisting of electrons and protons, causing auroras in our atmosohere, and protecting the Solar system from cosmic rays.

Glossary

Solstice
The longest and shortest days of the year in non-equatorial locations, this marks the points at which the Sun is either the highest or lowest in the sky.

Spectroscopy
Using a prism to split up the light from the star into a 'rainbow' of colours can tell us a lot about what chemical elements can be found in the star and how fast it is moving. We can also tell if there is more than one star even if the stars are too close together for us to be able to see them individually.

Spectroscopic binary
A binary star that can only be resolved using spectroscopy, rather than with visible light through a telescope.

Speed of light
A universal constant speed limit. Within a vacuum, light travels at 3×10^8 m/s, and is used to calculate the distance of a light year.

Sphere of influence
The region around a celestial body where its gravitational influence is the most dominant.

Spherical primary mirror
The primary spherical mirror has a central hole cut into it to allow the light reflected from the secondary mirror to be brought to a focus behind the telescope.

Spider
The secondary mirror is suspended by a device which traditionally had four arms or 'vanes', called a 'spider'. You can also find two or three vaned spiders. These hold the secondary mirror centrally over the primary and allow it to be aligned and adjusted in an operation called collimation.

Star cluster
A group of stars that are bound together by gravity.

Stellar atmosphere
The outermost region of a star, forming only a small amount of its mass, and sometimes a large portion of its size.

Supermoon
This is a full moon or new moon that occurs when the Moon is at its closest to Earth.

Supermassive black hole
A type of black hole thought to reside in the centre of most (or all) galaxies, and is thousands or billions of times larger than our Sun.

Supernova
A much large nova produced by a star when most or all of its material is expelled. This can be extremely bright, outshining an entire galaxy.

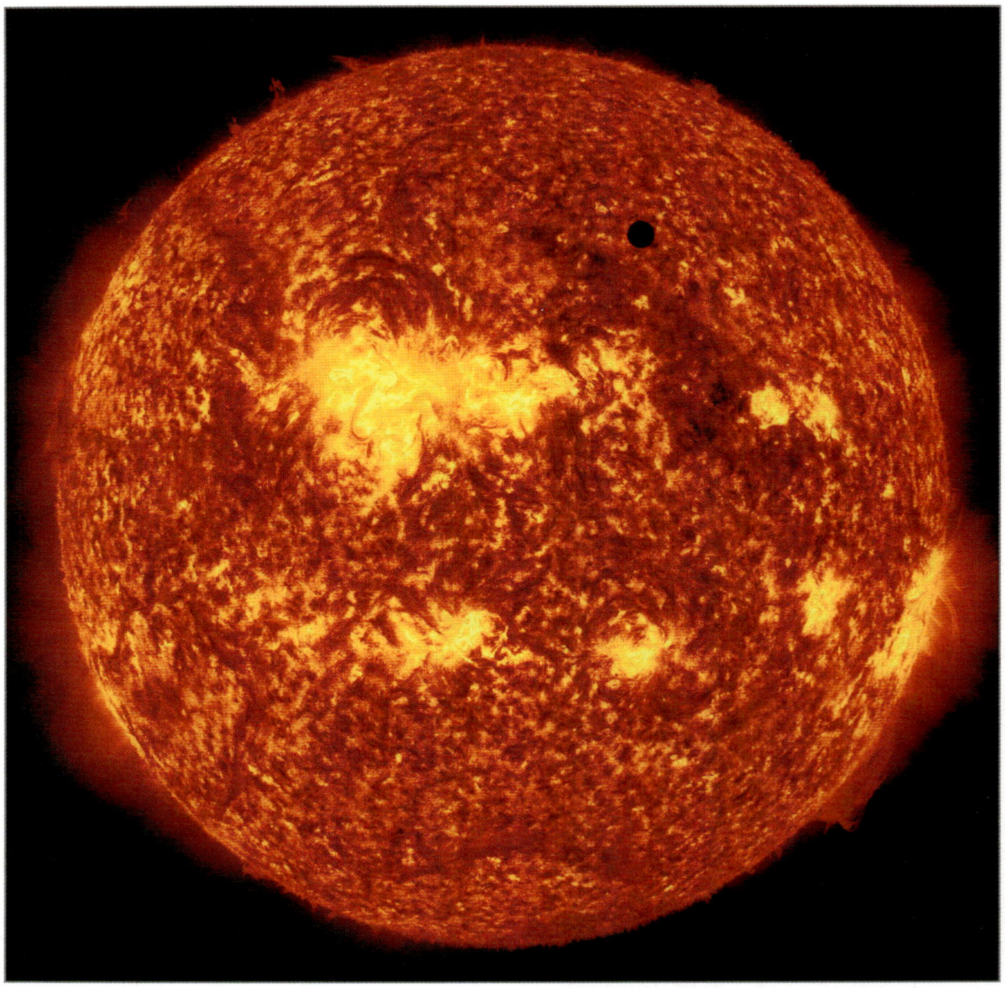

■ Transit refers to a smaller body passing in front of a larger one, such as a planet passing in front of the Sun

Sunspots
These are regions of complex magnetism on the Sun. You can see them as dark blotches with a dark centre and lighter outer either by projecting the image through a telescope or by using a 'white light' filter as described in this article. The reason sunspots are darker than the rest of the disc of the Sun is because they are cooler. They travel across the disc of the Sun as it rotates and grow and shrink as the magnetic fields change.

Synodic period
The time take for one object to complete its orbit around another. This is calculated as compared to relevant background stars.

Syzygy
Defined as the straight-line configuration of three bodies in a gravitational system, this is what happens during a solar or lunar eclipse.

T

Terminator
As the sunlight moves across the face of the Moon we see the dividing line between night and day on the surface. This is known as the terminator and is a great place to view through a telescope wherever it is on the lunar surface due to shadows throwing features into relief.

Terrestrial planet
The four rocky planets that orbit the Sun inside the asteroid belt, including Earth as well as Mercury, Venus and Mars.

Tidal acceleration
The effect of tidal forces from an orbiting moon, causing the moon's rotation to initially stop, and the planet's rotation to slow.

Tidal forces
Gravity is stronger the closer you are to the source, so the force on one side of a body is stronger than the other. On Earth, tidal forces cause the oceans to rise towards the Moon, causing a high tide.

Tidal locking
Due to tidal acceleration, most moons are tidally locked to their planet – they rotate at the same speed they orbit, meaning we only see one side of the Moon.

Trans-Neptunian Object
Objects beyond Neptune in the Solar System, such as Pluto, the Kuiper belt and more. Sometimes called plutoids.

Transit
The opposite of an occultation – when a smaller body passes in front of a larger body. An example would be when a planet passes in front of the Sun.

Trinary stars
A system of three stars orbiting each other, much like a binary star.

True horizon
The actual horizon of the planet Earth, as opposed to one that is defined by gravity experienced by the observer.

True North
The classical North Pole, the point at which the Earth rotates around. This is used in relation to the celestial pole.

U

Umbra
Parts of the shadow caused when a body is in front of a light source. The umbra is specifically the darkest shadow cast behind the body.

V

Variability
Some stars vary considerably in apparent brightness. Others only slightly. This is most commonly due to physical properties of the star. In some cases, more than one physical process creates a strange variability, but often the period can be determined by measuring the star's brightness each night for a long time.

Variable star
At first glance all stars seem to shine with a steady brightness, however, the light output of many will vary, increasing or decreasing brightness.

Variation period
The amount of time it takes for a star to change from its maximum to its minimum brightness and back again. For some variable stars this can be a matter of days or even hours, for others it can extend to years.

Visible spectrum
The portion of the electromagnetic spectrum that the human eye can see, from red to violet.

Visual back
This is the hole at the rear of the telescope through which the light is brought to a focus. It consists of a threaded ring which can accept all manner of accessories including diagonal prisms to enable comfortable viewing through an eyepiece and also cameras for recording what you see.

Visual binary
A binary star which we know exists because we can see it, rather than need evidence from other parts of the em spectrum.

Vortex
A powerful spin set up in a gas or fluid around an axis, rather like the effect when stirring a cup of tea! A hurricane is a type of vortex where clouds swirl around the 'eye' of the storm.

Voyager probes
Two probes which were launched in the late 1970's to fly past the outer planets and take photographs. They made many remarkable discoveries during the course of their journey.

W

Waning moon
Part of the Moon's phases where it's disappearing from sight after a full Moon.

Waxing moon
As a Moon approaches full, it's described as a waxing moon.

White dwarf
A star which has neared the end of its life and collapsed down to a small hot ball of gas perhaps only the size of the Earth but with the same mass as our Sun.

X

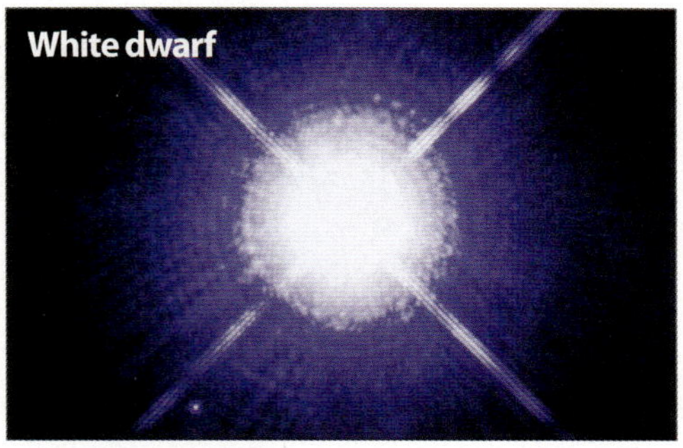

Y

Z

Zenith
The direction vertical above a location with respect to gravity, the opposite of nadir.

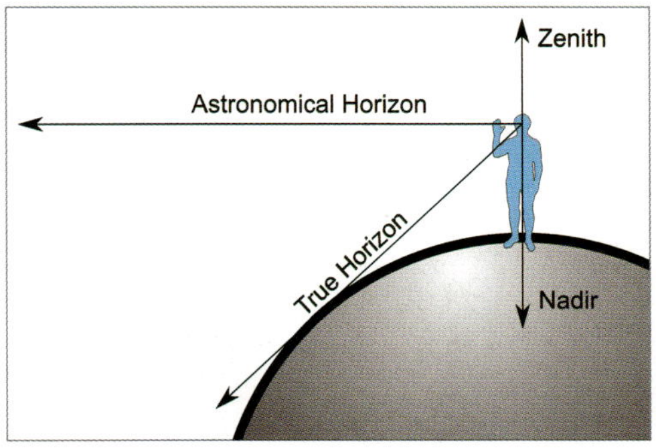

Zone of avoidance
Refers to the area of the night sky obscured by the Milky Way, limiting the amount we can observe in its direction.

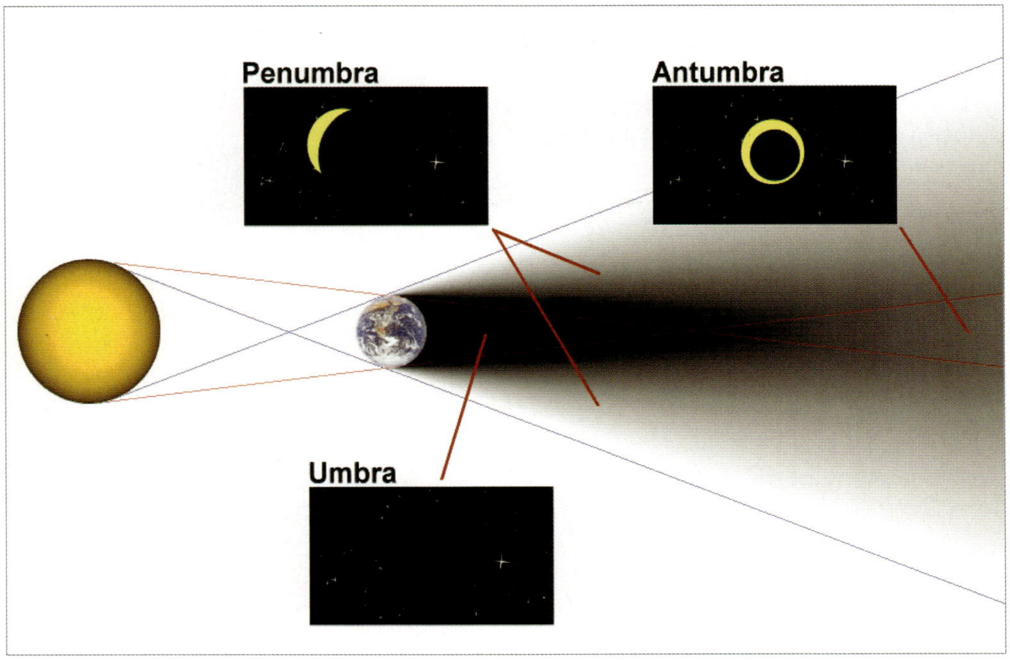

■ An umbra is the dark shadow caused by a body passing in front of a light source

Astronomy society directory

Unsure if there's an astronomical society near you? Here are some of the best clubs and societies

So you're ready to learn about the night sky, get advice on the latest telescopes and meet other astronomy enthusiasts. The next step is to find a club or society in your area where your hobby can truly begin to develop, and our directory is one of the best places to start, listing some of the major societies across the globe.

Many astronomical societies carry out the same activities from observational evenings to regular gatherings where talks are given. However the facilities that you might have access to will most likely vary from country to country with some societies boasting the use of observatories and university equipment. And, depending on which hemisphere you're in, you will see differing night sky objects and constellations on your weekly, or monthly, trips out under the stars with your group.

"Find a club or society in your area where your hobby can truly begin to develop"

United States of America

Marie Drake Planetarium
Town/City: Juneau, Alaska
Web: http://www.mariedrakeplanetarium.org

University of North Alabama Planetarium and Observatory
Town/City: Florence, Alabama
Web: http://www.una.edu/planetarium/

University of Arizona Astronomy Club
Town/City: Tucson, Arizona
Web: http://uaastroclub.org

Astronomy Club of the University of California
Town/City: Davis, California
Web: http://www.physics.ucdavis.edu/resources_for_undergraduates/astronomy_club.html

Colorado Springs Astronomical Society
Town/City: Colorado Springs, Colorado
Web: http://csastro.org

Central Florida Astronomical Society
Town/City: Longwood, Florida
Web: http://www.cfas.org

Atlanta Astronomy Club
Town/City: Atlanta, Georgia
Web: http://atlantaastronomy.org

Hawaiian Astronomical Society
Town/City: Honolulu, Hawaii
Web: http://www.hawastsoc.org

Amateur Astronomers of Central Iowa
Town/City: Marshalltown, Iowa
Web: http://www.amateurastronomersofcentraliowa.org

Idaho Falls Astronomical Society
Town/City: Idaho Falls, Idaho
Web: http://www.ifastro.org

Astronomical Society at the University of Illinois
Town/City: Illinois
Web: http://uias.astro.illinois.edu

Indiana Astronomical Society
Town/City: Urbana, Indiana
Web: http://www.iasindy.org

Kansas Cosmosphere and Space Center
Town/City: Kansas
Web: http://www.cosmo.org

Kentuckiana Astronomical Society
Town/City: West Point, Kentucky
Web: http://nightsky.jpl.nasa.gov/club-view.cfm?Club_ID=1169

Boston University Astronomical Society
Town/City: Boston, Massachusetts
Web: http://www.bu.edu/astronomy/other-pages/buas/

Central Maine Astronomical Society
Town/City: Whitefield, Maine
Web: http://maineastro.com

Eastern Michigan University Astronomy Club
Town/City: Ypsilanti, Michigan
Web: http://www.emich.edu/physicsastronomy/

Minnesota Astronomical Society
Town/City: Minnesota
Web: http://www.mnastro.org

Astronomical Society of Kansas City
Town/City: Minneapolis, Missouri
Web: http://www.askc.org

Rainwater Astronomers Association
Town/City: French Camp, Mississippi
Web: http://www.rainwaterobservatory.org/rainwater/

Cape Fear Astronomical Society
Town/City: Wilmington, North Carolina
Web: http://www.capefearastro.org

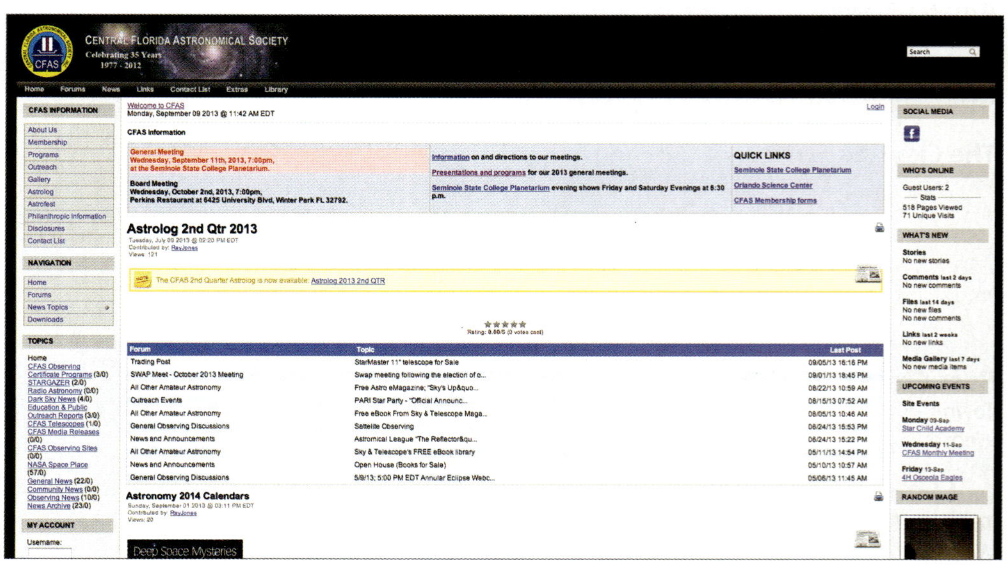

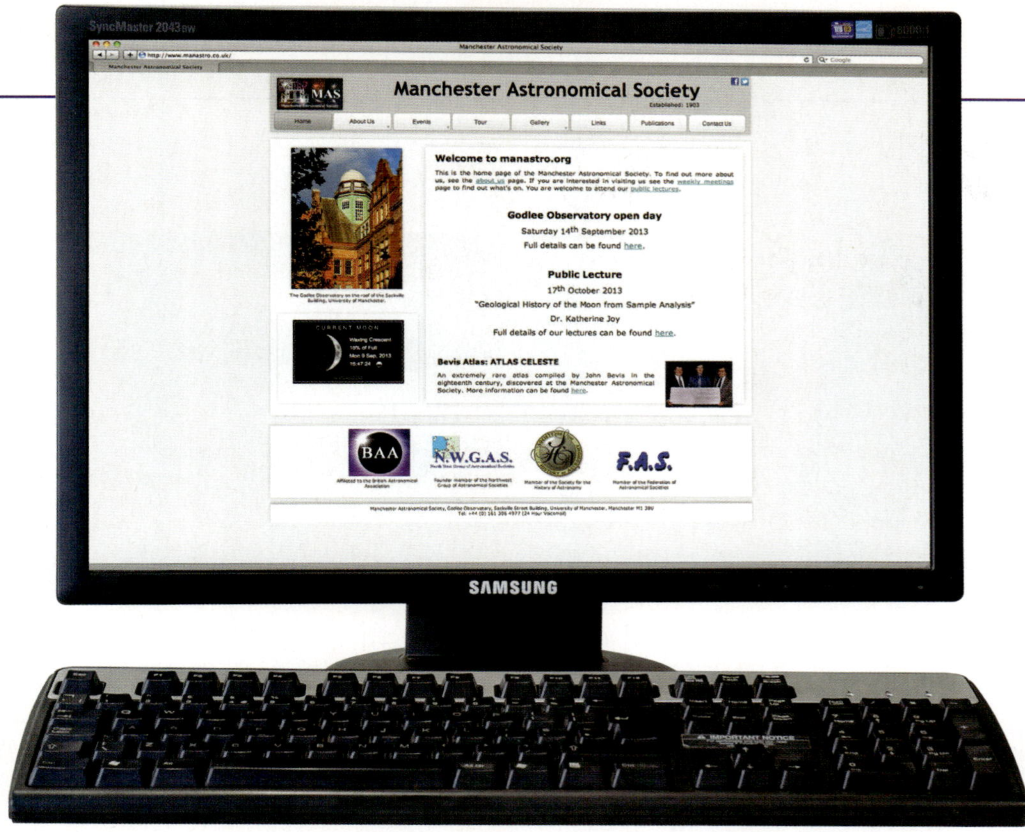

Northern Skies Astronomical Society
Town/City: Grand Forks, North Dakota
Web: http://www.und.edu/org/nsas/

Omaha Astronomical Society
Town/City: Omaha, Nebraska
Web: http://www.omahaastro.com

New Jersey Astronomical Association
Town/City: High Bridge, New Jersey
Web: http://www.njaa.org

National Public Observatory
Town/City: Radium Springs, New Mexico
Web: http://www.astronomy-national-public-observatory.org

Astronomical Society of Nevada
Town/City: Reno, Nevada
Web: http://www.astronomynv.org

Amateur Astronomers Association of New York
Town/City: New York
Web: http://www.aaa.org

The Cleveland Astronomical Society
Town/City: Cuyahoga Heights, Ohio
Web: http://www.clevelandastronomicalsociety.org

Oklahoma City Astronomy Club
Town/City: Oklahoma City, Oklahoma
Web: http://www.okcastroclub.com

Rose City Astronomers
Town/City: Portland, Oregon
Web: http://www.rosecityastronomers.org

Ladd Observatory
Town/City: Providence, Rhode Island
Web: www.brown.edu/Departments/Physics/Ladd

Penn State Astronomy Club
Town/City: University Park, Pennsylvania
Web: http://php.scripts.psu.edu/clubs/up/astro/index.php

Carolina Skygazers
Town/City: Rock Hill, South Carolina
Web: http://carolinaskygazers.org

Black Hills Astronomical Society
Town/City: Rapid City, South Dakota
Web: http://ggladfelter.net/BHAS/

Tamke-Allan Observatory Astronomical Society
Town/City: Harriman, Tennessee
Web: http://www.roanestate.edu/obs/

Central Texas Astronomical Society
Town/City: Waco, Texas
Web: http://www.centexastronomy.org

Utah Valley Astronomy Association
Town/City: Lindon, Utah
Web: http://www.uvaa.org

Astronomy Club of Virginia Tech
Town/City: Blacksburg, Virginia
Web: http://www.phys.vt.edu/~jhs/astroclb/

Vermont Astronomical Society
Town/City: Williston, Vermont
Web: http://vtastro.org

Seattle Astronomical Society
Town/City: Seattle, Washington
Web: http://www.seattleastro.org

Cheyenne Astronomical Society
Town/City: Cheyenne, Wyoming
Web: http://home.bresnan.net/~curranm/

United Kingdom and Ireland

Milton Keynes Astronomical Society
Town/City: Haversham, Buckinghamshire
Web: www.mkas.org.uk

Bristol Astronomical Society
Town/City: Bristol
Web: http://www.bristolastrosoc.org.uk/www/index.php

Cambridge Astronomical Society
Town/City: Cambridge
Web: www.caa-cya.org

White Peak Astronomy Observing Group
Town/City: Ashbourne, Derbyshire
Web: http://www.wpaog.co.uk/

Macclesfield Astronomical Society
Town/City: Macclesfield, Cheshire
Web: http://www.visualsense.com/_mas/

Cornwall Astronomical Society
Town/City: Mabe Burnthouse, Cornwall
Web: http://www.cornwallas.org.uk/

Tiverton and Mid-Devon Astronomical Society
Town/City: Tiverton, Mid Devon
Web: http://www.tivas.org.uk/

Wessex Astronomical Society
Town/City: Wimborne, Dorset
Web: http://www.wessex-astro.org.uk/

Clacton and District Astronomical Association
Town/City: Clacton-On-Sea, Tendring
Web: http://www.clactonastronomy.co.uk/

Cotswold Astronomical Society
Town/City: Cheltenham
Web: http://www.cotswoldas.org.uk/

Manchester Astronomical Society
Town/City: Manchester
Web: www.manastro.co.uk

Reading Astronomical Society
Town/City: Woodley, Reading
Web: http://www.readingastro.org.uk

Southampton Astronomical Society
Town/City: Upper Shirley, Southampton
Web: www.southampton-astronomical-society.org.uk

Isle of Man Astronomical Society
Town/City: Isle of Man
Web: www.iomastronomy.org

Directory

Vectis Astronomical Society
Town/City: Newchurch, Isle of Wight
Web: http://www.wightastronomy.org/

Mid-Kent Astronomical Society
Town/City: Canterbury, Kent
Web: www.mkas-site.co.uk

Blackpool and District Astronomical Society
Town/City: Blackpool
Web: www.blackpoolastronomy.org.uk

Leicester Astronomical Society
Town/City: Leicester
Web: www.leicesterastronomicalsociety.co.uk

Lincoln Astronomical Society
Town/City: Lincoln
Web: www.lincolnastronomy.org

Croydon Astronomical Society
Town/City: Croydon
Web: www.croydonastro.org.uk

Flamsteed Astronomical Society
Town/City: Greenwich
Web: www.flamsteed.info

Liverpool Astronomical Society
Town/City: Liverpool
Web: www.liverpoolas.org

Norwich Astronomical Society
Town/City: Norwich
Web: www.norwich.astronomicalsociety.org.uk

Irish Astronomical Association
Town/City: Belfast
Web: http://irishastro.org.uk/

Nottingham Astronomical Society
Town/City: Nottingham
Web: http://nottinghamastro.wordpress.com/

Abingdon Astronomical Society
Town/City: Abingdon, Oxfordshire
Web: www.abingdonastro.org.uk

Aberdeen Astronomical Society
Town/City: Aberdeen
Web: www.aberdeenastro.org.uk

Astronomical Society of Glasgow
Town/City: Glasgow
Web: www.astronomicalsocietyofglasgow.org.uk

Astronomical Society of Edinburgh
Town/City: Edinburgh
Web: www.astronomyedinburgh.org

North Staffordshire Astronomical Society
Town/City: Newcastle-under-Lyme
Web: http://www.northstaffsas.co.uk/

Shropshire Astronomical Society
Town/City: Rodington, Shropshire
Web: http://www.shropshire-astro.com/

South Somerset Astronomical Society
Town/City: Taunton
Web: http://ssas.fateback.com

Guildford Astronomical Society
Town/City: Guildford
Web: www.guildfordas.org

East Sussex Astronomical Society
Town/City: Bexhill-on-Sea, East Sussex
Web: http://www.esas.org.uk/

Stratford-upon-Avon Astronomical Society
Town/City: Alderminster
Web: www.astro.org.uk

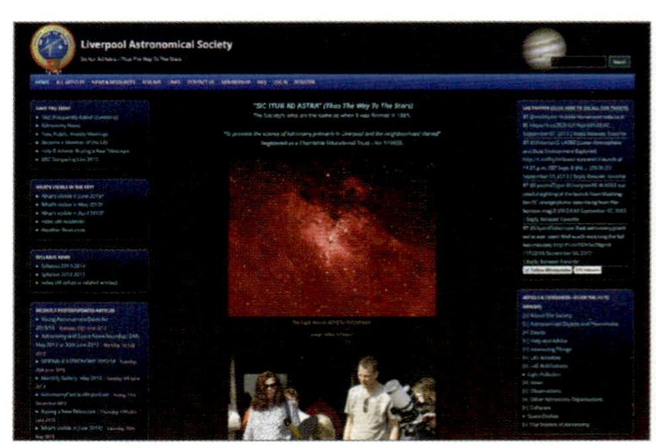

Newcastle Astronomical Society
Town/City: Newcastle
Web: www.newcastleastronomical.org.uk

Wiltshire Astronomical Society
Town/City: Seend, Wiltshire
Web: http://wasnet.co.uk/

Worcester Astronomical Society
Town/City: Worcester
Web: www.worcesteras.freeserve.co.uk

University of Birmingham Astronomical Society
Town/City: Birmingham
Web: www.astrosoc.org.uk

York Astronomical Society
Town/City: York
Web: www.yorkastro.co.uk

Sheffield Astronomical Society
Town/City: Fulwood, Sheffield
Web: www.sheffieldastro.org.uk

Cardiff Astronomical Society
Town/City: Cardiff
Web: www.cardiff-astronomical-society.co.uk

Gwynedd Astronomical Society
Town/City: Bangor
Web: http://www.gwyneddastronomysociety.co.uk/

Swansea Astronomical Society
Town/City: Swansea
Web: www.swanastro.org.uk

Leeds Astronomical Society
Town/City: Leeds
Web: www.leedsastronomy.org.uk

Bradford Astronomical Society
Town/City: Bradford
Web: www.bradfordastronomy.co.uk

Iceland

Stjornuskodunarfelag Seltjarnarness
Town/City: Seltjarnarnes
Web: http://www.astro.is

Belgium

Andromeda Dendervallei
Town/City: Hofstade
Web: http://www.andromeda-site.tk

Germany

Astronomische Vereinigung Weikersheim e.V.
Town/City: Weikersheim
Web: http://www.astronomieschule.de

France

Association AstroQueyras
Town/City: Saint-Vran
Web: http://www.astroqueyras.com

Spain

Astrobanyoles
Town/City: Banyoles
Web: http://www.astrobanyoles.org

Italy

Gruppo Astrofili di Padova
Town/City: Padova
Web: http://padova.astrofili.org/

Australia

Astronomical Society of Western Australia
Town/City: Subiaco
Web: http://aswa.info

Costa Rica

Asociacion Costarricense de Astronomia
Town/City: Rios
Web: http://www.acodea.org/index.php

Canada

Astro Club Borealis
Town/City: New-Brunswick
Web: http://www.umce.ca/astroclubnb/

India

The Bangalore Astronomical Society
Town/City: Bangalore
Web: http://www.bas.org.in/Home/

Cyprus

Kition Planetarium and Observatory
Town/City: Larnaca
Web: http://www.bas.org.in/Home/

Netherlands

Dutch Astronomical Society Noord-Drenthe
Town/City: Assen
Web: http://www.vwsnoorddrenthe.nl/

Chile

Sociedad Metropolitana de Astronomia Aficionada
Town/City: Santiago
Web: http://www.smaa.cl/